The Idea of Disarmament!
Rethinking the Unthinkable

Alan Geyer

Foreword by Lawrence D. Weiler

The Brethren Press, Elgin, Illinois
and
The Churches' Center for Theology and Public Policy, Washington, D.C.

THE IDEA OF DISARMAMENT!

Copyright © 1982 by The Brethren Press, Elgin, Illinois 60120
Printed in the United States of America

Cover design by Rich Nickel

Library of Congress Cataloging in Publication Data

Geyer, Alan F.
    The Idea of Disarmament!

    Includes index.
    1. Atomic warfare—Religious aspects—Christianity. 2. Disarmament—Religious aspects—Christianity. 3. Atomic warfare—Moral and ethical aspects. 4. Disarmament—Moral and ethical aspects. 5. Peace (Theology) I. Title.
BR115.A85G49   261.8'73   81-24212
ISBN O-87178-397-5   AACR2
ISBN O-87178-396-7 (pbk.)

TO JOANNE

a superpower

who is always disarming

Contents

Foreword

The history of post-World War II efforts to contain and reverse the arms race, particularly in the nuclear field, is clearly a discouraging one. The number of nuclear chips on the table of this dangerous international poker game that fallible humans play has increased from two at the time of Hiroshima to approximately 50,000 today. While in earlier years some successes were achieved, the arms race has accelerated and is now largely out of control. The danger of nuclear war, accidental, inadvertent or deliberate, has thus increased to ominous proportions. The complacent or self-righteous ones who would argue otherwise cannot point to any case in history where an arms race did not end in war.

If this be so, and if we are currently witnessing a massive increase in military expenditures and a confrontational approach to US-Soviet relations, is there not something rather quixotic in a book such as this? I think not, for a variety of reasons.

As Alan Geyer rightly believes, it is not a time for despair or for cynicism concerning disarmament possibilities. There are still some potential East-West flash points in the world. The North-South issues will be with us for years to come. However, a preoccupation with immediate political problems and an absence of a sense of history has seemed to blur our view of one significant structural improvement in the international order that offers some hope.

For the past thirty-five years, most of the serious conflicts in both Europe and the Third World have been the direct result of the world's efforts to settle, either *de jure* or *de facto,* the unwritten peace treaties of World War II, which left a disrupted world without an agreed political order. The conflicts stemming from those disagreements were both major causes of the early escalation of the arms race and the dangerous fuses that threatened to ignite the nuclear arsenals. With a few exceptions, the peace agreements of World War II have, with genuine or grudging acceptance, been achieved. This development needs to be viewed alongside that related post war "achievement," the survival throughout this turbulent period of that imperfect and still evolving structure, the United Nations system. In this case, survival itself has meant institutionalization and strengthening of the basis for international order.

Peace is never a static condition, but these preconditions for

international order have given us an improved foundation for dealing with the nuclear threat — if, that is, there is political will and
wisdom to do so, for many of our leaders have mind-sets that remain in the earlier period, and think about nuclear weapons in
ways that preclude rational efforts to control them.

Even the discouraging record of the efforts to control the arms
race reveals certain positive elements. We have learned that it is
possible to construct agreements in complicated negotiations, such
as the ABM Treaty; even among the supporters of the SALT
negotiations, there was at the beginning little optimism in this
regard. And we have learned that agreements have "worked" and
have, with some minor exceptions on both sides, been adhered to
by the parties. These are new elements which will not go away,
whatever the hostility to the process that is held by some of our new
cold warriors.

Moreover, even the increased US-Soviet tensions, dangerous
and inhibiting to the control of the nuclear threat as they are, do
not foreclose progress. Agreements in this field have more often
been contributors to an improved international climate rather than
the product of it — contrary to the current wisdom of the "realists."
If there is a perceived mutual need that can be met and a will to act,
international tranquility is not a precondition for agreement.

At the time of the first US-Soviet arms control agreement, the
Hot Line, Soviet sensitivity to making a bilateral agreement with
the US was such that the signing itself was not done in a public
ceremony. The limited Test Ban Treaty followed by less than two
years the Berlin blockade and was only a year after the Cuban
missile crisis. The Vietnam war produced such tensions in Soviet-
US relations that, at Soviet insistence, the emerging agreed draft
texts of the Non-Proliferation Treaty were never submitted to other
negotiating states as joint US-Soviet documents but rather as
separate US and Soviet texts, separate but with identical wording.
And the later successful negotiations on the SALT I agreements
were conducted even while Moscow's aid to the Vietnamese was
prolonging that American ordeal and while American aircraft were
bombing Hanoi and mining Haiphong harbor.

Hopeful possibilities for action still exist. And it is precisely
because of the present situation that critical new thinking and new
involvement by citizens are needed. The danger has increased. The
inevitable social tensions in the body politics of democratic nations
that are being produced by the massive peacetime shifting of
resources to the military sector raise serious future threats to civil

military relationships. And there is increasing awareness of the moral and rational bankruptcy of much of current nuclear weapons policy.

It is in recognition of this latter point that Dr. Geyer has devoted so much attention in this book on disarmament to nuclear weapons policy and doctrines of deterrence and counter-force, as well as to what the hypnotic preoccupation with nuclear weapons and strategy has done to our capacity for rational perception and diplomatic conduct. Thinking about nuclear weapons is a pre-requisite to effective thinking about nuclear disarmament.

Almost all government officials, at least until they leave office and begin to reflect, pay lip service to one variation or another of what have been the traditional doctrines. But my own judgment, after watching internal arguments over disarmament policy for many years, is that the basic reason for differing views by officials looking at the same set of facts is the different ways in which they think about nuclear weapons. It never really gets into the position papers, but it is there. And it needs to be brought out more into the open, among citizens as well as officials.

This book is a wide-ranging and long overdue effort to critique the myths and theories of the managers of the arms race. Dr. Geyer is not a dilettante, as unfortunately too many disarmament ad-vocates have been. He is a long-time and serious scholar. Perhaps as a result of this, he writes with some informed anger and passion. Some may feel there is overkill in some of his criticism, but he drives his points home without the equivocation and obfuscation that characterizes much of the writing on these topics. And he is very critical of some officials, including this writer, who have been involved in past disarmament efforts.

He means to start a debate and rethinking on basic issues, recognizing that his own answers may be inadequate. He wants to make us think and offers "new political and moral paradigms for understanding where we are and where we are tending." He correct-ly perceives that the basic issues of disarmament are political in nature and addresses the politics of disarmament and the role of the public. The fact that achievement of the two most significant arms agreements, the Limited Test Ban Treaty (because it was the first) and the ABM Treaty (because it was the most significant), was largely the result of public concern and debate is testament to the importance of this topic. And in a long neglected area, in which he also has special expertise, Dr. Geyer seeks to outline a theological reconstruction for churches to enable them to become more effectively involved in this most moral of political problems.

If all this were not enough, Dr. Geyer seeks to relate the bilateral strategic arena to multilateral disarmament diplomacy and the conflict between the largely bilateral East-West agenda and that relating to long term North-South issues. In most of the governmental bureaucracies, officials working in these two general areas are strangers to each other. It is indeed useful to have a writer familiar with strategic issues deal with questions of multilateral diplomacy and North-South issues.

Some "experts" may not like this book, but if there are people who have suspicions that things are coming apart under the momentum of the arms race, the views of such experts should be an additional reason for reading it. The relative absence of new ideas in this field is one of the tragedies of the past thirty years. But this book is really a call for critical thinking and serious involvement by an informed public. That is as it should be, for whether we control the nuclear arms race or permit it to foreclose the future will be largely determined by the indifference or the involvement of the people.

Lawrence D. Weiler

Preface

Two decades ago a trilogy of books by a most imaginative man was devoted to making nuclear war thinkable and manageable. Herman Kahn's *On Thermonuclear War, Thinking About the Unthinkable,* and *On Escalation: Metaphors and Scenarios* set the pace for the cerebrations of the early 1960s on these topics. These volumes are back in style in the 1980s because once again nuclear weapons have become "usable" and nuclear war not only "thinkable" but "winnable" — at least in the minds of some well-placed politicians and strategists.

This book, too, is concerned with making the unthinkable thinkable and with the metaphors and scenarios that will encourage thinkability. But it starts from a different direction: its purpose is to make disarmament thinkable. Not let's-dump-all-our-nukes-into-the-sea disarmament but a reversal of the arms race and a renewed vision of the political requisites of peace. Yet the anxieties and myths of our time make that task very difficult. The 1980s are marked not only by rapid accumulations of redundant weapons but by regression to the worst of Cold War animosities and threats.

Disarmament has become "bad politics" not because it is unwise but because foolish men have gained such inordinate political power. The American public is awash with ignorant dogmas and downright lies about their security problems, partly because the New Right has acquired a vast arsenal of financial and intellectual resources which have come to dominate foreign policy debate, political campaigns, much of the media, and now the national security bureaucracy. This is not, however, to scapegoat the New Right or the Russians or anybody else but to appeal that we be transformed by the renewal of our own minds.

This is more of a think-book than a fact-book. It is more concerned with ideas, good and bad, than with what George Kennan calls "military mathematics." It is written by the proprietor of a think tank who is appalled at the ideological captivity and influence of some other think tanks in the making of public policy in the United States. To make disarmament thinkable is to offer some new political and moral paradigms for understanding where we are and where we are tending.

Moreover, this book is an argument for the necessity of

nuclear disarmament. It is inescapably a critique of certain doctrines such as deterrence, counterforce, linkage, bargaining chips, and ICBM vulnerability. It is an argument for a much more salubrious understanding of security. It is an argument against viewing the arms race exclusively as a reaction to international events — and for discovering the domestic dynamics of the arms race as they pulse through politics, economics, technology, and culture. It is an argument for affirming the primacy of American responsibility for reversing the arms race, without minimizing Soviet complicity in it or the shenanigans of many other states.

This book is not primarily an argument for the high probabilities of nuclear war. It is the conviction of those probabilities, however, which prompts the writing. In the mid-1970s both the Harvard-MIT Arms Control Seminar and the Stockholm International Peace Research Institute (SIPRI) provided sober forecasts of those probabilities by the 1990s — forecasts which neither political nor technological trends of the past several years have done anything to discount. A 1980 study by political scientist Louis Beres of Purdue University, spookily titled *Apocalypse: Nuclear Catastrophe in World Politics,* systematically surveyed the scenarios of disaster and concluded that "a thermonuclear holocaust that has burned the world into oblivion" is "all too likely." Such a reading of trends is admittedly controvertible. Policy-makers in the early months of the Reagan Administration sharply discounted the likelihood of nuclear war even as they prepared to boost military spending to $1.5 trillion over the next five years, proceeded with Trident, cruise, MX, and Euro-strategic missiles, and simultaneously resurrected the neutron bomb, ABMs, and the B-1 bomber.

I hope this may serve as a mediating book: an approach to foreign policy which may have something to say to professionals in both governmental and academic communities, yet prove instructive to concerned citizens. My intellectual habits are incurably cross-disciplinary. I have sought to create an integrative work bridging a variety of disciplines and sub-disciplines: defense and disarmament, politics and technology, diplomatic and domestic institutions, bilateral and multilateral circles, national security and economics, military strategy and theology. That is a preposterously pretentious list unless I admit that these are only flimsy pontoon bridges which must soon be replaced by better bridge-builders.

There can hardly be a more theological topic than this question of the survival of the human race. But Christian theologians have been strangely disengaged from this question for nearly two decades, as have their churches. There are some spirited new beginnings toward disarmament and peace throughout the land and I hope these pages may reinforce them. A demanding new agenda in what I have called "the Third Nuclear Age" awaits serious theological work. It would therefore be fatuous to write this book deductively as an exercise in applied theology. Rather, the most faithful approach is to become immersed in the political and technical struggles over disarmament policy — and only then to ask what theological reconstruction is required to nerve a new generation of Christians to do, at last, the things that make for peace.

Dutch Catholic theologian Edward Schillebeeckx told the World Council of Churches Public Hearing on Nuclear Weapons and Disarmament in Amsterdam, November 1981, that theologians do not even know what they are talking about theologically unless they join in a fresh encounter with non-theologians. A new "non-theological prior cognition" was required in order to grasp "the autonomous immanent logic of the spiral of armament and the military and economic structure of manufacturing nuclear weapons." Public opinion and its manipulation, the relation of East-West issues to North-South issues, the survival of humankind in its totality — these provide further themes for analysis and reflection. Schillebeeckx concluded that, "setting all ideology aside," the theologian is obliged to see that humanity's "threatening real enemy is the autonomous spiral of armament itself. The theologian must analyze the rationality of this whole field in its structural setting."

The method of this inquiry is essentially that proposed by Schillebeeckx. Non-theological cognition precedes theological confession. In a sense, this ultimately becomes a book on basic theology. It may be as close to "Geyer's Dogmatics" as I shall ever come.

This provisionally secular, pre-doctrinal rather than post-doctrinal style may also open these issues to a wider public which is bound to share a common fate with Christians in nuclear matters.

I write as a sometime political scientist, a somewhat marginal ethicist, and a completely unsuccessful activist. A small sample of my defeats sprinkles these pages without, I pray, dampening the argument too much. I write, moreover, as a wounded veteran of dozens of international conferences on disarmament: UN General Assembly sessions, Non-Proliferation Treaty review conferences, academic and ecclesiastical summits and exchange programs. Yet it is precisely the human encounter in and around such events which has contributed most to my own sense of priorities in nuclear disarmament.

These international adventures help to explain my resolve to keep using the word "disarmament" itself, for all the rest of the world uses it and has used it throughout this century. It is a mark of resurgent isolationism in the US, as well as our macho national security jargon which fails to hide our insecurity, that even peace advocates are often loath to utter the word. But my concern runs deeper than keeping the word disarmament alive so that Americans can speak plainly to other peoples: it is that the very idea of disarmament as a purpose and a process may be doomed if we cannot even keep the word alive. I want to do whatever I can to restore the legitimacy and utility and even the power of the word. That commitment has nothing to do with pacifism, for I write as a non-pacifist never wholly persuaded that nations should eliminate all military force.

This book had its incubus in five happy years on the Political Science and Peace Studies faculties of Colgate University, where teaching on arms control and disarmament was particularly satisfying and whose former colleagues are colleagues yet. Special opportunities to develop my main ideas were provided by lecture series whose sponsors greatly honored me by invitations to address our common concerns: the Colliver Lectures at the University of the Pacific, the James Gathings Lectures at Bucknell University, the Staley Lectures at Mary Baldwin College, the World Order Lectures at Muhlenberg College, and the Ora Huston Lectures at Bethany Theological Seminary. My theological themes were tuned up by privileged presentations to the following international conferences: the Korean-US Consultation, Stony Point, 1977; the World Council of Churches Conference on Disarmament, Glion, 1978; the World Conference on Religion and Peace, Princeton, 1979; the Japan-US Consultation on Militarism, Okinawa, 1980; the Meeting of Church Leaders from the Federal Republic of Germany and US Lutheran Bishops, Minneapolis, 1981; the World Council of YMCAs, Estes Park, 1981. I am indebted for life to two organizations which have done most to nurture me in the legitimacy of theological and ethical discussion of politics and foreign policy: the Council on Christian Approaches to Defense and Disarmament (CCADD) and the Council on Religion and International Affairs (CRIA). I am grateful to CRIA for permitting me to publish here revised portions of articles on the United Nations and the Non-Proliferation Treaty which were first published in *Worldview* in September 1975 and September 1978. Several portions of Chapters 4-6 are revisions of material originally published in occasional papers of the Churches' Center for Theology and Public Policy.

I am deeply grateful to Fred Swartz, Clyde Weaver, and their colleagues at The Brethren Press for their shared sense of urgency about these issues, their robust commitment to the timely publication of this book, and their kindness and competence at every stage of the publishing process.

The Disarmament Policy Panel at our Churches' Center for Theology and Public Policy, chaired by Edward Doherty, has been a very present help in a time of international troubles. Lawrence D. Weiler, a former government official with unsurpassed seniority in disarmament affairs, an unflagging sponsor of governmental dialogue with academics and NGOs, and co-editor of *International Arms Control* (1976), most kindly yielded to my request that he write the foreword. My wife Joanne has heard and read and heard again and typed most of the manuscript, while others in the household have variously helped and painfully endured the production process. None of these creditors can possibly be blamed for the fact that this volume will fall somewhat short of solving all global problems and may even aggravate some of them. *Mea culpa.*

Alan Geyer

CHAPTER 1

The Third Nuclear Age

It is imaginable that we might destroy 200,000,000 Russians in a war. . . . It is not only imaginable, it is imagined. It is imaginable because it could be done in a moment, in the twinkling of an eye, at the last trumpet.
—Thomas C. Schelling in *Arms and Influence*

The Atom Bomb: Winston Churchill called it "the Second Coming in Wrath." Some would argue, even on into the 1980s, that history and politics hadn't really been changed very much by the Bomb. But Arthur Koestler proposed that the calendar itself be transformed from A.D. to P.H.—for Post-Hiroshima. By that reckoning 1982 is 37 P.H.

Whatever the historical divide between pre-nuclear and post-nuclear eras, the P.H. years themselves may be divided into three periods of contrasting disarmament trends:

1. 1945-60: marked originally by an American nuclear monopoly, then by proliferation and disarmament propaganda during the Cold War of the 1950s. This was the First Nuclear Age.

2. 1960-74: marked by the first serious efforts at negotiated disarmament, which produced numerous treaties and an era of détente—although nuclear arsenals continued to multiply. This was the Second Nuclear Age.

3. 1974- : marked by a many-faceted new nuclear crisis after a brief period in which the world had become increasingly complacent about and neglectful of nuclear issues. This is the Third Nuclear Age.

This latter and most dangerous period of post-Hiroshima history has experienced serious disintegration of the non-proliferation systems. It has been traumatized by the demise of détente. It has been dominated by a "qualitative" arms race which began with MIRVs (multiple warheads that can be independently targeted) and continues unabated with counterforce weapons. Its particular perils fully qualify it to be called the Third Nuclear Age. But these perils cannot be understood without reference to the two earlier periods. (A more complete history of nuclear arms and disarmament, which is beyond the scope of this study, may be found in Chalmers M. Roberts, *The Nuclear Years: The Arms Race and Arms Control 1945-70,* and Michael Mandelbaum, *The Nuclear Question: The United States and Nuclear Weapons 1946-1976.)*

The First Nuclear Age (1945-60)

The First Nuclear Age can hardly be regarded as a time of sustained seriousness about disarmament. The US was too convinced of the advantages of a nuclear monopoly—and then, at least nuclear superiority—and too complacent about its technological genius to submit to any honest-to-goodness controls. The Soviet Union was too paranoid about threats to its own security and too determined to catch up with the US to do much more than promote propaganda for disarmament, even while building up its own strategic arsenals.

It is possible that Bernard M. Baruch, who presented a US plan for international control of atomic energy to the United Nations on June 14, 1946, was utterly serious about the plan. His opening remarks remain very quotable:

> We are come to make a choice between the quick and the dead.
> . . . Behind the black portent of the new atomic age lies a hope which, seized upon with faith, can work our salvation. If we fail, then we have damned every man to be the slave of Fear. Let us not deceive ourselves: We must elect World Peace or World Destruction.

But the Baruch Plan was almost bound to fail because it would have permitted a continuing US monopoly of atomic weapons technology while imposing on the USSR a permanent position of inferiority. The proposed Atomic Development Authority confronted the Soviets with the prospect of a Western-dominated agency in which they would have no veto power. Given the early rumblings of the Cold War in 1946, that was hardly a prospect the Russians were willing to trust. It seems likely that major US policymakers anticipated a Soviet rejection. They knew that the Soviets, with good reason, had suspected the Hiroshima bomb as a demonstration to them as well as to the Japanese. A tale told at that time recounted the assurance of a State Department official to a certain general aghast at the thought of sharing any nuclear authority or technology with the Russians. The official said, "Don't worry! If they accept, we can always kill it in the Senate."

Princeton historian Martin J. Sherwin, in a well-documented study of atomic development during World War II, concluded that President Franklin Roosevelt "consistently opposed international control and acted in accordance with Churchill's monopolistic, anti-Soviet views." This commitment to "the diplomatic role of the atomic bomb," Roosevelt's "most secret and among his most important decisions," reveals a skepticism about prospects for postwar US-Soviet cooperation and an anticipation of the Cold War. By contrast many of FDR's science advisers did argue for international control of atomic energy but were kept uninformed of the Roosevelt-Churchill commitment to an anti-Soviet monopoly.[1] In the early weeks of the Truman presidency after Roosevelt's death on April 12, 1945 — weeks preoccupied with planning the A-bombing of Japan — "what little commitment there was among high officials for the international control of atomic energy all but vanished."[2] On this account, it seems most unlikely that the Baruch Plan represented a fully credible commitment by the Truman administration to international control.

The Soviet counter-proposal offered by a young Andrei Gromyko in 1946 was for immediate outlawry and destruction of all atomic bombs, followed by a limited system of inspection and control which included a veto power. That, of course, was equally unacceptable to the US.

Thus the first international effort at nuclear disarmament failed. And thus began the gamesmanship of disarmament in which the US and USSR sought to out-maneuver each other with grand schemes for disarmament which might win propaganda battles because each would force the other side to take a negative stand. In 1960 Joseph Nogee described this game which dominated the 1945-60 period in these mischievous terms:

> Every plan offered by either side has contained a set of proposals calculated to have wide popular appeal. Every such set has included at least one feature that the other side could not possibly accept, thus forcing a rejection. Then the proposing side has been able to claim that the rejector is opposed to the idea of disarmament *in toto*. The objectionable feature may be thought of as the 'joker' in every series of proposals.[3]

A variation of this game occurred when one side made a show of adopting the other side's former position, thus calling its bluff. It was a deeply cynical game on both sides — and both sides knew it.

In March 1950, the Soviets sponsored a World Peace Congress which produced the original "Stockholm Appeal" for an "absolute ban on atomic weapons." Signed by millions of peace enthusiasts, that Appeal offered no provision for inspection or enforcement — and just happened to come along at the same time the Soviets were proceeding with the development of their hydrogen bombs. (Twenty-five years later, as the Soviets were moving rapidly to build up their heavy missile forces, a "New Stockholm Appeal" was unleashed, with a very one-sided view of the arms race.)

During the 1950s, the US government alternated between its own grand gestures toward disarmament and very harsh attacks on private citizens or opposition candidates who offered any serious disarmament proposals. President Eisenhower's "Atoms for Peace" plan of 1953 and "Open Skies" plan of 1955 were notably lacking in feasible provisions for either arms control or Soviet cooperation. In 1957, when Eisenhower's disarmament aide, Harold Stassen, seemed on the threshold of success in negotiating an aerial inspection scheme based on parity, he was publicly humiliated by Secretary of State John Foster Dulles who forced his resignation not long after. Stassen's own seriousness cannot be doubted. Whatever the Secretary's own views on disarmament, Dulles was particularly responsive to Konrad Adenauer's stubborn insistence that all disarmament should be postponed until after German reunification.

Stassen's forced retreat, however, was offset by three other developments during 1957 which pointed toward the end of this somewhat farcical First Nuclear Age:

1. Appeals for the cessation of poisonous nuclear testing, including Adlai Stevenson's 1956 proposal labeled "dangerous" by Eisenhower, led to the convening of the first Pugwash Conference of Soviet and American scientists, thereby beginning an influential if unofficial channel of annual disarmament discussions.

2. Publication of Henry Kissinger's *Nuclear Weapons and Foreign Policy,* commissioned by a study group of the Council on Foreign Relations, stimulated strategic criticism of the Eisenhower Administration's "massive retaliation" doctrine and helped to make "arms control" thinking fashionable.

3. The launching of Sputnik on October 4, 1957, was a shocking introduction to imminent prospects of combining space technology with nuclear weapons. That was at once a stimulus to the missile race, a sobering restraint upon the propagandistic excesses of the disarmament game, and a harbinger of satellites which might make arms control verification feasible at last.

The Second Nuclear Age (1960-74)

The 1960s showed both continuities and discontinuities with the age of monopoly and propaganda. A new sobriety about the arms race and the imminence of parity with the Soviets informed the Kennedy Administration's approach to disarmament. To be sure, there were contradictions between that administration's missile buildup and its establishment of the US Arms Control and Disarmament Agency (ACDA) in 1961, as there were between the general negotiating principles of the McCloy-Zorin Agreement of 1961 and the brandishing of nuclear threats in the Cuban missile crisis of 1962.

As the new ideology of arms control was installed, the very idea of disarmament was subjected to more sophisticated and "scientific" criticism, although the McCloy-Zorin Agreement professed adherence to the eventual goal of "general and complete disarmament" set by the United Nations. These contradictions have never really been resolved. They have, in fact, been perpetuated in the hybrid name of the Arms Control and Disarmament Agency. The Senate-House Conference Report on ACDA's establishment in 1961 rationalized these differences by declaring: "The sequence of the words in the title indicates that arms control is the first step toward the ultimate objectives of disarmament." At this writing, there is some sentiment within the Reagan Administration for dropping the word "disarmament" from that title—if the total abolition of the agency cannot be managed.

To be sure, "arms control" and "disarmament" are often used interchangeably, even in this book. However, polar differences between two contrasting ideologies have persisted since the early 1960s. At the risk of some oversimplification, we may schematize these differences as follows:

Arms Control	Disarmament
1. Continuing strategy of nuclear deterrence.	1. Alternative security policies to deterrence.
2. Parity of strategic weapons, whether at increased or decreased levels.	2. Reduction and elimination of all mass destruction weapons.
3. Rationality in weapons deployment and use.	3. Renunciation of the resort to force.
4. Superpower prerogatives.	4. Rights of all nations and importance of UN.
5. Emphasis on stability.	5. Emphasis on change of institutions and attitudes.

Tilting more toward arms control than to disarmament—and traumatized by the Cuban missile crisis—the superpowers in the 1960s pursued nuclear negotiations on three tracks:

1. There was an effort to halt nuclear testing—which led to the Limited Test Ban of 1963, ending all atmospheric testing for those who signed the treaty.

2. There was an effort to halt the spread of nuclear weapons to other states—which led to the Non-Proliferation Treaty of 1968. To my mind, that is the single most important disarmament agreement yet concluded.

3. There was an effort to wind down the vertical proliferation of nuclear weapons by the superpowers themselves, or at least to slow down its winding up—which led to the SALT (Strategic Arms Limitation) Talks, beginning in November 1969.

It was the apparent progress on these three tracks of nuclear disarmament which promoted a widespread complacency on nuclear issues as we entered the 1970s—that is, this apparent progress plus several other factors:

(a) a political climate of détente;

(b) the assumption that nuclear energy was being safely developed for peaceful purposes;

(c) the assumption that oil would continue to be a cheap and unlimited source of energy;

(d) the assumption that nuclear war itself had become "unthinkable" because of the almost-absolute persuasiveness of the strategic doctrine of "Mutual Assured Destruction"—which produced the wicked acronym MAD and which, essentially, meant that war would be avoided by mutual deterrence;

(e) a negative factor: the absorption of the American public in the Vietnam War from 1965 to 1973, to the neglect of disarmament, development, and almost all other foreign policy issues.

The new nuclear crisis seemed to come upon us all at once about 1974, not that everyone would perceive its many dimensions at the time or even now.

The Third Nuclear Age (1974-   )

Behold how many nuclear happenings simultaneously launched the new nuclear crisis, the Third Nuclear Age!

1. India demonstrated its nuclear-weapon capacity with a test explosion in May 1974, provoking Pakistan and other Asian powers to new nuclear ambitions.

2. Leaked CIA reports of Israeli nuclear weapons were denied

by neither Israel nor the CIA. Taiwan, South Africa, and other countries were soon suspected of possessing, or moving to possess, nuclear weapons. For the first time since 1945, the world could not be sure which nations were nuclear powers.

3. The oil crisis and quadrupling of prices in 1973-74 spurred many countries toward nuclear energy and prompted a fierce new competition among industrialized countries for new nuclear customers. Perhaps as many as 30 countries would be capable of producing nuclear weapons by the 1980s. European nations concluded export deals with nations like Brazil and Pakistan not party to the Non-Proliferation Treaty. A new "London Suppliers' Club" would soon find itself in tension with the NPT and vexed by the fragility of Western consensus.

4. Conventional arms exports to the Middle East were also spurred by the "petro-dollars" generated by the oil crisis. While US policy-makers rationalized that such exports might divert regional temptations to nuclear weapons, the volume of the new arms trade increased regional tensions and (as we shall see in Chapter 4) may have become a powerful new dynamic in the nuclear arms race.

5. The hazards of "peaceful" nuclear energy were increasingly dramatized in the mid-1970s: nuclear accidents such as commercial passenger flights caught with insecure packages of plutonium; resignations of security officials who charged the government with lax nuclear safety standards and deceitful information policies; government shutdowns of nuclear power plants because of defective cooling systems; protests by scientists and action groups against further nuclear development. It was in that same pivotal year of 1974 — a year almost totally absorbed in Watergate — that the Atomic Energy Commission was abolished and replaced by two separate agencies at last: one for nuclear development and one for nuclear regulation. And all this happened years before Three Mile Island.

6. It was in 1974 that Congress held hearings on US forces in Europe, partly because of increasing costs of maintaining 200,000 troops and the thousands of weapons, leading to an aggravation of balance of payments problems, and partly because the US was engaged in Mutual and Balanced Force Reduction (MBFR) Talks with the Russians in Vienna. But there was an unexpected sensation. At the very time that Greece, Turkey, Italy, Spain, and Portugal were simultaneously experiencing serious political unruliness on NATO's "southern flank," it was also revealed that the US had 7,000 loosely guarded tactical nuclear weapons in Europe, many in

those most unstable countries. Some defense analysts testified that this wide deployment of nuclear shells, mines, and bombs was of no real military value to the US but that its inadequate protective systems made it the greatest single threat to US security.

7. The spectre of nuclear terrorism by revolutionary or criminal groups or college sophomores first emerged critically in 1974-75 and was put on the UN agenda where it has yet to be decisively confronted. This new threat of theft, leading either to blackmail or detonation, of tactical nuclear weapons or fissionable materials intended for "peaceful uses" was underscored by revelations that not all nuclear materials supposed to be in US inventories could be accounted for. A new unknown factor was the question as to what groups may have already acquired nuclear devices for terrorist purposes.

8. About the same time, studies by ACDA indicated that the consequences of nuclear war might include not only blast and radiation but also a critical depletion of the ozone layer which serves to protect human life from the sun's lethal ultraviolet rays.

9. In 1974 Secretary of Defense James Schlesinger gave fresh impetus to the revival of counterforce doctrines which Robert McNamara had discarded a decade before but which would now rationalize all the new strategic technologies of the 1970s: Trident missiles and submarines, cruise missiles, Mark 12-A warheads, MX, and the move from MIRVs to MARVs (from "multiple independently-targeted re-entry vehicles" to "maneuverable re-entry vehicles"). Critics charged that the new-old doctrines would make nuclear war much more likely; others, including European allies and the Soviet Union, were troubled by a new uncertainty as to what the actual shape of US security policy had become and even by a new suspicion of uncertainty within the US policy establishment itself—perhaps affected by Watergate.

10. It was discovered by the mid-1970s that there had actually been more nuclear tests since the 1963 Test Ban Treaty than before it, albeit mostly underground tests, and that thousands of additional nuclear warheads were being added to both US and Soviet missiles while the SALT talks were being conducted in the name of détente. In fact, the SALT talks were licensing further escalation. Even the Vladivostok accords of 1974 between Ford and Brezhnev which, with some cutbacks and infinite refinements were to become the basis of SALT II, would not have prevented further escalation.

11. The new multilateral forums of the 1970s—the Non-Proliferation Treaty Review Conferences of 1975 and 1980 and the

UN Special Session on Disarmament in 1978 — proved essentially impotent to halt the nuclear arms race. They did provide valuable summits for surveying the new nuclear crisis in its totality. They assembled some new disarmament machinery and launched innumerable research projects. But faced with the new realities of global bargaining, they resulted in diplomatic stalemates between the nuclear and non-nuclear states. Both vertical and horizontal proliferation were increasingly out of control.

12. And finally, by the late 1970s, the continent of Europe — that one place in the world where détente and peaceful coexistence had recorded dramatic achievements only a few years before — Europe was now caught up in a brand new regional arms race over the "modernizing" of theater nuclear weapons. On the Soviet side: Backfire bombers and SS-20 mobile missiles (missiles with multiple warheads which are tripling the total of Soviet warheads in some locations in Central Europe). On the NATO side: new ground-launched cruise missiles (GLCMs) and Pershing II missiles capable of directly attacking Soviet territory from close range, just a few minutes away, for the first time.

Taking stock of all these happenings we may, in bewilderment, simply ask: why? What has been let loose in this world to cause such an array of difficulties in just one policy area, nuclear policy? How can anyone understand all this, much less control it?

The nuclear arms race is, indeed, out of control. The new nuclear crisis is, moreover, much more than a matter of defense and disarmament — if it bears any relationship to defense at all in a defenseless world. It involves basic issues of energy, economics, environment, health, international trade, international law enforcement — not to mention psychology, philosophy, ethics, or theology. It is a cross-disciplinary crisis intellectually and morally. It cuts across all the existing bureaucratic and legislative structures of US government. It raises an ultimately sobering question: can any coherent nuclear policy be developed which can cope with these many pressures, all of which are connected with each other?

The greatest disaster of 1974 was not Watergate and the resignation of a disgraced president. It was the coverup of the new nuclear crisis. It was a coverup for which many governmental and non-governmental persons must share the blame. Some knew better but did not speak. Some knew something about one or another of these problems and made some noise about it. Some kept reading and hearing about one or another of these problems but did nothing. Millions of otherwise literate and even very professional people seemed to know nothing at all about it. But almost nobody was prepared to tell the whole story: a Third Nuclear Age had arrived. In retrospect, it seems like the Third Coming in Wrath.

The rest of this book tries to tell that story in terms of the ideas and institutions which are making theologians of us all. It aims at a point where hope will overcome despair.

CHAPTER 2

Nuclear Dogmatics I: Deterrence

*Science has torn from nature a secret so vast in its poten-
tialities that our minds cower from the terror it creates.
Yet terror is not enough to inhibit the use of the atomic
bomb. The terror created by weapons has never stopped
man from employing them.* — Bernard Baruch, Address
to UN Atomic Energy Commission, June 14, 1946

Military historian Walter Millis once observed that every
generation's theories of warfare have tended to make "amazing accommodations to mythologies appropriate to the time." Present
obsessions with "proper doctrine" (a favorite term of Henry Kissinger's) largely involve "the ingenious updating of ancient myths,
incantations, and propitiatory objects that have their roots in
prehistoric time." Millis noted that even the names of nuclear
missiles (Thor, Atlas, Nike-Hercules — to which we must add
Poseidon and Trident) suggest "an almost conscious recognition of
the mythical cast of war, and seem to carry a hint of invocation to
power far beyond that contained in the instruments themselves."
He added that "the computer-endorsed" scientific and
psychological myths associated with nuclear deterrence are this
generation's doctrinal patina covering the underlying primitivism
of its conceptions of power.[1]

When doctrines tend to subjugate wisdom to primitive
mythology and subsume peace and security under a perpetual reign
of absolute terror, we may well call them dogmas in the most pejor-
ative sense. The quest for disarmament inescapably requires the
hard mental toil of demystifying and demythologizing the military
dogmas sanctified by this generation's unrelenting fear of eternity.
The dismantling of mistaken ideas is a prerequisite to the dismantling of weapons systems.

The dominant doctrines about security and disarmament in the
United States are largely the product of think tanks: research
centers in the gray areas between universities and the military
establishment, often managed by corporations, peopled primarily
by civilians. The most influential strategic thinkers of the US since

1945 have not been military officers: they have been civilian scientists and social scientists like Bernard Brodie, Edward Teller, Albert Wohlstetter, Henry Kissinger, Herman Kahn, Thomas Schelling, Robert McNamara, Alain Enthoven, James Schlesinger. That fact should temper our disposition to view the armed services themselves as the prime formulators of national security policy.

Serious proposals for nuclear disarmament can hardly win their way in a strategic vacuum. They must confront established ideas of national security and set forth better ideas of national security. Disarmament requires as much strategic wisdom as any military doctrine — and probably more. It is precisely the downgrading of disarmament to the more security-conscious jargon of arms control, itself reduced to a minor sub-category of nuclear deterrence, which has cut the nerve of real progress toward disarmament and security. This chapter and the next explore some of the implications for disarmament of strategic military doctrines.

The moment has come not only to subject counterforce ideas and weapons to critical resistance but to look more deeply into the most basic premises underlying all nuclear weapons and to expose their unwisdom. That means a fresh and comprehensive critique of the dominant strategic idea of the post-World War II decades: nuclear deterrence.

In its most elemental sense, deterrence is prevention. It is not, however, prevention by the actual exercise of force. It is rooted in the common and legitimate human experience of fear in the face of serious dangers. When those dangers are so serious that they discourage a contemplated course of action, deterrence has occurred.

Deterrence is the manipulation of fear. It is the deliberate promotion of fear as a weapon of dissuasion.

Indeed, to know when fear is appropriate is to begin to be wise. At many levels of life, deterrence and prudence are intimately connected.

However, in nonmilitary realms like parenting, bureaucratic management, and law enforcement, the question must forever be pressed as to whether the manipulation of fear is an adequate or always appropriate policy. Personality disorders, bureaucratic inefficiency, and criminal pathology all disclose the limits and even the counterproductivity of policies which are preoccupied with threats and shows of force. Most psychologists and political philosophers would agree that coercion has its limits in every society. Deterrence is a form of coercion which intends to avoid the application of force by threatening to apply it.

Given the universality of deterrence in this elemental sense, there is an ancient history of military deterrence. Thucydides and Machiavelli were much attracted by the virtues of showing force without having to inflict it. Such a strategy presupposed a capacity for rationality which has always been central to deterrence theories: adversaries, when reflecting upon the costs or risks of attack, would calculate that the benefits would not be worth the total consequences of the attack. The balance of power diplomacy of the 19th century was predicated on the doctrine that shifting combinations of military powers could dissuade any single power from launching a major war. There are striking affinities between nuclear deterrence based on "mutual terror" and European diplomacy of 100 or 150 years ago.

There is even a modern but pre-nuclear literature on deterrence which reflected the new technologies of total war, especially air attacks with blockbusters and incendiaries. It was when the capabilities of offensive weapons to overwhelm any conceivable defense became apparent that strategic thinking moved to a new frontier: the manipulation of terror. For it then became possible to threaten suffering and devastation on a vast scale without having to defeat ground or naval forces.[2]

It is this continuing advantage of offense over defense — in fact, the relegation of defense to irrelevance in strategic conflict — that has been the dominant fact of military technology in the nuclear age. Strategies of nuclear deterrence, whatever their variations, exploit fear of retaliation by weapons of mass destruction against which there can be no secure defense. Deterrence has thus become the manipulation of absolute terror.

Strategic Doctrines and Empirical Reality

Before looking at the origins and limits of nuclear deterrence doctrines we may well raise several problematical questions about the influence of strategic ideas on political action.

It is far from clear that strategic ideas themselves produce new nuclear weapons. The history of weapons development in the US suggests an opposite pattern: technical innovation tends to precede any meaningful strategic purpose. The ideas then are invoked or concocted to rationalize new weapons systems. That has been the case with ABMs, MIRVs, and cruise missiles — three of the most destabilizing innovations in the arms race, all "weapons systems in search of a mission" and rationalized in the most inconsistent and ground-shifting fashion.

A second disturbing question — a question that vexes our European allies as well as our adversaries — is whether there is clarity or confusion at the highest levels of US policy-making. All through the 1970s, in both Republican and Democratic administrations, the nuclear doctrines of the US government seemed to slip and slide between deterrence and counterforce, between parity and superiority, between détente and "nuclear war fighting." Both formal policy pronouncements and responses to inquiries produced disconcerting intimations of incoherent ideas in the heads of presidents, secretaries of state and defense, and ranking military chiefs. In an extraordinarily candid public revelation, President Carter's Soviet affairs adviser Marshall Shulman told the Arms Control Association in December 1979 that US defense policy had become increasingly irrational and that the basic problem was lack of coherent political leadership "at the top" — a statement which marked the increasing separation of Carter from his chief Soviet and arms control experts, as well as Shulman's fall from grace.

A third question is closely connected with the second: whether there is any basic correlation between strategic doctrines and the actual deployment of US military forces. Such a correlation is gravely doubted by Benjamin S. Lambeth of the RAND Corporation who reports that each new administration "dismantles the conceptual architecture" of its predecessors as a kind of political ritual. In the untidy scramble over budgetary politics and contradictory claims as to cost-effectiveness of weapons systems, there results a "virtual flea market of conflicting influences and pressures that affect American defense decision-making." Lambeth concludes lugubriously: "It is not unreasonable to ask whether the United States has even *had* a strategic doctrine worthy of the name in recent memory."[3] At least, we must recognize that there has been a recurring gap between the *declaratory policy* of governmental pronouncements and the *operational policies* of strategic targeting and weapons deployments.

Of course, a demand for coherent strategic doctrine can lead to escalation of the arms race as well as to reversing it. What the above observations remind us, however, is that there is no clinical, super-political bureau in which pure doctrine rules in splendid rationality. That reminder should guard us against the confident claims of nuclear deterrence theorists concerning the rationality of US and Soviet policy-makers — a topic to which we shall return below.

The Origins of Nuclear Deterrence

The ultimate meaning of "total war," a term much used during World War II, was not revealed until the A-bombing of Hiroshima and Nagasaki. When the world saw at last that one weapon could destroy a whole metropolis — and then foresaw that a few weapons could obliterate a whole nation and a finite number of weapons could annihilate the human species — total terror offered new possibilities for strategic military doctrine.

In the first atomic year of 1945, Bernard Brodie wrote the intellectual charter for nuclear deterrence:

> The first and most vital step in any American security program for the age of atomic bombs is to take measures to guarantee to ourselves in case of attack the possibility of retaliation in kind. . . . Thus far the direct purpose of our military establishment has been to win wars. From now on its chief purpose must be to avert them. It can have almost no other useful purpose.[4]

This transmutation of military force from winning wars to preventing wars has always been the most attractive moral feature of deterrence doctrine. The threat and scope of retaliation have been the most abhorrent features.

Several developments — political, military, and technological — in the late 1940s and early 1950s moved deterrence toward official promulgation and codification.

The emergence of the Cold War, a foreign policy of containment, and the creation of new national security bureaucracies (all in 1947) provided powerful stimuli to strategic brainstorming.

The frustrations of an indecisive Korean War, fought for limited objectives with conventional weapons but at great cost, prompted a resolve to be more punitive in future encounters with Communist forces.

But it was the technology of nuclear fusion (hydrogen bombs) after 1950 — a quantum leap beyond fission's "usable" atom bombs — which actuated the full totalitarian potential of deterrent threats.

The harsh pronouncements of nuclear deterrence by the early Eisenhower administration had three special roots:

1. Secretary of State John Foster Dulles, in his ideological and moralistic zeal, gave deterrence a punitive ferocity. On January 12, 1954, Dulles spoke of "massive retaliatory power" as "a great capacity to retaliate, instantly, by means and at places of our own choosing." That language, unfortunately, presupposed a nuclear

monopoly which no longer existed — and reflected a chronic habit of underestimating Soviet technology which would not be broken until Sputnik more than three years later.

2. Behind the rhetoric of Dulles was a rather unsubtle, hardline Joint Chiefs of Staff, headed by Admiral Arthur Radford who shared the Soviet-baiting-and-underestimating disposition of Dulles.

3. President Eisenhower himself, abetted by Secretary of Defense ("Bigger Bang for a Buck") Charles Wilson, viewed massive retaliation as a strategic posture which could realize big budgetary savings in conventional forces. Thus the initial tendency, shared across the top of that administration, to view nuclear threats as adequate to cope with any Soviet challenge, nuclear or conventional.

These distinctive features of deterrence-as-massive-retaliation provoked a legion of nuclear strategists in the mid-1950s to articulate more moderate and nuanced doctrines of deterrence, emphasizing *flexibility* and *survivability*. The concern for flexibility stressed a revitalized Army and "proportional" and "graduated" responses to Soviet forces. (The Air Force had been more enamored of its "superiority" and therefore of "absolutist" notions of deterrence.) The concern for survivability harked back to Brodie's 1945 anticipation of the need for a safe and secure retaliatory force. It was Herman Kahn who anointed such a force a "second strike capability."

These moderated and nuanced doctrines would carry over into the early 1960s and receive their most official articulation in the tenure of Robert McNamara as Secretary of Defense in the Kennedy Administration. But there was another momentous development in military technology which really set the stage for the super-sophistication of the McNamara period: the space race, inaugurated by Sputnik in 1957. Missile technology promised greater range, swifter weapons, reduced warning-time from hours to minutes, and the probable nullification of defensive weapons altogether.

Now deterrence re-emerged with a new sense of bi-polarity and mutuality. In fact, there was apprehension that the US assumption of strategic superiority had yielded to vulnerability to a preemptive Soviet "first strike." While research and development on both Minuteman ICBMs and Polaris submarine-missiles had started in the 1950s, it was Polaris that dramatically symbolized the new technology of invulnerability and survivability in the 1960s. Both programs were greatly spurred by the Kennedy campaign assumption of a "missile gap." (The fact that such a "gap" could not be found by the new administration hardly inhibited production and deployment.)

For McNamara, *survivability* was thus reaffirmed as the essence of deterrence—that is, the survivability of missiles in their Polaris launchers and their hardened ICBM silos. Strategic stability meant according the Soviets a legitimate, survivable "second strike" capability of their own—a good thing, it was felt, since it might reduce any anxious Soviet tendencies toward a preemptive "first strike." By 1966 or 1967, the USSR did acquire a second-strike capability.

Thus the age of "mutual deterrence" had arrived—that age foreseen in 1955 by Winston Churchill when, by a "process of sublime irony, safety will be the sturdy child of terror, and survival the twin brother of annihilation." McNamara's prescription of secure retaliatory forces on both sides became known as "Mutual Assured Destruction" (MAD).

While McNamara had briefly courted the notion of "counterforce" nuclear weapons—weapons aimed at military targets with minimal civilian casualties—he soon abandoned that notion as a strategic illusion. The destruction of cities and the annihilation of millions would be inevitable in a nuclear war. McNamara quantified the US "second strike" capability as inflicting "unacceptable levels of damage" on the USSR: a minimal destruction of 50 percent of Soviet industrial capacity and killing of 25 percent of Soviet population (more than 50 million deaths).

In the post-McNamara years, MAD continued to be the dominant notion of nuclear deterrence. Arms controllers throughout the 1970s tended to hold fast to MAD, even while confronting a revival of counterforce advocates. The latter became ascendant in the last two years of the Carter Administration and, in an even more assertive style reminiscent of Dulles and Radford, in the Reagan Administration. The troubled relationship between deterrence and counterforce doctrines will be explored in the next chapter.

A Critique of Nuclear Deterrence

The critique of deterrence is not exclusively a matter of external assault upon its defenders. Among the most persuasive objections to deterrence ideas are those pressed by its advocates upon one another. My own awareness of this intramural criticism has been especially helped by the late Bernard Brodie's profoundly thoughtful book, *War and Politics,* and by the papers on "The Future of Strategic Deterrence" for the 1979 annual conference of the International Institute for Strategic Studies (London). The Institute itself (to which I have belonged since 1965) originated in a circle of strategic critics of the doctrine of massive retaliation. There are many signs of moral sensitivity and political wisdom among some deterrence advocates. Such signs include the following:

(a) Insistence on preventing war because nuclear war would be intolerable;

(b) Concern to avoid provocative and destablizing new nuclear weapons systems;

(c) Resistance to such strategic temptations as "counterforce," "first strike," "nuclear superiority," and "war-winning;"

(d) Steadfast support for arms limitations;

(e) Conviction that, while the threat to use nuclear weapons may be profoundly evil, their actual use would be intolerable;

(f) Acute sensitivity to legitimate Soviet security needs and therefore to the need for strategic stability;

(g) Emphasis on the enhancement of rationality in decision-making and in communications with adversaries;

(h) Acceptance of the irreversibility of nuclear know-how and the probable persistence of some nuclear threats;

(i) Realism about the extremities of human aggressiveness and brutality in much international conflict and therefore a moral seriousness about security needs.

It is because of such positive moral and political qualities that some deterrence advocates should be cordially regarded as coalition allies of disarmament groups on many issues. Many of the liabilities of deterrence theory in its grossest forms cannot fairly be attributed to everyone who advocates some limited and provisional role for nuclear weapons.

Nevertheless, what deterrence dogmatists have done is to legitimate an unending dependence upon nuclear weapons and to frustrate the development of wiser and more humane security policies for the United States and the world. Both the dogmas and the legitimacy of nuclear weapons must therefore be called into question in the most thorough possible analysis.

I profoundly believe that the refutation and displacement of deterrence as our prime national security doctrine are necessary for the following twenty-one reasons:

1. *There is no single body of coherent deterrence doctrine.*

Proponents of deterrence hardly constitute a monolithic or agreeable company. Beyond their common acceptance of some nuclear weapons as a component of national security, they think and act in the most various and contrary ways.

Some *deterrence minimalists* favor drastic nuclear reductions to a level of a few hundred or a few dozen strategic weapons, believing that numbers hardly matter. They can point to China as a country with only a few hundred warheads that has renounced "first use" altogether, that de-emphasizes the decisiveness of nuclear weapons in war, and that seems effectively to have deterred both US and USSR.

Others we may call *deterrence centrists:* devotees of parity between the superpowers, which means more or less keeping up with the Russians — but settling for "nuclear sufficiency" or "essential equivalence" where numbers do not exactly match, and supporting strategic arms limitation.

Still others are *deterrence maximalists,* pushing for new counterforce weapons which would reclaim strategic superiority or a "margin of safety" for the US and force the Soviets to negotiate on American terms. Most of the criticisms which follow apply more to deterrence centrists and maximalists than to minimalists.

Some proponents emphasize the importance of absolutely certain retaliation to make deterrence credible: clear evidence of will and intention are said to be indispensable. Robert McNamara as Secretary of Defense insisted that the will to use "our assured-destruction capability" must be "unwavering."[5] Thomas Schelling's *Strategy of Conflict* (1960) suggested that saying "we may or may not retaliate, but even we don't know for sure" may actually be more credible than threatening a certain and total assault.[6] Oxford's Michael Howard has set forth "Healey's Theorem" (named for former UK Defense Minister Denis Healey): "If there is one chance in a hundred of nuclear weapons being used, the odds would be enough to deter an aggressor even if they were not enough to reassure an ally."[7]

Some proponents are in the forefront of disarmament movements; others have vigorously opposed SALT II and a Comprehensive Test Ban as treasonous appeasement of the Soviets. Some, like Robert McNamara and Herman Kahn, have advocated large-scale civil defense programs as essential to deterrence; others, like Thomas Schelling, have argued that civil defense would increase the expectations and the risk of war. Some, like Bernard Brodie, have claimed that nuclear weapons make large-scale conventional forces obsolete; others, like Maxwell Taylor, have argued that excessive reliance on nuclear retaliation has made the US vulnerable to limited wars without adequate conventional forces for either deterrence or defense.

2. *Deterrence is an idea peculiarly open to speculative license and promiscuous rationalizations.*

As a seductive pseudo-science, deterrence theory has provided a gold mine for hundreds of professional careers and an infinite arsenal for foreign policy rhetoric. If the theoretical variations and mathematical games are limitless, so are the policy rationalizations.

In a recent book reminiscent of David Halberstam's *The Best and the Brightest,* which lamented the misapplied brilliance of Kennedy-era leaders in Vietnam policy, James Fallows observes:

> The 'best' minds of the defense community have been drawn toward nuclear analysis, but so were the best minds to be found in the monastery, arguing the Albigensian heresy, in the fourteenth century. A novel theory about how the Kremlin might respond to nuclear strikes may be advanced, may make the author's name, and may lead to billions in expenditures without entering any further into the domain of fact than did the monks' speculations about the nature of God.[8]

While that quotation may reinforce prejudices against theological meddling in military topics, it also rightly challenges the intellectual credibility of deterrence strategists. Indeed, the epithet "nuclear theologians" most commonly refers not to seminary professors who dabble in strategic issues but to professional military or arms control theorists whose ideas are repudiated by other theorists whose ideas may be just as ill-founded, if not more so.

Lawrence Freedman, director of policy studies at London's Royal Institute of International Affairs, has called deterrence "a gift to strategists in that its nature and workings remain so elusive and so imperfectly understood as to permit endless speculation with little danger of empirical refutation, and justifying the maintenance of almost any military capability on the grounds that it might be doing good and we could well be worse off without it."[9]

In the past five years, a particularly licentious variation of deterrence has been increasingly invoked to justify new nuclear weapons systems: we may well call it the *dogma of promiscuous perception.* A leading proponent has been Paul Nitze: Pentagon and State Department veteran, ringleader of the anti-SALT Committee on the Present Danger, now Reagan negotiator on European nuclear forces. This view holds that more nuclear forces are needed to offset the "perception" of US military weakness—whatever the actual strategic balance may be. If the United States is perceived by the Russians to be weak, so the argument goes, this country becomes vulnerable to intimidation. If allies perceive the US to be weak, they will become more vulnerable to Soviet intimidation or seduction. So new missile systems, which may not be objectively required, are said to be subjectively necessary. This argument from perception increasingly won over Secretary of Defense Harold Brown in the last two years of the Carter Administration—and captivated the White House as well.

It is not only the licentiousness of the perception dogma that must be exposed: it is the source of the very idea of US military inferiority. Who has done the most to promote the perception of US weakness? The very same persons who have promoted the dogma itself. In proclaiming the military inferiority of the US, they have relentlessly undermined the confidence of the American public and its allies in the US armed forces and have risked serious Soviet miscalculations. Thus they have largely manufactured the crisis which they propose to overcome by the senseless multiplication of nuclear weapons. As Richard Barnet has written: "Once the purpose of military spending is to create 'perception,' and weapons are procured primarily as symbols, there is never enough."[10]

Deterrence, in practice, thus reveals the same traits as those still-hallowed doctrines of "national interest" and "national security": little if any clear and meaningful content and much vulnerability to manipulation from almost any policy perspective.

3. *Deterrence claims of beneficent historical influence cannot be substantiated.*

The most confident assertions have been advanced to the effect that it is deterrence which has prevented nuclear war for the past thirty-five years. But such assertions could well be prime examples of the logical fallacy *post hoc ergo propter hoc:* the unwarranted assumption that a happening was caused by a prior happening—or, in this case, that a non-happening was caused by a prior happening. A variety of historical hypotheses could be offered as reasons why nuclear war has not happened since Hiroshima and Nagasaki: a disinclination to fight any major war after the suffering and devastation of World War II, economic constraints, overextended military forces, deep-seated feelings of insecurity and inferiority, ideological revulsion, respect for world opinion. We do not have easy access to the motives and calculations of

US policy-makers, much less of those in the Kremlin.

If the mere existence of nuclear weapons presumably has had some inhibiting effect, we can hardly know just what that effect has been—much less if it was caused by rational calculations of strategic balances or imbalances. Memoirs of the Cuban missile crisis of 1962 reveal that some US policy-makers had high expectations of nuclear hostilities, yet were not inhibited from supporting military action or nuclear threats directed at the Soviet Union.

Laurence Martin, a nuclear strategist now serving as vice-chancellor of the University of Newcastle-upon-Tyne, highlights this uncertain and controvertible reading of nuclear history in this acknowledgment: "Least of all do we understand—indeed, in principle we cannot—whether or why past strategies of deterrence have been successful."[11]

And we must say that, even if deterrence could be shown to have a pacifying effect in the past, there is no proof it will do so in the future. In fact, certain historical trends like nuclear proliferation may simply make deterrence obsolete at best. At worst, one might well conclude that the historical influence of deterrence strategies has been to magnify the probabilities of nuclear war in the future.

4. *Deterrence dogmas reflect American cultural excesses tending to political absolutism and doctrinal messianism.*

It was at a US government briefing prior to the 1978 UN Special Session on Disarmament that the counselor to the Arms Control and Disarmament Agency, Adam Yarmolinsky, described deterrence in the idolatrous terms it has too long enjoyed: "Nuclear deterrence is the absolute bedrock of national and international security."

"Absolute bedrock"—those words indeed reveal the absolutist categories which have too typically characterized American messianism when projected onto the whole world. The fact that Yarmolinsky was a strong advocate of arms control hardly diminishes the force of his statement to a gathering of nongovernmental leaders largely committed to nuclear disarmament. After all, "disarmament" could not really be expected to get rid of nuclear weapons!

While some dependence on nuclear weapons is hardly an American monopoly, the distinctively American brands of deterrence and arms control theory enjoy much less than universal enthusiasm, even among close allies. Soviet Foreign Minister Gromyko knew how to provoke chuckles all around when he chided Vice President Mondale (President Carter's stand-in) for his inability to pronounce the word "disarmament" and his addiction to "arms control" at the 1978 UN Special Session on Disarmament. It is precisely this mean subservience of "arms control" to deterrence which severely inhibits US ability to communicate with the outside world on the issues of disarmament.

Curt Gasteyger of Geneva's Graduate Institute of International Studies traces the main characteristics of American-style deterrence to the early postwar years when military superiority seemed assured, yet when the US posture was one of total confrontation with Soviet power, permitting no dialogue and no serious thoughts of disarmament. Thus did historic circumstances reinforce the "doctrinal messianism" of deterrence which "originated and developed in a hostile world that left little, if any, room for accommodation."[12]

Gasteyger also notes that even the more moderated notions of "mutual deterrence" which emerged after 1960 were essentially American projections not really shared by the Soviet Union, whose sense of "mutuality" was at any rate impaired by its confrontations with China. The point is not that the USSR is uninhibited by nuclear weapons: it is that the elaborate doctrinal edifice of "mutual deterrence" may not satisfy other countries where they really live. Gasteyger suggests that the American concept of nuclear deterrence may be nothing more than a *chimera:* a mythical fire-breathing monster not dwelling anywhere in historical reality.

5. *Deterrence dogmas reinforce the isolationist and reactive traits of US diplomatic behavior.*

In their massive study, *Deterrence in American Foreign Policy* (1974), Alexander George and Richard Smoke expressed the hope and the expectation that deterrence would play a much less dominant role in US diplomacy. If their expectation may have been premature, their hope was well founded — given a government still burdened by isolationist habits of thought and conduct. George and Smoke lament the fact that the United States has lacked,

> except in the vaguest terms, any vision of how it wishes world politics to develop over the long run. The result is the widely observed 'reactive' character of US foreign policy, a tendency to do little until a challenge to the status quo arises, and then to deal with it as a threat. Deterrence is an influence policy peculiarly appropriate to these attitudes.[13]

That historical assessment is shared abroad by Laurence Martin, who faults American-style deterrence for its neglect of conventional and essentially political threats to security: "Perhaps the fact that speculation about nuclear strategy began in a country that had only a few years previously pursued an isolationist foreign policy helped to foster this neglect."[14]

Here, too, the objection is not necessarily to nuclear weapons as such: it is to the blinders and distorted perceptions which dogmatic deterrence brings to international politics. A deficiency of historical awareness combines with a poverty of vision to fixate most deterrence theorists on immediate notions of threats as discrete events, stripped of their cultural and political texture. Here, too, like too many narrow calculators of national interest, deterrence apologists chronically covet short-term victories at the expense of long-term disasters. That, we must remember, is precisely how the Nuclear Age began.

Thirty-seven years after Hiroshima, we may well assess the first A-bomb decision not simply in the context of bringing World War II to an end, but in the longer historical view of political and technological consequences. As nuclear perils multiply rapidly all around us, who would now make the same decision if the realities of the 1980s could have been anticipated in 1945? In fact, some scientists did have such historical imagination in 1945. An official Committee on Social and Political Implications, chaired by Nobel Prize chemist James Franck, submitted its report to Secretary of War Stimson on June 11, 1945, declaring:

> The use of nuclear bombs for an early unannounced attack against Japan is inadvisable. If the US were to be the first to release this new means of indiscriminate destruction upon mankind, she would sacrifice public support throughout the world, precipitate the race for armaments, and prejudice the possibility of reaching an international agreement on the future control of such weapons.[15]

But these realistic visionaries were overridden by more immediate (and ill-founded) calculations of military necessity. Yet they foresaw with remarkable clarity what the postwar world would be like if the bombs were dropped.

We can neither undo nuclear history nor forget nuclear technology. We can begin to think with greater wisdom and imagination about the mushroom-clouded future of the whole human family.

6. *Deterrence dogmas have been preoccupied with technical fixes on primarily political problems.*

The messianism and isolationism which have debased strategic nuclear thought have been alloyed with other vitiating tendencies in some think tanks. What Henry Kissinger long ago called "the flight into technology" has been characteristic of most deterrence theorists.

Strategy is properly a political discipline: a study of ways of influencing the behavior of other states or peoples. Yet most deterrence advocates have either shunned or slighted political analysis, preferring the abstractions of mathematical models and psychological games.

Bernard Brodie, himself a seminal deterrence strategist long immersed in the think-tank ethos, testified that the most prominent systems analysts had been richly trained in highly theoretical economics. What they brought to deterrence studies, however, was an insensitivity to and an intolerance of "political considerations that get in the way" of their theory and calculations. They were conspicuously weak in diplomatic and military history as well as contemporary politics. Brodie was straightforward in naming Alain Enthoven, Malcolm Hoag, Henry Rowen, and Albert Wohlstetter as examples of these liabilities.

The most thorough and most persuasive intellectual attack on deterrence theorists' flight into technology is political scientist Philip Green's *Deadly Logic: The Theory of Nuclear Deterrence,* first appearing in 1966. Green meticulously takes apart the "pseudo-sciences" of systems analysis and game theory, concluding his weighty volume with the judgment that such deterrence studies constitute "a disservice not only to the scholarly community but ultimately to the democratic political process as well."[16] The scrupulousness of Green's attack does not inhibit him from using terms like "intellectual bankruptcy," "intellectual imperialism," and "pseudo-quantification" to characterize the state of deterrence theory. Altogether, *Deadly Logic* is a searing disclosure of the moral and methodological faults of the think-tank sub-culture.

7. *Deterrence dogmas have been obsessed with militaristic escapes from political responsibility.*

We have earlier noted that the dominant strategic conceptualizers have been civilians, not military men. Bernard Brodie observed that the military do not put much premium on intellectual excellence: that their whole training is "toward a set of values that finds in battle and in victory a vindication" and that exalts loyalty, not a capacity to criticize dogmas as outdated nor a capacity to reflect on ultimate purposes; that the resort to force and a primitive view of adversaries tend to dominate military circles; and that most senior officers have experienced decades of isolation from civilian politics.[17]

In the very last paragraph of *War and Politics,* Brodie pointed to the frustrations of military officers over constraints on the use of nuclear weapons and particularly over "the fact that some people are trying to defuse them." While younger officers may have a somewhat better understanding of world affairs, Brodie concluded that firm civilian control over the military is as imperative as ever, especially in nuclear affairs.[18] Earlier, he had written that "the professional military officer knows no more than the rest of us about the strategy of thermonuclear war, and he and all of us should be clear that he does not."[19]

Yet civilian control over the military is no guarantee of political wisdom, as we have seen. In fact, it is precisely the alliance between technical and military elites which tends to put deterrence dogmas beyond the effective reach of public criticism. The public is manipulated by the rituals of anti-Communist rhetoric, the mystique of toughness, and the obsession with force which reinforce the idolatry of deterrence. In this domestic crucible of the unending Cold War, military options persistently crowd out diplomatic responses to international conflict.

8. *Deterrence dogmas tend to oversimplify Soviet motives.*

Fixations on technical and military options block out perceptions of the human reality of adversaries. This block-out makes it almost impossible to imagine that the Soviets could be constrained by bitter memories of twenty million deaths, pulverized cities, and scorched earth in World War II. Or that Soviet technocrats could devoutly wish to be relieved of the pressures of the arms race so that the chronic shortcomings of their industrial, agricultural, and consumer goods sectors could have a better chance of being overcome. Or that Soviet strategists could be plagued with nightmares over the logistical problems of sustaining secure supply lines and political compliance through unruly satellite areas, should they be even tempted to contemplate an assault on Western Europe. Or that the Politburo itself could seriously wonder how it could ever manage a productive and pacific occupation of Western Europe and North America. Or even that Soviet leaders might have some moral scruples against killing tens of millions of Americans.

George Kennan and other Kremlinologists have repeatedly

highlighted the essential conservatism and caution of the Brezhnev coalition, notwithstanding Soviet willingness to exploit targets of opportunity in areas peripheral to their basic security interests.

With regard to both the European theater and the intercontinental arms race, however, deterrence theorists have been obsessed with the most preposterous scenarios instead of the most probable ones.

Bernard Brodie castigated the civilian systems analysts of the McNamara period for their absorption in such fantasies as the "Hamburg grab"—a presumed Soviet strike with massive conventional forces which would suddenly surround this great city only thirty miles from the East German border and then virtually dare NATO to start a nuclear holocaust in reply. Brodie reported that this scenario kept popping up, not because any serious Kremlinologist ever "presumed to detect in the Soviet eye a special hankering" for Hamburg but because the tactic imagined "seemed to provide a perfect example" of a purely theoretical contingency that "needed to be guarded against."[20]

The Cuban missile crisis in that same period generated an unprecedented discussion of Soviet motivations in the crucible of immediate nuclear terror. What especially bothered Brodie was that the Joint Chiefs of Staff kept pressing for military force as "the only thing the Soviets understand"—a familiar and enduring crudity which keeps frustrating thoughtful policy analysis. This JCS posture, Brodie wrote, reflected

> a primitive outlook upon our opponent, who naturally respects us for our power just as we respect him for his power. But that is not the same thing as saying that the *application* of force is the only thing he will understand. It is hard to think of any generalization of comparable breadth that would not apply equally to the US as to the Soviet Union, which, obviously, is not to deny that the two countries are very dissimilar in several important political and sociological respects.[21]

To brutalize completely the image of enemies by claiming that force is the only thing they understand—and to attribute to enemies the extreme irrationality of unrelenting aggressiveness—is to contradict one of the other major tenets of deterrence: confidence in the rationality of the adversary. Neither assumption is well-grounded in human psychology or history.

The 1980s dawned with two particularly pernicious dogmas rationalizing new classes of nuclear weapons in terms of the most unlikely Soviet behavior: "ICBM vulnerability" to a Soviet first strike and the "theater nuclear imbalance" in Europe. Nothing is more dangerous in these scenarios than the possibility that new US weapons deployments could enhance prospects for a self-fulfilling prophecy: the most alarmist hawks in the Soviet system may now be bolstered in a post-Brezhnev era when arms control is discredited and preemptive strikes become more serious temptations. These promiscuous extensions of deterrence will be further discussed below. They are so ominous that they deserve extended review.

9. *Deterrence dogmas provide no guidelines for the actual conduct of war.*

Since the very purpose of deterrence is to prevent war, the theory is clearly not designed to help policy-makers manage hostilities if war should break out, for whatever reason. Former Chairman of the Joint Chiefs of Staff Maxwell Taylor, who continues to be optimistic about the efficacy of nuclear deterrence, confesses that "there is no conceivable way of hedging adequately against a failure of deterrence."[22]

The actual use of nuclear weapons in a retaliatory strike would, of course, demonstrate that the policy of deterrence had failed. Moreover, the weapons of annihilation designed for total terror would hardly be "usable" for any rational political or strategic purpose and might quickly bring on a senseless holocaust. Awareness of their uselessness might paralyze leaders from making any military response. On the other hand, prior deployment of more "usable" counterforce weapons could well make the outbreak of nuclear hostilities even more likely because such weapons might provoke the adversary into a preemptive strike. Any sense that the other side's nuclear inhibitions have been lowered is just about the most dangerous development in a moment of high strategic tension. It makes the game of "nuclear chicken" even more irrational and unpredictable, even though the "usable" weapons may be designed to enhance the "rational" conduct of war.

We must not be forced into a false choice between "useless" and "usable" nuclear weapons; neither kind makes any dependable contribution to our security.

Counterforce advocates like Fred Iklé (former director of the US Arms Control and Disarmament Agency, now director of policy planning for the Pentagon) are right, however, in criticizing some deterrence theorists for slighting the risks of accidental war. Iklé's concern is with the gross immorality and irrationality of an all-out retaliatory strike which might result from technical miscues or personal aberrations. This hazard increases with pressures toward a swift launch-on-warning policy, especially as anxiety mounts over the vulnerability of land-based missiles—and the dangers of false alarms strain fail-safe systems.[23]

However, other deterrence theorists such as Wolfgang K. H. Panofsky have been as concerned as Iklé about the risks of accidental war and the folly of a launch-on-warning policy. Panofsky emphasizes the continual reduction of nuclear weapons themselves as a prime means of reducing chances for accidental war, while Iklé looks to technology to produce new and less vulnerable weapons.[24]

10. *Nuclear weapons, even in years of presumed strategic superiority, have not spared the US from humiliating defeats.*

In the early hours of the Senate Foreign Relations Committee hearings on the SALT II Treaty in July 1979, Senator Howard Baker of Tennessee exhibited an embarrassing misunderstanding of history. After claiming that US military power had drastically declined during the 1970s (that decade during which separately targetable US missile warheads actually multiplied five times), he spoke nostalgically of the 1945-1970 period when the United States could and did "work its will in the world." Senator Baker was then given a scolding and a sound history lesson by Senator Joseph Biden of Delaware, who pointed out that in China, Hungary, Cuba, Vietnam, and Czechoslovakia, the United States had not found its nuclear arsenal useful in preventing communist hegemony. Senator Baker soon retired from the hearings and remained frequently absent thereafter.

In short, there never was a time when the US could convert its strategic prowess into effective force in most theaters of international conflict. The great paradox of our foreign policy is that, as our power to destroy the world has multiplied many times over, our political influence has steadily declined—ever since Hiroshima. Deterrence, in practice, has not solved any fundamental foreign policy problems.

11. *Nuclear weapons states themselves are likely to be the primary targets in a nuclear war.*

Those states which have actually deployed nuclear weapons for the sake of deterrence are just the states most likely to be devastated if deterrence fails. It is precisely the weapons designed to prevent nuclear attack on the United States which might become the only provocation to a Soviet nuclear attack and the major targets of such an attack—especially if those weapons increasingly suggest to the Soviets that the US is moving toward a first strike capability. That is a danger which will intensify if the US moves ahead with landbased MX mobile missiles: weapons whose power and accuracy will threaten the Soviets' retaliatory forces but may also lower Soviet restraint and multiply vulnerable populations in this country.

The very possession of nuclear weapons, therefore, is potentially a unique source of insecurity and suicidal conflict. Such apprehensions account for the increasing unwillingness of Western European populations to be "protected" by the stationing of weapons which may increase their vulnerability to annihilation. A nuclear-free Norway may be at least a marginally safer country than Germany if nuclear war breaks out in Europe.

Surely the insecurity of both Israel and Iraq, of India and Pakistan will be compounded as these nuclear-prone countries increasingly provoke their adversaries to contemplate preemptive strikes. Israel's strike against the Osirak reactor on June 7, 1981, not only exposed the vulnerability of Iraq: it provided one more dramatic example of a brilliant military exploit which will redound to Israel's long-term insecurity. Politically, if not yet strategically, Israel is now more vulnerable than ever to nuclear attack in the face of Arab hostility.

12. *Masses of civilians are held hostage by nuclear deterrence to the decisions of political elites over whom they may have no control.*

The decision-makers of the superpowers are not themselves the most likely victims of a nuclear attack. They will have deep shelters and ample stocks of food, water, air, medical supplies, and other good things—doubtless at a great distance from primary target areas.

There is a terrible irony in this predicament for the citizens of a totalitarian state like the Soviet Union. US hostility to the USSR is presumably based largely on convictions of incompatibility with totalitarianism—yet it is the powerless people and not the Politburo who would suffer most. The nuclear weapons of the United States are aimed, psychologically, at half a dozen men in the Kremlin with escape hatches. But they are aimed, physically, at tens of millions of repressed subjects.

Nearly three decades ago, the French super-scholar Raymond Aron wrote in his *Century of Total War:* "It will be indispensable, but singularly difficult, to convince the masses in the Soviet Union that the West bears no ill will except toward their tyrants, if atom bombs unite in death Stalinists and their opponents: women, children, and the secret police."[25]

If Aron's sentiments betray his acceptance of deterrence, albeit with a sense of political awkwardness if not tragedy, it is precisely this issue which did most to convert an erstwhile think-tank strategist from deterrence to radical rejection thereof: Lewis C. Bohn. In Bohn's view, the "gravest defect of nuclear deterrence" is this hostage predicament of uncountable millions:

> The ordinary people whom this policy commits us to bomb if war comes would bear no responsibility for that war; nor would they have harmed us in any way. The scores of millions of men, women and children in Soviet (or Chinese) target cities who would be vaporized, burned, pulverized or irradiated by our nuclear response, and the scores of millions more who would be left wounded, ill, orphaned and homeless, do not have the political power or physical ability either to launch war against the US or to prevent their leaders from doing so. They could not even know of their government's decision for such war before it was taken; those who survived might not even learn of it afterward. . . . Whatever our destruction of these civilians was called, it would not be retaliation. In its action on powerless populations, our nuclear deterrence force is in fact precisely the dreaded first strike force, no matter in what sequence the nuclear blows fall.[26]

While counterforce critics of deterrence like Fred Iklé and Paul Ramsey also invoke this sense of horror over nuclear hostages, the devastating weapons they propose for military targeting would hardly spare these same powerless people.

13. *Deterrence dogmas presuppose a bilateral model of world politics at a time of uncontrolled nuclear proliferation.*

If the probabilities of nuclear war are rising and if, as I believe, proliferation is a more and more likely catalyst to nuclear war, the relevance of strategic doctrine to proliferation is an issue second to none in national security policy. The reality of a balkanized world of many poor but over-militarized states, as described by military historian Harvey A. DeWeerd, is increasingly unmanageable by the major powers and threatens to suck them into local nuclear wars.[27]

It is just here that compartmentalized approaches to public policy are most glaringly exposed. Deterrence theorists are largely strangers to the world of multilateral diplomacy in which defenses against proliferation must be reconstructed. The superpowers simply can no longer control the nuclear options of other countries, if they ever could: the accessibility of nuclear know-how and materials is too great. They can, however, help to develop the kind of equitable structures of security and technology in which other countries will want to participate.

Similarly, the energy and nonproliferation policies of the United States, and administrations of both parties, have been fixed upon technical and industrial schemes dominated by the West instead of facing up to the political preconditions of global controls on nuclear policies.

So: neither deterrence theory nor nuclear export controls can provide adequate security against the most plausible nuclear threats. Moreover, the mutual insulation between the bilateral SALT talks, dominated by strategic doctrine, and the inescapably multilateral Non-Proliferation Treaty has been so thick that the political currents which should flow between them have been shut off.

It is just this hiatus in deterrence thinking which most disturbs Hedley Bull's mind about the future of strategic doctrine: two-power assumptions in a world of many-sided nuclear threats. The "high posture" doctrine, which holds that proliferation can best be discouraged if the superpowers maintain a big lead in nuclear capacity over would-be competitors, is breaking down as hierarchies of power crumble in both East and West and as nuclear technology circulates widely and rapidly. Bull concludes that the best course in the long run

> is to work against all nuclear proliferation, that which has already taken place as well as that which may occur in the future, however difficult this may be. This requires us to take every opportunity to push nuclear weapons—and the doctrines and practices of nuclear deterrence associated with them—as far into the background of international political relationships as possible.[28]

Bull proposes new institutional structures in which non-nuclear states might have direct access to basic information about nuclear weapons and policies—albeit assuming the continued deployment of such weapons by the superpowers. In my view, such institutions would not cope with political realities unless they are accompanied by meaningful nuclear disarmament.

14. *Superpower preoccupation with nuclear weapons offers bad role models for other nations on the threshold of nuclear weapons systems.*

It is not just bifurcated policies and inadequate multilateral structures which expose the irrelevance of nuclear deterrence to proliferation: it is the double-standard of nuclear responsibility.

If *we* need nuclear weapons for our security — if the real point in possessing nuclear weapons is to enhance political power and prestige — if being a nuclear-weapon state is to be granted special prerogatives and exceptions in international institutions, why should we expect other nations to repress their own ambitions for security, prestige, and prerogatives along similar lines? If nuclear deterrence is good for *us,* why should we regard it as bad for everybody else? And if we finally conclude it might be good for many other countries, too, can we really imagine a safer and more secure world with dozens of nuclear-weapon states? (Some Chinese and French strategists have imagined just that!)

This contradiction in the relation of nuclear strategy to world politics is but another indication of how out of touch with realities some "realists" can get.

The nuclear double-standard is a heavy moral liability for the United States — and a liability which increasingly exacerbates US relationships with non-nuclear states, especially in the Third World. B. C. E. Nwosu of Nigeria, chief science officer in the Ministry of Education, made plain his moral contempt for nuclear hypocrisy in an address at the Massachusetts Institute of Technology in 1979:

> Developing countries should seek to keep all their technology options open. . . . They have to choose their friends wisely. Any country that tells you that nuclear energy is bad but refuses to share with you the secrets of commercial solar energy or other alternative technologies should not be taken seriously. Any country that sits on thousands of megaton bombs and harasses you about the dangers of nuclear proliferation should not be considered a friend.[29]

This increasingly bitter issue of equity in both security and energy relationships has dominated the 1975 and 1980 review conferences for the Non-Proliferation Treaty, as Chapter 5 will document.

15. *Nuclear-weapon states deprive non-nuclear states of their rightful autonomy in matters of their own security and survival.*

The totalitarian nature of nuclear weapons mocks the pretensions of sovereignty and self-determination in a world in which nationalism remains a vital social force.

Even the superpowers cannot realistically hope to muster a

reliable defense against strategic missiles, although ABM (anti-ballistic missile) enthusiasts keep reviving that illusory hope. Whatever the efficacy of deterrence itself, "defense" has become a misnomer in the scenarios of nuclear conflict.

But it is not only the permeability of any nation-state directly targeted by nuclear missiles that exposes the degraded status of sovereignty: it is the vulnerability of any state at all to a large-scale nuclear conflict in which it may not even be an actor. A state which has renounced all nuclear weapons for itself under the Non-Proliferation Treaty—and which may also have refrained from any military alliance with one of the superpowers, thus doubly entitling it to be free from nuclear attack—is still a potential victim of lethal radioactive debris and severe ozone depletion. Winds and ultra-violet rays have astonishingly little respect for national boundaries.

It is this loss of autonomy which has caused non-nuclear states increasingly to press their claims for an equitable share in decision-making about nuclear technology and weapons. "No annihilation without representation" has become a far-from-whimsical slogan even for allies within the major military blocs, for they are especially vulnerable targets to direct nuclear devastation.

The question as to who makes strategic nuclear decisions cannot morally be regarded as a purely domestic matter of politics, elections, command-and-control: it is inescapably an issue of planetary import and species survival. The transnational dimensions of nuclear doctrine and decision-making remain very far from being articulated into structures of adequate accountability.

16. *Nuclear weapons have not kept the peace by preventing conventional wars since 1945.*

The optimism of some early notions of deterrence extended to the prevention of conventional as well as nuclear wars. Bernard Brodie and John Foster Dulles, while differing from one another in many respects, shared that optimism. Other strategists, especially from the mid-1950s through the 1960s, took a contrary view: that nuclear weapons would make conventional wars even more likely because policy-makers would tend to be preoccupied with, and virtually paralyzed by, their own strategic forces.

The official articulation of containment doctrine in NSC-68, April 7, 1950—a document much more aggressive and militaristic than George Kennan's 1947 "Mr. X" vision of containment—showed some sophistication in recognizing the severe limits of deterrence. The clear implication of NSC-68 was that "the imminent mutual neutralization of nuclear forces would render them less and less relevant to deterring anything but each other, and pointed to the consequent need to deter lesser threats by more conventional preparations for direct defense."[30] But then the subsequent seductions of Massive Retaliation in the 1950s obscured that bit of wisdom in NSC-68.

Doctrine aside, there have been dozens of conventional wars in the world since Hiroshima — wars marked by tens of millions of casualties and immeasurable suffering — so that the efficacy of deterrence is once more impossible to substantiate.

Potentially, nuclear war is the worst imaginable conflict. Actually, it has been sub-nuclear wars which have done all the killing since 1945.

17. *Strategic nuclear preoccupations divert attention and resources from economic and social threats to national security and international development.*

The superpowers are vulnerable to many things besides direct nuclear attack — and many more probable things. Their growing vulnerability to energy shortages, cut-offs of strategic minerals, eco-catastrophe, economic disaster, and political terrorism calls for a much more rounded vision of national security than is offered by nuclear deterrence.

The fact that the United States has invested more in deterrence doctrines than the Soviet Union or any other country can no longer conceal the fact that the United States is now caught up in an adverse balance of vulnerability with regard to non-nuclear problems. Curt Gasteyger's analysis of the limits of deterrence points to the coupling of strategic nuclear dogmas with the dogma of "linkage" as a source of escapism which repeatedly turns away from difficult economic and social tasks. It is "linkage" which attempts to connect almost any foreign policy problem with US-Soviet rivalry and which holds back on arms control or other agreements because of alleged bad conduct elsewhere in the world. But Gasteyger observes that "to invoke linkage looks more often than not like an attempt to take refuge on the more familiar ground of the East-West contest, where responsibilities are clear and culprits more easily identified than in those volatile areas over which one has little or no control."[31]

Whatever the imminent threats to the US in these non-nuclear areas, it is the articulation of our national security in concert with that of a world-community-of-shared-risks that has so largely eluded our strategic nuclear thinkers. It is here that the Brandt

Commission report of 1980 makes a salutary contribution to our fuller understanding of what security and survival really require.[32]

18. *Deterrence dogmas are negatively preoccupied with threats to the neglect of positive inducements to mutual security.*

Roger Fisher's *International Conflict for Beginners* (1969) observes that "in this era of nuclear weapons and deterrence" the Pentagon has "become quite sophisticated about making threats" but has "no comparable sophistication regarding the making of offers."[33]

It may not be the Pentagon's business to be sophisticated in the making of offers—but it surely is the business of civilians in the foreign policy establishment to be sophisticated in the ways of positive diplomacy. The lopsided truth is that deterrence, at best, is only the negative, reactive side of US diplomacy while the more constructive side is languishing in a dismal state of underdevelopment. The fact that "détente" has dropped out of acceptable public speech in America reflects at least two things: a regression to chauvinistic Cold War attitudes and a recognition that détente itself was never persuasively developed into a major credible component of foreign policy. Not by Nixon, not by Kissinger, not by Ford, not by Carter, and certainly not by Brzezinski who wore out secretaries of state and arms controllers and Soviet specialists by his unsophisticated anti-Soviet hostility. We have hardly suffered from an excess of détente: we have had far too little of it.

The threat to retaliate with nuclear weapons has evoked strenuous ethical and even theological exertions to legitimize deterrence as a lesser evil than the actual use of nuclear weapons. This distinction between *threat* and *use,* seemingly so obvious in terms of consequences, raises difficult questions about credibility if the threat isn't based on an actual *intention* to retaliate. Michael Walzer's *Just and Unjust Wars,* after declaring that nuclear weapons are "morally unacceptable," yet justifies deterrence as at least temporarily falling "under the standard of necessity."[34] But that is where he leaves this matter, without making clear his own position on the ethics of intention or use. Even an unambiguously clear justification of threats which rejects the actual use of nuclear weapons is hardly enough to redeem deterrence theory ethically— not if the preoccupation with threats itself is recognized as a badly flawed approach to diplomacy.

At stake in this discussion are the most fundamental assumptions about the behavior of nations. The final chapter of the Alexander George-Richard Smoke study of *Deterrence in American*

Foreign Policy is titled "From Deterrence to Influence in Theory and Practice." Their 600-page review of case studies highlights the narrowness and negativism of deterrence theory and practice. A more adequate theory of political influence, they insist, must focus on initiatives which generate incentives and inducements. It is "inadequate merely to deter unfavorable change; one must also create and/or guide change in favorable directions." The latter is actually the more demanding work of diplomacy, requiring much more than a response to the immediate situation and a search for means to cope with it. The policy-maker must begin with "a model or image of his desired future international reality" and reason back from it to present choices "in order to devise appropriate strategies" to achieve long-term objectives. Here again, the reactive character of US diplomacy historically has been reinforced by deterrence rather than transformed.[35]

The concluding sentence of George-Smoke is worth quoting in full:

> The challenge to U.S. foreign policy remains, therefore, one of finding a longer-term image of a desirable world order — a genuine international community — which will be acceptable domestically and which can enlist cooperation among the nations; and of finding *all* the mechanisms of inter-nation influence, emphatically including inducement strategies, that can take us to this goal.[36]

19. *Deterrence dogmas presuppose an extravagant confidence in political rationality.*

There is a literally absurd contradiction at the heart of deterrence theory: a simultaneous dependence upon absolute terror and absolute reason. The logical and psychological difficulties involved in living with this nuclear contradiction are very great for the average sensitive citizen, as Erich Fromm, Jerome Frank, and Robert Jay Lifton have indicated. Deterrence theorists themselves, however, exhibit a sublime confidence in the rationality of decision-makers entrusted with managing a security system based on the most grisly fear: the fear of total annihilation. As Karl Deutsch has pointedly observed, these theorists first propose "that we should frustrate our opponents by frightening them very badly and that we should rely then on their cool-headed rationality for our survival."[37]

The mental health and prudent judgment of political and

military leaders in the crucible of unprecedented Doomsday pressures, not to mention the hysteria of the general public or the volatility of the physical environment if nuclear weapons have actually exploded, can hardly be taken for granted in any of the countries possessing nuclear weapons.

Yet Henry Kissinger, among many other deterrence theorists, has stipulated just such a requirement for effective nuclear strategy:

> The opponent must be rational, i.e., he must respond to his self-interest in a manner which is predictable. . . . In weighing his self-interest, the potential aggressor must reach the conclusion the 'deterrer' is seeking to induce. In other words, the penalties of aggression must outweigh its *benefits.*[38]

This application of quantitative models of cost-benefit analysis would seem to be of dubious dependability in a rapidly escalating nuclear crisis. The megalomania which propels some leaders into high office, the paranoia and sheer fatigue which too often accompany the pressures of ultimate responsibility, the onset of senility in aging elites, and the isolation from adequate intelligence and counsel which has marked even American presidents over the past two decades all indicate the hazards of such a presumption of rationality.

A presumption of irrationality and unpredictability may be the beginning of wisdom in nuclear diplomacy. Even where leaders maintain what Karl Mannheim called "functional rationality" — the capacity to choose the *means* of action — they may lose entirely their "substantial rationality" — the capacity to choose appropriate *ends.*[39] Such a loss means the demise of ethical sensibilities. What is "rational" in an instrumental context may be intrinsically irrational — a common mark of paranoia. In fact, that is what paranoia is all about: highly systematized delusions projected from inner hostilities.

Philip Green's preface to *Deadly Logic* notes that "no self-enclosed system of strategic logic is proof against contamination by the quite different, nonrational drives of the very political system which originally generates it."[40] Green helpfully cites social psychologist Thomas Milburn's critique of deterrence — a critique which emphasizes that threats tend to increase political cohesion among adversaries, tend *not* to change motives but rather to increase anxiety and hostility, and generate the kind of stress which impairs perspective and judgment.

Even the immediate success of deterrence, which means frustrating an adversary, can generate less pacific and more aggressive behavior in the long run. The massive Soviet missile build-up of the 1960s was spurred by the temporary humiliations of the Cuban missile crisis.

There is yet another shadow on nuclear rationality having nothing to do with external threats. Decision-makers with nuclear arsenals at their disposal may confront a personal crisis in which they become unhinged by temptations to provoke a self-serving or suicidal foreign policy crisis. Secretary of Defense James Schlesinger reportedly had such apprehensions about Richard Nixon in the last days of the Watergate trauma and took special precautions to screen any impulsive strategic decisions.

20. *Deterrence dogmas reveal a subhuman and truncated philosophy of human nature.*

If deterrence theorists' absolute presumption of rationality seems to exalt cerebral powers to superhuman levels, their punitive preoccupation with threats seems to degrade *homo sapiens* to subhuman levels. This lack of a coherent and credible portrait of human nature is perhaps the most fundamental flaw in the whole body of deterrence dogma. The workings of the human brain are much more mysterious and unpredictable than most strategists have imagined.

The mechanistic models of terror and conflict advanced by some nuclear thinking suggest comparison with the works of rat psychologists who never manage to lift their vision to the level of the love and creativity of which human beings alone are capable — except for their Creator who made them that way. Only if violence itself is the ultimate of law of life does deterrence theory make much sense.

Hedley Bull has taken Western strategic analysis to task for its portrait of "strategic man," a character he regards as a cousin of the "economic man" presupposed by classical economic theory. In a good-humored understatement, Bull asserts that

'strategic man' does not provide the key to human behavior at all times and in all places. If we are to apply deterrence theory to a host of international political situations other than that of the Soviet-American conflict at the time of the Cold War, we have either to develop a conception of a genuinely universal 'strategic man' or abandon the concept.[41]

The dehumanizing premises of deterrence tend to be turned on adversaries with particular animosity, making strategy itself clumsy and prudent diplomacy all but impossible. We have previously noted the chronic tendency to oversimplify Soviet motives. Now we must underscore the moral and spiritual liabilities of deterrence in obscuring the adversary's shared identity with us in the same species. If we cannot locate our enemies within a common framework of some sort, there is really no hope for peace. George Kennan's address in accepting the Albert Einstein Peace Prize in 1981 described deterrence as the idea "which attributes to others—to others who, like ourselves, were born of women, walk on two legs, and love their children, to human beings, in short—the most fiendish and inhuman of tendencies."[42]

Deterrence theory not only tends to base strategy on subhuman assumptions: the strategy prescribed tends to debase human existence itself, even while threatening to bring on Doomsday.

As a deterrence maximalist, pleading for "more of everything," Herman Kahn has insisted that "we must be prepared against every kind of war and prepared to wage any kind should deterrence fail." But Kahn's approach, complains Harvard's Stanley Hoffmann, "condemns the world to the 'burrow' Kafka describes in his nightmarish story, a burrow dug by an animal in quest of peace and security. Constant noises of mysterious origin keep the poor beast rushing in perpetual anguish in whatever direction the knocking seems to come from."[43]

What human values can possibly be made secure by such a "security" policy, even if it could be proved, as it cannot, that nuclear war itself could be prevented thereby?

21. *Deterrence dogmas make nuclear disarmament illegitimate and impossible.*

Two decades ago, the United States and the Soviet Union approved a "Joint Statement of Agreed Principles for Disarmament Negotiation," since known as the McCloy-Zorin Agreement. That statement committed the superpowers to the goal of "general and complete disarmament" (GCD) and to the elimination of nuclear stockpiles and delivery systems. It was anticipated that the process of disarmament should follow "an agreed sequence, by stages" and that all measures should be "balanced." The agreement thus did more than set a utopian goal: it set forth the main guidelines for a strategy of disarmament.

The Test Ban Treaty of 1963 recommitted the superpowers to

"general and complete disarmament" and to the discontinuance of the production and testing of nuclear weapons. The Nuclear Non-Proliferation Treaty of 1968 reaffirmed the goal of "general and complete disarmament," the "earliest possible . . . cessation of the nuclear arms race," and "effective measures" toward nuclear disarmament. The SALT I ABM Treaty of 1972 declared the intention to end the nuclear arms race and to proceed "toward reductions in strategic arms, nuclear disarmament, and general and complete disarmament."

Thus by rhetoric and by instruments of international law, the United States has repeatedly committed itself to nuclear disarmament and, ultimately, to general and complete disarmament.

The dogmas of deterrence, however, do not envision the elimination of nuclear weapons but their deployment in perpetuity. True believers in the dictum that "nuclear deterrence is the bedrock of national and international security" can hardly commit themselves to nuclear disarmament.

The program of arms control intimately connected with deterrence is committed to maintaining the stability of the "nuclear balance," not to arms reductions as such. Theoretically, it tends to be diffident or agnostic to whether the balance rises or falls. Indeed, it imagines that there can still be stability at higher and higher levels of deployment. Arms control in practice, as the SALT process testifies, readily tends to increases in nuclear stockpiles and even totally new strategic systems. With candor but approval, McGeorge Bundy recently declared: "Arms control is best understood as a modest reinforcement to strategic stability, even as an element of strategic deterrence."

This, however, is the Gordian knot that must be cut: the strategic disdain for disarmament interlocked with the co-optation of arms control by deterrence. If it is now a truism that disarmament must be credibly articulated as a security policy, the truth must dawn that deterrence can no longer dictate the terms of security.

Whatever the efficacy of deterrence against the Soviets, it has been extremely effective in blocking genuine progress toward nuclear disarmament. Its static notions of stability, while repeatedly invoked to deploy more and bigger weapons systems, clearly thwart any visionary strategy for disarmament itself.

So: the advocates of disarmament must think clearly and speak plainly about this final incompatibility of goals between them and most advocates of deterrence, even if they become allies in the struggle for particular short-term objectives like SALT II or opposition to MX.

An Ambivalent Footnote on Deterrence

The preceding critique is obviously meant to point to this conclusion: nuclear deterrence doctrines are not only inadequate guides to national security but, in most forms, are unwise and self-defeating. In the short run and at the very least, they must be stripped of their absolutism, isolationism, technical fixations, excessive negativism and hyper-rationalism. In the long run—but a run which must start in the immediate future—deterrence must be displaced by a much wiser vision of security policy.

These fearsome topics, however, require even more than refutation of doctrines and a vision of alternatives. They impel us to survey the political landscape around us and to choose the most promising path through the jungle of mutual terror to the higher ground of genuine security.

That path may be charted most clearly by some who remain deterrence moderates or minimalists. For the hardest political choices likely to be put before the American public in the 1980s are not between retention and renunciation of nuclear weapons: they are choices between escalation and de-escalation of the arms race. Indeed, the imminent political danger is that deterrence moderates will soon be overwhelmed by maximalists who confront only collapsing resistance to new offensive missiles, Euro-strategic missiles, and space warfare.

In such a political jungle thick with predatory interests, bureaucratic alliances, perverse mythologies and even willful lies, those politicians who can make a credible case for restraining the arms race will need all the help they can get. The repudiation of deterrence can hardly be made a prerequisite of political acceptability. Indeed, we shall need all those moral and political qualities shown by some advocates of deterrence and mentioned at the outset of this critique—including their resistance to "nuclear war fighting," opposition to new deployments, support for arms limitations, and awareness of legitimate Soviet anxieties.

There is, after all, some residual wisdom in deterrence ideas. Elemental deterrence is a well-nigh universal human experience. Fear of aggression can be healthy and even essential to survival. If power balances are never mechanistic and automatic, there are persistent tendencies toward countervailing power in most political relationships—not least because those who are most aggressive tend to overreach themselves unless they are confronted with some kind of powerful resistance. Nuclear deterrence can be faulted for its empirical shortcomings on the nature of political power — but not for insisting on power itself as an element of dissuasion.

There is also this residual truth in nuclear deterrence: as long as nuclear technology is available to any government or non-governmental group, it will be a potential inhibitor to decision-makers. The hard question for *deterrence-as-theory,* however, is whether a whole security strategy should stand as a super-structure on that inhibitory potential.

Whatever political accommodations disarmament advocates make to deterrence moderates should not obscure the need those very moderates have for more radical pressures to offset more chauvinist pressures. Therefore, tactical compromises should not preclude—indeed, they will require—an enduring insistence upon alternative security strategies.

Ultimately, the issue is not what kinds of nuclear weapons we need nor how many of them: it is how best to overcome the demonic myth that our security requires nuclear arms at all. The choice must not finally be put between two competing brands of nuclear doctrine: it must open up a third way which recognizes that weapons of mass destruction are massively irrelevant.

CHAPTER 3

Nuclear Dogmatics II: Counterforce

Even if war should begin as a counterforce war, it would quickly expand into a war against cities and people. Because many cities are close to missile bases and airfields, it has been estimated that some thirty million Americans would be killed in a first counterforce-type strike. The first bombs to fall would knock out most communications and reconnaissance facilities. Neither government could know whether the other was 'playing the game,' which forces were still in existence, and what its own men were doing. In such confusion, total war would be almost inescapable. — Ambassador James Wadsworth in the *Saturday Review,* July 28, 1962

Deterrence is not the only doctrine which rationalizes the unending production and deployment of nuclear weapons. There is an unruly offspring of deterrence called "counterforce" which is increasingly usurping the strategic authority deterrence has maintained for three decades. British science writer Nigel Calder's recent investigation into *Nuclear Nightmares* concludes that, in both the US and USSR, the proponents of preparation to fight and "win" nuclear wars have "largely displaced those who were only interested in deterring war. The 'unthinkable' has become most thinkable and calculable, and the concept of deterrence is crumbling fast."[1] Whether or not the edifices of deterrence are crumbling fast, any serious study of strategic dogmas and their disarmament implications in the 1980s must assess the resurgent counterforce phenomenon.

While counterforce ideas, like deterrence, come in sufficient variety to require cautious generalizations, the core concept is a targeting doctrine. The prime targets are military: bases, launchers, airports, arms industries. "Counter-city" or "counter-value" targeting, usually associated with MAD, is rejected in these arguments:

1. Attacks or threats on civilian population are immoral;

2. Decision-makers are likely to be inhibited from actually choosing such immoral options, even after an enemy attack, thus

weakening the credibility of deterrence;

3. The targeting of the enemy's own deterrent forces is a more effective threat than the targeting of cities;

4. Deterrence strategies as such provide no guidance for the waging of war if war breaks out;

5. We need weapons which are "usable" and which therefore make a nuclear war "winnable," at least in inflicting more devastation upon enemy forces while achieving some "damage limitation" on our side;

6. The development of counterforce weapons by the Soviet Union exposes the vulnerability of our deterrent forces, thus requiring a "countervailing" capability on our side.

The Origins of Counterforce

The ascendancy of such dogmas in the 1980s should not obscure their historical antecedents, not only in the nuclear age but in earlier centuries. The moral criteria of classical "just war" theorists, especially *non-combatant immunity* and *proportionality,* have been invoked in support of targeting doctrines which focus on military objects. The desire to provide decision-makers with other options than the all-or-nothing formula of massive retaliation emerged with the strategic critics of the 1950s. The concern over the vulnerability of US deterrent forces to a pre-emptive strike dates at least back to the RAND Corporation's "basing study" of 1954, by Albert Wohlstetter and others, which highlighted the potential vulnerability of strategic air bases to Soviet attack. (Laurence Martin calls this study the "dawn of counterforce.") An early missile age version of counterforce was briefly entertained by Robert McNamara (until he came to regard it as based on a false promise of sparing civilian casualties). In the 1970-76 period, President Nixon, Secretary of Defense James Schlesinger, and Arms Control Director Fred Iklé all set forth highly moralized arguments for new counterforce weapons — without, we must add, fully clarifying their relationship to deterrence.

For more than a decade, in fact, it has been difficult to find any evidence of corporate clarity in the nuclear thinking of the US national security establishment. The answers to the following very serious questions are far from clear:

What is the present status of deterrence in relation to counterforce? Is counterforce basically a maximalist form of nuclear deterrence? Or is it minimalist in imposing severe constraints upon the capabilities of weapons and choice of targets? Is counterforce a supplement to deterrence or a repudiation of it? Has counterforce already displaced deterrence in the doctrinal dynamics of the arms race? What are the implications of counterforce for strategic stability, parity, arms control and disarmament?

The most authoritative articulation of counterforce to date came late in the Carter Administration and reflected both the confusion and drastic policy shifts within it. Presidential Directive 59, the text of which has not been made public, outlined a "countervailing strategy" for "limited nuclear war," featuring weapons capable of precise targeting on military forces and political leadership, rather than massive retaliatory attacks on cities and industries. The doctrine commissioned a "secure strategic reserve"—which term apparently comprised the MX missile, new SLBMs (sub-launched missiles), and both ALCMs and GLCMs (air- and ground-launched cruise missiles).

PD 59 thus attempted to legitimize a new generation of counterforce weapons which had been in the research-and-development stage for years but had previously lacked clear strategic rationales. The technologies, as usual, had preceded the political purposes. Moreover, a new high-technology strategic bomber and advances in computers, radars and optics for new ABM programs (which could scrap the ABM Treaty of 1972) had been waiting in the wings for political signals to proceed.

Thus the Carter Administration—begun with some inclinations toward a minimal deterrent force of a few hundred nuclear weapons, resurrected hopes of disarmament toward the goal of zero nuclear weapons, and pledges of reduced defense spending—concluded with a counterforce commitment of such magnitude that the Reagan campaign and Administration had to strain to top it. The fact that PD 59 was disclosed just five days prior to the Democratic Convention of 1980 prompted suspicions that domestic political calculations loomed larger than Soviet threats. At any rate, two years of tough anti-Soviet rhetoric in the second half of the Carter term, crafted largely to shore up a faltering presidency, were reified in military policy. PD 59 consolidated and rationalized all those trends of the 1970s toward the actual production and deployment of new counterforce weapons. What had been "bargaining chips" and experimental programs were now to become standard equipment for "fighting" and "winning" nuclear wars.

Yet the confusion remained. In fact, the confusion was compounded by a letter sent from Secretary of Defense Harold Brown to NATO defense ministers on August 8, 1980, two days after Richard Burt disclosed the existence of PD 59 in a *New York Times* article. Secretary Brown's letter contained a deeply troublesome contradiction: it asserted that the new countervailing strategy was "designed to enhance deterrence . . . if deterrence fails." One does not have to be a devotee of deterrence to wonder if PD 59 signaled the undoing of deterrence itself by a policy that might make nuclear war more likely rather than less so.

James Fallows claims that US policy since the 1960s has been a consistent mix of "counterforce" and "counter-city" targeting and that PD 59, therefore, did not represent a significantly new departure.[2] It may be more accurate, however, to emphasize the vacillations and incoherence of strategic doctrine and to view PD 59 as a regression to ideas of the early 1960s which made a comeback in the early 1970s.

If arms control has been too largely reconciled to deterrence, no credible reconciliation between arms control and counterforce has yet emerged. In fact, the ascendancy of counterforce in the Reagan Administration was so dominant in its first year that only the vaguest of suggestions were offered as to whether or how or when a new round of arms control would become possible. It is this ascendancy which makes a thorough critique of counterforce doctrines and weapons a most urgent task on the disarmament agenda.

A Critique of Counterforce

1. *Counterforce magnifies the most serious liabilities of deterrence.*

Doctrinal messianism, technical and militaristic fixations, oversimplification of Soviet motives, excessive bilateralism in the face of proliferation, neglect of grievous economic and social problems, preoccupation with threats to the neglect of inducements, extravagant confidence in crisis rationality—all of these tendencies are hardly diminished by counterforce. They are powerfully reinforced by a quantum leap to new heights of dogmatic abstraction and political illiteracy. As Calder puts it: "The sophistication about 'limited war,' 'counterforce options,' and the like leads back to exchanges just as bloody-minded but more deadly and less controllable than 'mutually assured destruction' at its most facile."[3]

On the other hand, the most valid criticisms of deterrence strategy by counterforce promoters are hardly compensated for by counterforce alternatives. The professed repugnance at targeting cities is more than offset by the widespread devastation bound to follow a major counterforce attack. The lament about the lack of deterrence guidelines for the actual conduct of a nuclear war, especially an "accidental war," is converted into a strategy which makes nuclear war, even accidental war, more likely than ever.

2. *Counterforce appeals to a specious moral argument about civilian hostages.*

In the actual conduct of any war, there must always be a humane presumption of minimizing casualties and suffering. The principle of non-combatant immunity in Christian tradition, while savagely violated in every modern war, remains an indispensable moral imperative.

It is the invocation of that principle in the service of counterforce that chronically obfuscates a rounded view of the moral issues at stake. No strategic nuclear weapon can be made accountable to non-combatant immunity in any meaningful sense. Counterforce proponents may bewail the degree to which MAD holds civilians hostage but the professed precision of their targeting doctrine hardly spares those same civilians. "Pinpoint nuclear attacks," in any credible scenario, will still annihilate millions of people.

The most immediate political purpose of PD 59 was to provide a strategic excuse for the MX. Any notion that MX would be a humane weapon was totally belied by its projected characteristics. Each of ten warheads on one MX would have a minimum of 335 kilotons (and perhaps as much as 600 KT) of explosive power. That minimal power is over twenty times that of the Hiroshima A-bomb, variously estimated at 12-15 KT. Therefore, the total power of just one MX (with its ten warheads) would amount to more than two hundred times that of the first A-bomb (which probably killed at least 100,000 people). That is hardly a "clean" missile. It certainly is a missile incapable of respecting the principle of non-combatant immunity.

At a recent international conference, I found myself engaged in a discussion of counterforce weapons with a ranking officer from the US Joint Chiefs of Staff. With great earnestness, he urged me to appreciate the moral superiority of such discriminating weapons. He knew the just war tradition quite well. He invoked non-combatant immunity as a justification for MX. What he did not know at all, to our mutual embarrassment, was the specifications for MX. When they were described, he modestly allowed that he himself had been so enamored of the moral arguments for counterforce that he hadn't actually done his homework on the weapons themselves.

It is not just weapons specifications that nullify the moral case for counterforce: it is the actual location of prime military targets. If those targets were entirely isolated from urban areas, there would still be many millions of casualties from radioactive fall-out in any nuclear war. What is unavoidable, however, is the close conjunction of hundreds of military targets with densely populated areas. A recently unclassified government report revealed that a US retaliatory strike on military targets alone — that is, a counterforce strike — would hit metropolitan Moscow with sixty nuclear warheads. Millions of civilian deaths would surely result. McGeorge Bundy, citing this report, adds that "our own strategic plans have always been focused mainly on military targets."[4] That claim, from a former insider in the national security establishment, raises further vexing questions about the relationship of counterforce to deterrence, such as: "What's new?"

No Christian ethicist has labored more thoughtfully to justify counterforce doctrine than Paul Ramsey of Princeton University. Ramsey's seriousness about noncombatant immunity leads him to rule out intentional attacks on civilians. The unintended victims of nuclear attack are victims under the scholastic principle of "double effect." Had Ramsey's argument stopped there, it might be faulted primarily for its lack of empirical seriousness about nuclear devastation. But, as Michael Walzer shows, Ramsey adverts to an exceedingly scholastic and indirect doctrine of deterrence. In the end, Ramsey depends on "collateral civilian damage" to deter enemy attacks: "The entire burden of Ramsey's argument falls on the idea of death by indirection."

Schematically, Walzer sets forth Ramsey's "continuum of increasing moral danger" concerning nuclear attacks on civilians. The first of four points is Ramsey's own preference:

(a) the articulated prospect of collateral (and disproportionate) civilian deaths;

(b) the implicit threat of counter-city strikes;

(c) the "cultivated" appearance of a commitment to counter-city strikes;

(d) and the actual commitment.

Walzer's own inclination is to doubt that the differences make any real difference. He quotes British philosopher G. E. M. Anscombe in suggesting that Ramsey comes close to "double-think about double effect."[5]

Whatever the fairness of these criticisms, it must finally be pointed out that Paul Ramsey has made a strenuous effort to assimilate counterforce within a theory of deterrence and not to pose them as mutually exclusive alternatives. That, it must be said, is an increasingly dubious exercise in the political and military environments of the 1980s.

3. *Counterforce asserts an unwarranted confidence in the rationality of limited nuclear war.*

It was in reaction to Eisenhower-era massive retaliation that some strategists in the mid-1950s began to conceive of "limited nuclear war" as a necessary amendment to deterrence. Not only moral revulsion against unlimited holocaust animated their concerns: they believed deterrence itself had lost credibility because it failed to provide for intermediate military threats clearly not justifying the unleashing of the full nuclear arsenal. Henry Kissinger's *Nuclear Weapons and Foreign Policy* (1957) first articulated a "limited nuclear war" strategy based on a system of "graduated deterrence," featuring intermediate ranges of military force and tactical nuclear weapons. He believed that to reduce the totality of nuclear threat was to make it more credible. (Just three years later, Kissinger's *Necessity of Choice* retracted most of his enthusiasm for tactical nuclear weapons.) Kissinger's confidence in the rationality of graduated deterrence was not a product of systems analysis or game theory: it was a reversion to nineteenth century norms of civility and rationality.

Similar to Kissinger's ideas were those of Maxwell Taylor, who prescribed a strategy of "flexible response" in his 1960 book, *The Uncertain Trumpet.* Taylor's views were clearly formed on the turf of interservice rivalry. As Army Chief of Staff under Eisenhower, he had resisted the loss of control over the Jupiter IRBM (intermediate-range nuclear missiles) program to the Air Force. That meant depriving Jupiter missiles of their original field use as mobile missiles, based on trains, trucks, and barges. Taylor retired (briefly) to advocate a buildup of conventional weapons and revival of the Army Jupiter program, putting both under command of a Limited War Headquarters, paralleling the Strategic Air Command.

Both Kissinger and Taylor subsumed their limited nuclear war doctrines under a moderated and nuanced strategy of deterrence. But it was Herman Kahn's 1961 book, *On Thermonuclear War,* which first tied an aggressive confidence in the rationality of limited nuclear war to an advocacy of counterforce. Kahn's mechanistic models, formed by systems analysis and game theory, stressed technology, efficiency, and the utility of force in such a way that a "controlled counterforce war" was commended as a serious policy option. All this was made to seem tolerable by Kahn's incredibly low casualty estimates, optimism about civil defense, and baseless quantification of prospects for decontamination and recuperation. In Stanley Hoffmann's view, Kahn's proposal wrongly supposed that nuclear crises and wars could be "managed under coolly rational rules, not only by the leaders, but by whole populations."[6]

The limited nuclear war notions embodied in PD 59 and embraced by Reagan strategists suggest a reversion to the logic of Herman Kahn and a severe dissociation from political and psychological probabilities. This inability to take seriously the prospect of uninhibited escalation once the nuclear threshold has been crossed is one of the most perilous deficiencies of some current political and military leaders. It is not only the unpredictability of leaders confronting a disintegrating environment and a public traumatized by nuclear attack that tends to be slighted. It is forgetfulness of the totality with which both superpowers have waged their modern wars. The Korean and Vietnam wars were limited, true — but they never crossed the nuclear threshold and they did not involve direct superpower confrontations.

It is precisely the crossing of this nuclear threshold which most resolutely must be avoided if conflicts are to be kept under any semblance of control. Richard Rosecrance, a Cornell political scientist, has strongly argued against the utility of tactical nuclear weapons in Europe on the grounds that battlefield conditions would make political restraints highly improbable:

> Any kind of nuclear war is much more difficult to keep limited than a conventional conflict because of the lack of a 'fire-break,' a clear dividing point between conventional and nuclear weapons. Once nuclear weapons are employed in however limited a fashion, neither side could be sure that his opponent was staying withing fixed limits. On a battlefield it will be next to impossible to know precisely what yields an opponent is using or how many bombs have been employed. Because of collateral damage, limitations on targets or geographical areas could not be enforced . . . As strikes extended to tactical nuclear delivery systems deployed outside the immediate battlefield area, the question of strategic strikes would immediately be posed.[7]

The politically divisive NATO decision of December 1979 to deploy new theater weapons (discussed more fully below) partakes of this same counterforce rationalization of "limiting" nuclear war. Instead of firming up the nuclear threshold, however, that decision may well make escalation and total devastation more probable in the event of war.

Twenty years after Kahn's *On Thermonuclear War,* Maxwell Taylor would write an Op-Ed piece defending the efficacy of deterrence against counterforce arguments. A "limited strategic attack concentrated on a limited target such as our silo-based ICBMs" would not really amount to war "in any rational, Clausewitzian sense." Any major strategic exchange would be so devastating that victory and defeat would be "virtually indistinguishable, save perhaps that the victors might survive a bit longer than the vanquished."[8]

4. *Counterforce dogmas of "nuclear war-fighting" and "war-winning" make nuclear war "thinkable" and thereby increase its probabilities.*

It is bad enough to promote illusions about the rational conduct of nuclear war and the prospects for limiting its ravages: it is even more objectionable that counterforce dogmas tend to weaken the moral resistance to nuclear war itself. That nuclear threshold has been an enduring if precarious fact of the post-1945 world. It is perhaps the most significant moral constraint in human affairs of any kind.

The nuclear threshold is threatened by the resurging temptation to believe that nuclear weapons aren't really all that bad, after all: they are "usable" in some circumstances and the US must be prepared to use them to assure a meaningful victory in any war with the Soviet Union. To be confronted in the 1980s with ranking politicians and strategists (George Bush, Caspar Weinberger, Alexander Haig, Frank Carlucci, Fred Iklé, and presumably President Reagan) who urge the thinkability and winnability of nuclear war is a profoundly depressing thing, given the enormity of overkill in superpower arsenals. It was Carlucci who, during his confirmation hearings in the Senate Armed Services Committee after his 1981 nomination as Deputy Secretary of Defense, clearly affirmed his commitment to both a "counterforce capability" and a "nuclear warfighting capability." (The fact that Carlucci viewed the latter as "over and above" the former is further evidence of confusion as to just what counterforce itself really means in relation to both deterrence and the actual conduct of war.)

High-level confusion over the plausibility of "nuclear war-fighting" was painfully exposed on October 16, 1981, when President Reagan tried to explain his own position. Asked by a newspaper editor if a US-Soviet nuclear exchange could be limited, Reagan replied:

> I think, again, until some place—all over the world this is being, research going on, to try to find the defensive weapon. There never has been a weapon that someone hasn't come up with a defense. But it could—and the only defense is, well, you shoot yours and we'll shoot ours. And if you still had that kind of a stalemate, I could see where you could have the exchange of tactical weapons against troops in the field without it bringing either one of the major powers to pushing the button.

That statement stirred the sensitivities of Europeans about their "nuclear battleground" and generated consternation in NATO governments which US officials took days of special effort to subdue. If it became apparent that Reagan actually intended no change in policy, perplexity remained as to the nature of existing policy and of Reagan's effective command. That perplexity was compounded three weeks later when Reagan, confronted with a public dispute between Secretary of State Haig and Secretary of Defense Weinberger, confessed he did not know what NATO policy was concerning first use of nuclear weapons as "warning shots." The lack of coherent strategic policy which marked the Carter Administration thus marked the leadership of another President inexperienced in foreign affairs. Even more disturbing was the lack of clear evidence of awesome respect for the nuclear threshold.

Some deterrence thinkers have made this issue the firmest demarcation between themselves and counterforce advocates. Here, indeed, counterforce has tended to stray from the first principle of deterrence: the prevention of nuclear war. Bernard Brodie, more than two decades ago at the time when the Missile Age was just dawning and nuclear arsenals were quite modest by today's standards, strenuously objected to the war-winning fancies of his contemporaries: "A plan and policy which offers a good promise of deterring war is therefore by orders of magnitude better in every way than one which deprecates the objective of deterrence in order to improve somewhat the chances of winning."[9]

Those who reject deterrence because of its incompatibility with disarmament must surely make common cause with deterrence on this issue.

5. *Counterforce dogmas encourage unwarranted expectations of nuclear superiority.*

The age of nuclear parity arrived two decades ago when each of the superpowers had acquired a retaliatory second-strike force capable of inflicting intolerable devastation upon the other. That parity is no adequate foundation for national security but it is an irreversible fact, pending either significant disarmament or nuclear war. Neither defensive technology nor a counterforce first strike offers a credible threat to that equation.

In a 1968 *Foreign Affairs* piece on the strategic balance, Carl Kaysen testified to the durability of parity:

> We cannot expect with any confidence to do more than achieve a secure second-strike capacity, no matter how hard we try. This capacity is not usefully measured by counting warheads or megatons or, above the same level, expected casualties. Whether the result comes about with twice as many Americans as Soviet delivery vehicles—as has been the case in the past—or with roughly equal numbers, or even with an adverse ratio, does not change its basic nature.[10]

Kaysen's caution remains a basic text for both deterrence and disarmament advocates.

By contrast, counterforce proponents these days are trying hard to reclaim nuclear superiority for the United States. They are more inclined to count megatons and strategic launchers than the more consequential totals of warheads—but they are preoccupied with military mathematics. They tend to view the US as currently or imminently inferior to the Soviet Union in the arms race. They support a massive US buildup to recreate at least a "margin of safety" —a reasonable-sounding synonym for superiority.

Of special import—but serious dubiety—is the assertion that a prodigious buildup of counterforce weapons to advantageous margins is a requisite of renewed arms control. This idea holds that the Soviets must be intimidated into accepting US terms for a new SALT treaty and other arms control agreements. It is an idea which flies in the face of the whole experience of the past three decades, during which every escalation of military technology on the US side has been resolutely matched by Soviet escalation.

Yet this is the dogma that dominated the Reagan Administration's approach to arms control from its inauguration. In July 1981 Secretary of State Haig asserted that the US would not be ready to conclude any new arms control agreement until a new "position of strength" enabled the US to "demonstrate that we have the will and the capacity" to solve its security problems "without arms control." He referred specifically to the need for new weapons to offset the presumed vulnerability of US land-based missiles. The USSR, after emphasizing for six months the need to resume arms limitation talks, began to shift toward an even more blatant effort to build up its own strategic nuclear forces. Following the Haig statement on arms control, the Soviet armed forces chief of staff, Marshal Nikolai Ogarkov, declared that the USSR would counter every US effort to gain military superiority—although he added that such superiority was impossible anyway and that any nuclear conflict would be catastrophic for "the whole of mankind."

Thus the quest for strategic advantage—whether in deterring nuclear war, or presuming to win it, or pressuring adversaries into arms control negotiations—has proved to be increasingly senseless. Obsession with two current myths—ICBM vulnerability and European nuclear imbalance—provides the rallying points for counterforce dogma in the early 1980s. Those myths, as we have promised, will be reviewed separately because of their enormous implications in hyping the arms race.

There is no wiser word on this issue than that uttered by Henry Kissinger in a moment of exasperation in 1974:

> What, in the name of God, is strategic superiority? What is the significance of it politically, militarily, operationally at these levels of numbers? What do you do with it?[11]

Dr. Kissinger who, since retiring from the State Department in 1977, has wobbled unsteadily along the lines between deterrence and counterforce, later recanted that utterance in the course of very equivocal testimony on the SALT II Treaty in 1979.

6. *Counterforce weapons are provocative threats which increasingly tempt adversaries to contemplate a preemptive strike.*

The nuclear threshold is dangerously weakened not only by fatuous claims of benignity for counterforce weapons but also by their apparent malignity to adversaries. It is the technology that threatens most provocatively: the attempt to develop a capacity, however unattainable, to destroy all those arms on which the other side depends for its security. *We* may say that we need such a capacity to enhance our deterrence. *They* may say that we are preparing for a preemptive attack—which would intensify the pressure to beat us to the attack with whatever counterforce weapons they possess. Or, if *we* anticipate the possibility of *their* attack, we may jump the gun ourselves. Thus the probabilities of a nuclear war are magnified both by the notion that strategic weapons are "usable" by our side and by their implicit threat of a "disabling first strike" to the other side. It is this contradiction between the "humaneness" of weapons as *we* see them and the annihilation of deterrent security as *they* see them which could convert parity to holocaust.

Neither superpower would ever acknowledge a drive to achieve such a "first strike" capability. It would not only be indecent, it would be dangerous and probably catastrophic to admit such an intention. Yet both the US and USSR are developing missiles whose number, power, and accuracy provide precisely the technical characteristics required of first strike weapons. Confronted with such technological terror, neither side will find it easy to trust the good intentions of the other. As Calder sees it:

> When both superpowers are armed to the teeth with 'counter-force' nuclear weapons, the danger is not that either side is tempted in cold blood to make his strike, but that both are driven toward it by mutual fear. There may come a moment when, without any malice in your heart, you have frightened your opponent so badly you must hit him before he hits you. Nuclear deterrence becomes nuclear impulsion.[12]

In such a situation, even if optimistic projections of nuclear "victory" have been abandoned, the leaders on one side may become suddenly and irreversibly committed to the notion that only a preemptive strike can save their country from total annihilation.

7. *Counterforce weapons threaten to overwhelm the technologies of arms control verification.*

The superpowers' confidence in their own "national technical means" of verification (NTM) has been the keystone of strategic arms control. Those means include satellite photography, seismography, radio monitoring of telemetry from missile tests, missile-tracking ships, and reconnaissance planes. The Carter Administration, when it was actively promoting the SALT II Treaty, repeatedly expressed absolute confidence in the adequacy, even redundancy, of its NTM systems. In fact, Jimmy Carter and his aides never seemed to tire of repeating, somewhat over-enthusiastically: "We don't *have* to trust the Russians! We can trust our own means of verification."

If that kind of technical fix on the means of arms control raises political questions of US-Soviet relations just as serious as over-technicized military doctrines do — and if the verifiability of SALT II itself was a debatable issue — the counterforce drive raises a more ultimate question. Will the pace of military technology now so outstrip the pace of arms control technology that verification will be an insoluble problem in future strategic negotiations?

Counterforce weapons like MX and ground- and sea-launched cruise missiles are designed to feature just those characteristics of mobility, concealment, and deception which will frustrate Soviet intelligence capabilities. If the Soviets lose confidence in their own verification systems, they may not only be spurred to frustrate US verification: their mounting anxiety could only increase the pressures toward accidental war or preemptive strike. The US would doubtless experience a similar collapse of confidence in its NTM, with similarly unpredictable risks.

8. *Counterforce targeting of adversary leaders threatens any prospect for rational decision-making in preventing, controlling, or stopping nuclear war.*

If counter-city deterrence is repugnant because it holds masses of civilians hostage to nuclear threats while possibly leaving escape hatches for their leaders, counterforce strikes at a cardinal principle of arms control in targeting political leaders themselves. That principle holds that adversary leaders must be permitted to exercise rational control, communications, and negotiations if nuclear war is to be prevented or stopped at the earliest possible moment.

PD 59, by contrast, promised that adversary leaders, even in their bunkers, are to become prime targets of new precision weapons. Such a targeting doctrine, however, may be more appropriate to a strategy of deterrence than to counterforce, given the latter's propensities to make nuclear war more thinkable and more probable. If nuclear war actually breaks out, the power of adversary leaders to constrain their own forces, to communicate and to negotiate may be the only hope of avoiding a total slide into the abyss.

That hope is further diminished by the sheer geography of leadership targets. Most political and military leadership sites in the USSR are in Moscow and other centers of governmental control. Nuclear strikes on these targets would hardly reveal any consequential difference between "counterforce" and "counter-city" warfare — at least in the minds of surviving Soviet leaders still under attack. Their eyes and ears could hardly persuade them that the US was being scrupulously rational and restrained. Rather, as Colin Gray has observed: "Once executed, a very large strike against the Soviet political and administrative leadership would mean that the US had 'done its worst.' If the Soviet government, in the sense of a National Command Authority, were still able to function, it is likely that it would judge that it had little, if anything, left to fear."[13] In this, as in innumerable other respects, the mythology of counterforce intentions is belied by the realities of counterforce consequences.

9. *Counterforce dogmas escalate the vertical proliferation of nuclear weapons, thus impairing an already-faltering non-proliferation regime.*

The provocative tendencies of counterforce are not limited to the terrors of superpower conflict.

If deterrence is irrelevant to non-proliferation and legitimizes bad role models for nuclear-prone states, counterforce is a potent catalyst to the spread of nuclear weapons. To justify not only the retention of nuclear arsenals but their further multiplication by the superpowers is to heap contempt on those nations which have the potential for nuclear weapons but have heretofore restrained themselves from developing them.

Any national security doctrine which does not squarely confront the political and technological realities of proliferation is an isolationist trap. The timing of PD 59, whatever its connection with the Democratic Convention of 1980, was disastrous for the Second Review Conference of the Non-Proliferation Treaty in Geneva, also just five days later. The US position had already been made well-nigh-indefensible in that forum because of failure to ratify SALT II or to conclude a Comprehensive Test Ban—yet US good intentions to complete those agreements remained more or less believable until PD 59 and its "countervailing strategy" were disclosed. The fact that the US delegation in Geneva was taken completely by surprise, not to mention the astonishment of Secretary of State Muskie over his being "inadvertently" excluded from this decision for a new nuclear doctrine, compounded the virtually universal dismay.

Most serious of all, however, was the basic fact that PD 59 provided an authoritative rationalization for nuclear weapons proliferation by the US and gave the Soviets a new excuse to accelerate their own counterforce programs. It thereby catalyzed a great leap forward in the arms race. The whole notion of a balance of obligations, on which the Non-Proliferation Treaty rests, was rudely upset. The entire disarmament agenda was made to seem incredible. The Review Conference itself broke up in acrimony and disarray after four weeks of failure to close the gap between the superpowers and the non-nuclear weapon states.

There was one other Very Bad Thing about the disclosure of PD 59. It came on August 6, 1980 — the thirty-fifth anniversary of the bombing of Hiroshima.

Secretary Haig's July 1981 exposition of the Reagan Administration's arms control philosophy plainly reaffirmed this commitment to vertical proliferation. After all, Haig said, arms control should not be allowed to "restrict the advance of technology." But if arms control cannot restrict military technology, what can it do?

10. *Counterforce weapons lead to quantum increases in military budgets.*

Counterforce advocates typically seek to trivialize concerns about new weapons costs by pointing out that strategic arms in recent years have accounted for only a fraction of the cost of conventional weapons. That argument ignores the fact that, for the past decade, a host of new weapons systems have been primarily undergoing research and development. As the US moves toward actual production of MX, more Trident subs, new cruise missile systems, a new ABM system, and new strategic bombers, the costs of counterforce weapons will loom very large indeed. MX alone may well exceed $100 billion.

Minuteman Vulnerability and the Chain of Follies

It was the technology of the proposed MX missile that did most to evoke a new counterforce doctrine from the Carter Administration almost from its beginnings in 1977. Behind the military hardware itself was a highly theoretical issue which had been drummed up with increasing alarmism throughout the 1970s: the claim of "ICBM vulnerability." Reminiscent of the "missile gap" alarms of 1959-60, the aggressive attack by hardline strategists on this issue has had far-reaching consequences beyond reckoning.

The alleged vulnerability of Minuteman missiles became the pivotal dogma of the entire deterrence-counterforce-arms control debate. Not only did the go-ahead on MX emerge from that debate. The SALT process was delayed, discredited, and finally defeated. The détente of the 1970s was largely undone by this dogma. And the nuclear arms race escalated far out of control. It may be doubted whether any argument over any single weapon since the Hiroshima A-bomb has been more portentous in its results than this Minuteman dispute.

The dogma of Minuteman vulnerability envisioned an "open window" in the early-to-mid 1980s through which the Soviets might be tempted to launch or threaten an attack on US land-based missiles. That window would be opened because heavy Soviet missiles would predictably acquire the power, the number of warheads, and the accuracy to knock out the entire US ICBM force—or so it was said. The US, however, lacked both missile mobility and defensive weapons to guard against such an attack.

In the most desperate yet frequent scenario, ICBM vulnerability would enable the Soviets to launch a successful first strike—a counterforce strike targeted only on US ICBMs and destroying them all. The Soviets would not attack cities in this first round but would retain at least half their ICBMs for that purpose if the US retaliated. An American President, faced with the decision as to whether to launch a retaliatory second strike, would very likely be inhibited by fears of what a Soviet "third strike" would do to US cities: senseless devastation and slaughter. So: the Soviets would have a good prospect of destroying the whole US ICBM force with relative impunity. With such a prospect, it was imagined, they might not have to attack at all. They could simply threaten to attack and resort to nuclear blackmail.

At first, the Carter Administration showed signs of discounting such scenarios, largely because they were promoted by senators and lobbies opposed to SALT II, to which the White House was committed. The Committee on the Present Danger (headed by Paul Nitze and Eugene Rostow), the American Security Council (headed by retired General Daniel O. Graham), and Norman Podhoretz's neo-conservative *Commentary* magazine succeeded in dominating the strategic debate and intimidating the administration. At the end, Secretary of Defense Harold Brown had been captured by the vulnerability scenario, declaring that the Soviet Union would have within two years "the necessary combination of ICBM reliability, numbers, warhead yields, and accuracies to put most of our Minuteman and Titan silos at risk."

On further inspection, however, this argument from ICBM vulnerability is itself so vulnerable to sober criticism that the inability of the Carter Administration to stand against it is a matter of astonishment. Leaving aside the familiar tendency to dehumanize Soviet decision-makers and oversimplify their motives, we may well think through the scenario itself and note its fantasies.

What confidence could the Soviets actually have that their

attacking missiles would be 100 percent reliable and effective? Could they really assume that all or most of their missiles could be launched and their MIRV warheads released without electronic or computer breakdowns? Could they complacently believe that their missiles would avoid being thrown off course by the polar magnetic field, over which they have never tested their trajectories? How could they be sure that in a chaotically explosive environment they could avoid the problem of "fratricide": exploding missiles knocking other missiles off their intended course? Could they really expect that the US would simply leave all its ICBMs idle in their silos instead of launching them on warning? And if, despite these difficulties, they still managed to knock out 80 percent or even 90 percent of US ICBMs, would they really be prepared to accept the many millions of their own casualties that "only" 100 or 200 US missiles (with several hundred warheads) could surely inflict in a second strike? Aren't the Soviets aware that their own missile force, three-fourths of which is land-based, is more vulnerable than the US triad? By what faith or calculus could the Soviets suppose that, even if all US ICBMs were knocked out, the US would refrain from retaliating with the other two legs of the strategic triad — thousands of nuclear warheads on submarines and bombers? Do the Soviets not know that just one Poseidon submarine could destroy 160 Soviet cities, or (soon) one Trident submarine more than 300 cities? What pictures in their heads could possibly induce them to attack our land-based missiles?

The only contingencies in which such a Soviet assault is credible at all are (a) the insanity of leaders, or (b) fear of an imminent first strike by the US. Counterforce logic about ICBM vulnerability is thus circular and tends toward the ultimate self-fulfilling prophecy. Because we anticipate the possibility of a Soviet first strike, we shall proceed to deploy precisely those weapons which will make the Soviets fearful of a US first strike and may tempt them to preempt that prospect — unless we beat them to it by anticipating their fearful reaction to our counterforce weapons.

In reality, what we have most to fear is Soviet fear, not Soviet confidence. What the Soviets have most to fear is American fear, not our confidence. The fear-mongering promoted by the ICBM vulnerability dogma is one of the most perverse political phenomena in our modern history.

MX is not the only hardware rationalized by the ICBM vulnerability dogma. Cruise missiles were originally promoted as an offset to ICBM vulnerability, as a cheap alternative to MX, and as weapons less likely to spur the Soviets to expand their own strategic systems. Henry Kissinger supported cruise missiles in 1973 as "bargaining chips" rather than priority weapons—but the Pentagon's cruise missile patrons were never really prepared to negotiate away their investments in this exotic technology whose strategic purposes have yet to be consistently explained. Now we are getting both MX and cruise. Mark 12-A warheads in process of installation on three hundred Minuteman III missiles will double their power and their counterforce potential against Soviet missile silos.

Some of the particular problems concerning MX have already been noted: provocations to preemption, specious moralism about non-combatants, undermining of verification systems, and enormous costs. MX promises to be the most costly weapons system ever devised.

But there are yet other problems with MX. One is its promiscuous rationale, which flip-flops from a defensive excuse to an offensive license for a multi-megaton counterforce system. That rationale begins with an understandable (if misplaced) defensive concern to offset the vulnerability of fixed ICBMs—hence mobility of some sort on trains or trucks or planes or subs. But then the rationale shifts from mobility to offensive weapons characteristics: ten warheads on each missile, totaling upwards of four or five megatons of explosive—perhaps several hundred times the Hiroshima A-bomb. These counterforce first strike implications of MX thus go far beyond the initial defensive anxiety about fixed ICBMs.

The Reagan Administration's MX program, announced October 2, 1981, put off until 1984 any decision as to whether or how to make the missile actually mobile. What had been decided was to produce 100 MX missiles and to deploy at least 36 of them in existing ICBM silos. The offensive firepower of these weapons had now become more compelling than concern about Soviet attack, even though Reagan continued to speak of the "window of vulnerability." This surprising announcement, which stunned those politicians and military strategists who had always assumed that "vulnerability" must be countered by "mobility," promised many months and perhaps years of continuing controversy in Congress and the national security bureaucracies. Former National Security Adviser Zbigniew Brzezinski, who had strongly supported the Carter Administration's MX plan for 200 mobile missiles in 4,600 protective shelters in Utah and Nevada, protested that the Reagan plan not only failed to solve the vulnerability problem but was "destabilizing" because it threatened the Soviets with a first-strike weapon which was as unprotected as existing ICBMs. Similar objections were voiced by former Defense Secretary Harold Brown, General David Jones (Joint Chiefs Chairman), and Senators Jackson and Tower.

These objectors to the Reagan plan did not, however, speak to a more disturbing anomaly. While the vulnerability dogma was losing credibility, even within the Reagan Administration itself, the decision had been made to proceed with MX, after all. It was to be part of a $180 billion "modernization package" to enhance "deterrence." The package also included 100 B-1 bombers, Trident II missiles, and submarine-launched cruise missiles. True, the environmentalists of Utah and Nevada had won at least a temporary battle against deployment of mobile missiles in their states. But counterforce escalation, now based on even flimsier logic, was powerfully reinforced. The contradictions between deterrence and counterforce were sharper than ever. The arms race had been made still more perilous — unless the logic could be overturned.

This promiscuous relationship between MX and Minuteman needs to be exposed as part of a much more extensive chain of spuriously related weapons systems going back to the 1960s and now promising to extend to the end of this century — if Earth survives. Both the flimsy logic of each link and the tenuousness of the entire chain of rationalizations must be made plain if we are to understand how badly US security has been served.

The enormous size of the US offensive missile force (1,710 strategic nuclear launchers) was originally predicated on untruths about a "missile gap" at the beginning of the 1960s.

Both the ABM and MIRV decisions of the late 1960s were predicated on alarms about a Soviet missile defense system, said to be large and growing. (Although it must be remembered that Secretary of Defense McNamara, whose personal analysis of the arms race led him to resist the ABM, was obliged to announce it as an "anti-Chinese" missile defense — an excuse which made sense only in the political animosities of the Vietnam War, certainly not in the strategic equations between China and the US.) The US "needed" the multiple-warhead MIRVs to be able to penetrate Soviet missile defenses and to maintain our second-strike capability.

Then, when it became apparent that the Soviets had only a single ABM unit (around Moscow) and had no real confidence in their own defensive technology, MIRVs were justified as "bargaining chips" in negotiations with the Russians. Yet no serious effort was made to forestall MIRV deployment through the SALT I talks which began in 1969. In 1970, the Nixon Administration went full speed ahead with MIRV deployments on both our Minuteman ICBMs and sub-based missiles. Referring to these desperately shifting rationales for Minuteman III and Poseidon missiles back in 1970, veteran US government arms controller Adrian Fisher quoted Santayana's definition of a fanatic: "one who doubles his speed when he has lost his way."

The main function of "bargaining chips," in practice, has not been to negotiate a halt to the arms race at any stage: it has been to provide a rationalization for escalation when all other strategic logic fails. Even if we do not need new nuclear weapons for valid strategic reasons, we can say that we need them for diplomatic reasons. This argument assumes (a) that the Soviets will trust our intentions in good faith and (b) that our own government will retain the political will to stop weapons development or deployment when a diplomatic opening presents itself. These assumptions have proved unwarranted. The diplomatic tactic again and again has led to irreversible strategic deployments.

The MIRV decision not only exposed the doctrinal gymnastics on the US side: it showed up the follies on the Soviet side. It proved the prescience of arms controllers in the early 1960s who warned that any ABM "defenses" would turn out to be extremely provocative of new "offensive" missile systems. In the age of nuclear parity, they said, "defense" could be more threatening than "offense" because it might seem to nullify the utility of deterrent weapons. Superpower confidence in "assured destruction capabilities" would be shattered if those arms were deprived of their assurance of destruction. ABMs would therefore provoke a rapid multiplication of nuclear missiles on the other side in an effort to overwhelm the new defense and make deterrence credible again. Which is precisely what MIRVs were all about—that is, *if* the US could really take Soviet ABMs seriously. Whatever the final motives for actual US MIRV deployment, the Soviets had handed the Pentagon a timely excuse. The USSR's one ABM unit of fewer than one hundred noncredible defensive missiles around Moscow boomeranged badly: more than 5,000 additional nuclear weapons would be targeted on Soviet sites. Herbert York, the Pentagon's first Director of Research and Engineering, rightly judged that "the Soviet ABM program has been fantastically counter-productive and has had anything but a stabilizing effect."[14]

Once again, however, the US had grossly overreacted to a Soviet stimulus, largely because of faulty intelligence. Or, it may be said, another administration found a strategic excuse to appease the aggressive momentum of military technology within the national security bureaucracies.

The chain of folly did not end with MIRVs, however. In fact, it was precisely the MIRV decision which set the stage for the Minuteman vulnerability issue of the 1970s. For it was US MIRVs which provoked the Soviets into their own MIRV program. And the Soviets, with their fondness for bigness, began producing huge SS-18 missiles perhaps capable of mounting thirty or more warheads each. As Russian warheads multiplied and their accuracy improved, the survivability of Minuteman became an anxious question. In fact, the very MIRVing of US missiles suddenly seemed to make the nuclear arsenal vulnerable — for MIRVing meant the concentration of warheads on a finite number of ICBM sites, perhaps tempting the Soviets to consider that there could be a new payoff from a preemptive strike on the US. That is, if only Soviet minds would work the way some American strategists fancied they would!

Even the MX, ostensibly designed to offset those Soviet SS-18s, is not the end of the chain. For, in addition to Mark 12-A warheads and Tridents and cruise missiles and new bombers, there are bizarre new proposals for ABMs on the US side. The new ABMs would be designed to protect MX. (If a defensive missile system really *could* work, then we must ask why we need any MX at all.) Quite apart from the unprovable technologies of such "defenses," a regression to ABM after a decade of abandonment would complete the circle of senseless logic. A short history of the nuclear arms race since the mid-1960s would then read: the US needed ABMs against Chinese attack, MIRVs to penetrate Soviet ABMs, MX to protect our vulnerable MIRVs against their MIRVs, new ABMs to protect our vulnerable MX which is protecting our vulnerable MIRVs which are protecting our second strike capability which is vulnerable to an essentially non-existent Soviet ABM force.

That is the chain of follies to which we must connect the Minuteman vulnerability issue. It is a pattern of "reasoning" which exhibits speculative chaos and political blindness.

There are yet other problems with MX which are still being struggled over at this writing: the strategic dilemma as to whether it will only provoke more counterforce missiles on the Soviet side, the environmental dilemmas concerning any basing-mode on land or aircraft, the preference of General Maxwell Taylor and a corps of admirals for putting all strategic missiles out to sea instead of multiplying land targets which could bring down a rain of thousands of nuclear warheads on American territory. An underlying reality is pervasive congressional skepticism over virtually all the basing-modes proposed for MX. They have been so widely lampooned as Rube Goldberg contraptions that one observer has wondered whether the "giggle factor" might eventually defeat the entire system, even though few members of Congress had taken public stands against it. In times of economic austerity, however, the costs of MX could prove to be the most promising constraint. Annihilation may not matter: an unbalanced budget would be something really serious.

Theater Nuclear Imbalance

Almost completely overshadowed in 1979 by the Minuteman vulnerability issue, the SALT II debate, and the MX fight was yet another nuclear controversy: whether there existed a "theater nuclear imbalance" in Europe and, if so, whether NATO should deploy proposed new "Eurostrategic" weapons. In fact, there was almost no public controversy in the US over this question before NATO ministers on December 12, 1979, ambivalently accepted US proposals for 572 new theater nuclear weapons: 464 Ground-Launched Cruise Missiles (GLCMs) and 108 Pershing II Medium-Range Missiles (MRBMs). Not only had other strategic and arms control issues obscured the theater problem. The Iranian hostage crisis after November 4 and the early drumbeats of the 1980 elections made concentration on TNF (theater nuclear forces) "modernization" an exercise in which only a very few specialists and activists became engaged.

Yet the onset of a new nuclear arms race in Europe was a dismaying event which has split most of the major political parties of Western Europe, stimulated the most massive movements for disarmament since the 1950s, and very nearly wrecked NATO. In Europe, of all regions, where détente itself originated (although Richard Nixon and Henry Kissinger tried to claim credit for it) and where the achievements of détente were still highly prized, a dispute over the adequacy of NATO's thousands of nuclear weapons did much to revive the Cold War. Not that the Soviets were blameless: their own missile "modernization" with triple-warhead SS-20 MRBMs and their new Backfire bombers had provided the warrant for the NATO decision. However, the Russians had tried, and failed, to get theater weapons restricted by SALT I and then by SALT II. They had understandable reasons for believing that US "forward based systems" had long confronted them with a "theater nuclear imbalance."

President Brezhnev tried to head off the NATO decision with his announcement on October 6, 1979, that the USSR was prepared to reduce its total of theater weapons if NATO would refrain from proceeding with its new missiles. At the same time, Brezhnev announced token reductions of 1,000 Soviet tanks and 20,000 Soviet troops in East Germany. President Carter immediately rebuffed the proposal, dismissing it as "an effort designed to disarm the willingness of our allies to defend themselves." The allies, however, were much more disposed to put Brezhnev to the test in serious negotiations.

With regard to TNF issues and the entire post-Helsinki agenda of European security, European and American priorities have increasingly diverged since the late 1970s. The drafting of NATO communiqués has become ever more an art of concealing these divergences, especially between Germany and the US.

As Michael Howard put it:

> The question that was so often asked in the United States, 'what have we got out of détente?' was not often asked in the Bundesrepublik, where every family with relatives in East Germany knows precisely, in terms of communication and travel, how much their divided nation has benefited from the Ostpolitik initiated by Chancellor Willy Brandt. . . . It was these human contacts, as well as the increasing flow of trade with Eastern Europe, that the government of West Germany was anxious to preserve.[15]

To be sure, Chancellor Helmut Schmidt had been an early sponsor of new Euromissiles, at least as "bargaining chips" with the Soviets — a fact which increasingly divided his Social Democratic Party and undermined his political mandate.

The dogma which threatened to destroy détente in Europe was that of a "theater nuclear imbalance" — the regional counterpart of "Minuteman vulnerability" and the latest version of a "missile gap." Like MX, Euro-strategic weapons had counterforce implications. And, like "Minuteman vulnerability," the idea of a "theater nuclear imbalance" adverse to NATO requires considerable demythologizing. Three myths caught up in this dogma are exposed by the following questions:

1. *Was there really a nuclear imbalance in Europe in 1979 — or is there one now?*

NATO has long had thousands of tactical nuclear weapons for battlefield use to offset Soviet troop and tank deployments. And more:

(a) Pershing I nuclear rockets capable of striking 500 miles into Eastern Europe;

(b) Land-and-carrier-based fighter-bombers with nuclear bombs, capable of striking the USSR;

(c) Hundreds of nuclear warheads on several Poseidon submarines assigned to NATO, also capable of striking the USSR. Each Poseidon sub can carry up to 160 warheads; therefore each sub is theoretically capable of destroying 160 Soviet cities. Thus one submarine alone is a nation-destroying weapon;

(d) 192 nuclear warheads on four British Polaris submarines, soon to be replaced by four Tridents which will mean hundreds of additional British warheads. Plus 50 nuclear-armed Vulcan bombers;

(e) 132 warheads on French bombers, submarines, and land-based missiles — and France, too, is now "modernizing."

It takes the most abstract exercises in military mathematics to validate any claim of Soviet theater advantage in 1979 or 1980. The basic reality has been theater parity for many years: of course, the Soviet Union could pulverize Western Europe — just as NATO could pulverize the Soviet Union. Now, however, because the Brezhnev offer was spurned without being tested, the Soviets indeed are proceeding to deploy dozens of additional SS-20s during a three-or-four-year "window" before NATO's new weapons can be installed. So, by another of those self-fulfilling prophecies, there is a Soviet missile buildup in Europe.

2. *Isn't the whole notion of a "theater nuclear balance" artificial and absurd if we separate it from the thousands of intercontinental strategic weapons which both the US and USSR possess?*

This question is much more basic and pertinent than the first. No amount of bookkeeping on the balance of nuclear weapons in the European theater itself makes much sense if the overarching reality is intercontinental parity. The US will control Euro-strategic weapons just as surely as it will make the decisions about when or whether to fire ICBMs, SLBMs, or ALCMs. Continental boundaries, like the boundaries of nation-states, are meaningless in any nuclear conflict involving the superpowers.

Whether or not the US should have agreed with the USSR to address theater issues in SALT I or II, it is hardly conceivable that these issues can be split apart from a resumption of the SALT process. After all, the new Euro-strategic weapons could strike Soviet territory directly from European land-bases for the first time. In the unending asymmetry of US engagement in Europe, this means that US theater weapons could hit Russian cities in four or five minutes—but SS-20s could not reach American cities at all. Just as surely the Soviets could simply shorten the trajectories of their own ICBMs to compensate in the European theater for any TNF buildup on the NATO side. McGeorge Bundy, after opposing new Euro-strategic weapons as well as comparative weapons counts with SS-20s and *Backfires,* wrote that "in any moment of serious stress neither Washington nor Moscow is at all likely to regard such American weapons as a separately usable or clearly limited kind of force. Any American-controlled weapons that can reach the Soviet Union will almost surely be all alike to them both."[16]

There is no way to make Europe detachable from the rest of the world in nuclear matters, whether the political flash-points occur in Europe or on any other continent. That is, unless Europe becomes a Nuclear Free Zone—which is hardly what NATO and the Warsaw Pact are working on at the moment.

3. *Isn't it the intolerable risk of new theater nuclear weapons that they increase the illusion of being able to fight a "limited nuclear war"?*

Three months prior to the TNF decision, Henry Kissinger was in Brussels speaking to a conference sponsored by Georgetown University's Center for Strategic and International Studies with which he had become affiliated. While the American media were largely occupied with other topics, Dr. Kissinger made page one headlines all over Western Europe by his new prescription for a "flexible option." It seemed like his 1957 *Nuclear Weapons and Foreign Policy* all over again: what the US and NATO most needed was a capacity "to wage small-scale nuclear wars." Such a capacity would be more credible than "the threat of mutual suicide." It would be attainable if NATO would only decide to deploy those GLCMs and Pershing IIs. The former secretary of state seemed to be an advance man for the Carter Administration's Euro-strategic campaign.

Thus did Henry Kissinger make a claim to membership in the counterforce camp. In fact, the European theater is the most tempting region for counterforce thinkers to fantasize about "small-scale nuclear wars" in which there are only military targets and civilians are spared because the whole affair can be quite rationally managed and contained. But that may be because it is only in Europe that the US maintains large ground forces and still thinks in battlefield terms. The Reagan Administration's fond myth of the "integrated battlefield" of conventional, tactical, and strategic nuclear weapons deserves something less than reverence. The healthy suspicion that any nuclear war, especially one involving the superpowers, would probably become a "large-scale nuclear war" throwing off all restraints and escalating toward Götterdämmerung seems foreign to counterforce calculations. Herbert Scoville, Jr., former official of both the CIA and ACDA, said in 1981: "A nuclear war in Europe will be a catastrophe unparalleled in the history of our civilization. The hope that a nuclear war can be kept limited is groundless."

Beyond these exercises in de-mythologizing the dogma of a "theater nuclear imbalance," several further difficulties must be mentioned.

Just as a new land-based ICBM system like MX would greatly multiply American territorial targets for Soviet attacks, so would 572 new land-based missiles in Western Europe. Germans and Britons and Italians are about to become more vulnerable than ever to mass annihilation. If multiplying land targets in the US is a dubious strategy in view of the vast territorial advantages of the USSR, the concentrated populations of Western Europe have yet a stronger claim to be spared such nuclear targeting. Perhaps all of Europe's nuclear weapons, too, should be put out to sea before they are banished altogether.

The danger that counterforce weapons will undermine the technologies of verification is especially acute concerning cruise missiles which are small, mobile, easy to conceal, convertible to either conventional or nuclear warheads. Moreover, cruise missiles are particularly designed to avoid the radars of early warning and defense. The entire future of arms control negotiations could be jeopardized by GLCMs — and, perhaps all too soon, SLCMs (sea-launched cruise missiles). (Your reputation as an expert will be greatly enhanced if you pronounce those acronyms "Glickems" and "Slickems" instead of spelling them out.) While President Reagan's October 2, 1981 program for strategic "modernization" attracted most attention to its go-ahead on MX, B-1, and Trident II, Soviet verification technology was perhaps most threatened by the word that the US would deploy 500-600 SLCMs. The protocol of the unratified SALT II Treaty prohibited such weapons — but that protocol expired December 31, 1981.

Finally, Europeans themselves seem much more likely than

Americans to remember that their consent to GLCMs and Pershing IIs in 1979 was sealed with the promise that the new weapons would be "bargaining chips" toward serious negotiations to reduce theater weapons on both sides. The Reagan Administration has been pushed with increasing vigor by NATO allies to make good on that pledge by the Carter Administration. Preliminary US-Soviet talks began in Geneva, November 30, 1981, with Paul Nitze heading the US delegation.

Twelve days before those talks began, President Reagan set forth a "zero option" which Helmut Schmidt had urged upon him: the US would refrain from deploying its new Euro-missiles if the USSR scrapped all its SS-20s and even the older SS-4s and SS-5s they had replaced. It was a proposal designed to counter recent Soviet propaganda and also to placate NATO governments hard-pressed by new disarmament movements. Given weeks of advanced publicity about these political motives, it was hardly surprising that the Soviets initially rejected the "zero option" within hours of its announcement. Their complaint was that the Reagan proposal was only a propaganda ploy and that it totally ignored US forward-based systems as well as British and French nuclear weapons already targeted against the USSR. Early agreement therefore appeared extremely problematical. Some skeptics blamed both sides for playing the game of disarmament as cynically as it had been played in the 1950s. Yet the conciliatory tone of Reagan's address and Brezhnev's counterproposal for a moratorium on further SS-20 deployment seemed to indicate the first diplomatic opening since the Soviet assault on Afghanistan two years before.

In August 1981, President Reagan made a startling decision which unwittingly implied an alternative to negotiations as a way to forestall GLCMs and Pershing IIs: the decision to produce neutron bombs. While arguments would continue on the effects "enhanced radiation" weapons would have on deterrence and counterforce, this decision clearly overloaded the nuclear circuit in Europe. It came at a time when NATO politicians were still far from securing adequate public support for longer-range GLCMs and Pershings. Ironically, the general in charge at State, Alexander Haig, had argued strongly against proceeding with neutron weapons because of these political difficulties — but the civilian in charge of Defense, Caspar Weinberger, had discounted politics. Weinberger was enamored with neutron technology which might "save thousands of innocent civilians" in a nuclear war, though he hoped it would "add to the credibility of our deterrent." He declared that making such tactical decisions about warfare on European territory "cannot be turned over to even our closest allies."

Several NATO governments immediately protested the neutron decision. The ruling Social Democratic Party in Germany complained that it was an obstacle to East-West arms control and had provoked "new arguments" for anti-Americanism in Europe. German consternation was hardly assuaged by White House assurances that this was merely a "domestic" decision not requiring actual deployment in Europe — after all, the whole point of neutron weapons was to counter the imagined threat of a Soviet tank attack in Germany. Nor were Germans and other Europeans gratified by Weinberger's unfortunate charge that anti-neutron sentiment was "largely a tribute to the effectiveness of the Soviet propaganda campaign against this weapon." In truth, Weinberger and the White House had given the most hawkish of Soviets a propaganda bonanza, with every indication that the USSR would now proceed to produce the neutron bombs it had also experimented with some years before. The US decision was a classic case of uninhibited fascination with sophisticated technology which leads to the most unsophisticated politics. It also led to a crude camouflage of the diplomatic and moral issues. It showed a very high-level disrespect for truth. Yet its result might be a bizarre case of fratricide: a suddenly increased prospect that Euro-strategic weapons might be killed by the neutron bomb.

For the beleaguered disarmament constituency in the US, there is a new appreciation of trans-Atlantic links. This mythology of "theater nuclear imbalance" has galvanized millions in Western Europe to a new seriousness about the arms race. The largest anti-nuclear demonstrations in history were staged in most European capitals — demonstrations which clearly had much to do with the Schmidt-Reagan "zero option." The political consequences of this issue, in both Europe and America, are just beginning to register. Some Americans are increasingly looking to Europeans for aid in interpreting nuclear realities to the US public.

CHAPTER 4

Nuclear Dynamics: The Arms Race

The fact that the Soviets and the Anglo-Saxons have decided to discontinue nuclear tests on land, sea and in the air is satisfactory. . . . But the Moscow agreement does nothing to remove the terrible menace hanging over the world from the nuclear armaments of the two rivals — in particular, over the peoples which do not possess them. . . . If one day the Americans and Russians disarm — that is to say, if they destroy their nuclear armaments and ban the means of delivery — we shall wholeheartedly do the same. But, unfortunately, we do not seem to have reached that stage yet. And the sad Geneva Disarmament Conference will, as could have been foreseen, have sat interminably for nothing. France is only waiting for this vain play-acting to end. — President Charles deGaulle at a press conference July 29, 1963, commenting on the Limited Test Ban*

After being wafted about by airy strategic doctrines, we must face some very worldly questions. What really causes the nuclear arms race itself? Do missiles produce conflicts — or do conflicts produce missiles? What are the dynamics of cause-and-effect? Does our perception of causes point toward security policies which may reverse or even end the arms race? Or do we see a world of relentless hostilities in which the prosecution of the arms race is an infinite imperative? Or, again, do we foresee an end of the arms race only by a victory by one side or the other? But, after all, how many sides are there in the arms race?

The idea of disarmament must be grounded in answers to such questions. To think through these questions is to do as much clear-eyed historical analysis as possible. It is not really to dispense with ideas but it is to insist that ideas conform to the contours of reality. The problem, of course, is that the political landscape itself looks very different to different observers.

Our discussion of nuclear dogmas has repeatedly suggested the persistence of gaps between military ideas and empirical realities.

These gaps reflect not only the inadequacy of the ideas themselves. They reflect the fact that military technology typically outpaces the strategic ideologies which rationalize weapons innovations. They reflect confusion among policy-makers at the highest levels. And they reflect a more intentional divergence between declaratory policy and operational policies. Thus the US is now producing counterforce weapons with first-strike implications, even though first-strike intentions are denied. The perception of these gaps is crucial for the development of sound disarmament policies.

When we shift attention from doctrines to empirical realities, we do not really escape ideological controversies. Any effort to make politics meaningful requires a framework of meaning: a set of ideas which seeks to describe and analyze reality. The moral dilemmas of political leadership involve more than choosing among good principles: they require choices among conflicting pictures of reality. In fact, agreement on principles is often a much simpler matter than agreement on facts and their meaning. The facticity of foreign policy is typically more troublesome than the formulation of purposes. It is just such a disagreement about the facts, especially about the comparative powers of two hostile nations, which most commonly provokes a war. Any claim to be "realistic" is at least as suspect as any claim to be "moral."

A generation of "political realists" including Hans Morgenthau, Walter Lippmann, and Reinhold Niebuhr in the 1945-1970 period persistently poured skepticism on "idealistic" advocates of disarmament. The "reality" which they invoked insisted that the arms race was more a symptom than a cause of political conflict. Accordingly, the only "realistic" hope for eventual disarmament depended upon resolving basic political problems. Morgenthau regularly declared: "Men do not fight because they have arms, but they have arms because they deem it necessary to fight."

The opposite form of "realism" has emphasized the primacy of disarmament itself. Disarmament advocates like Britain's Nobel Prize winner Philip Noel-Baker have argued that armaments themselves, especially mounting accumulations of them, become prime causes of wars. (A comprehensive discussion of the causes of war is beyond the scope of this book. Two volumes which provide such a discussion are Dean G. Pruitt and Richard C. Snyder, editors, *Theory and Research on the Causes of War* [1969] and Geoffrey Blainey, *The Causes of War* [1973].)

What we must question here, however, is the chicken-or-egg polarity of competing "realisms," especially concerning the nuclear arms race. Whatever may have been true of conventional arms races in earlier generations, the dynamics of the nuclear arms race indicate a vicious circle of both causes and consequences. Military technology, particularly in matters of strategic nuclear weapons and their increasingly sophisticated delivery systems, has acquired a degree of autonomy which threatens to outrun the political capacities of either governments or international institutions to control.

The issues of disarmament may have less and less to do with the "realities" of foreign policy as such: they surely require much sterner forms of domestic discipline within our national political systems. For the problem of disarmament is no longer basically a matter of diplomacy and treaties — although we must continue to work for international accords wherever possible. Rather, the struggle for disarmament requires some changes in our own institutional styles and values without which diplomacy has little chance to make real peace. Disarmament is far more than a specialized, technical subject: it is the profoundest possible challenge to political imagination and cultural change.

Images of the Arms Race

The pertinence of this approach to nuclear dynamics may be vivified by examining a set of *alternative images of the arms race.* What, after all, causes the nuclear arms race between the super-powers?

One image, of course, is a *denial* that the arms race continues. Some persons speak of "nuclear parity" as if the race had actually ended. After meeting Secretary Brezhnev at Vladivostok in late 1974, President Ford announced that they had "capped the arms race." With the collapse of SALT II, the Vladivostok accord has yet to be firmly implemented. Moreover, that accord actually raised the permissible limits of offensive strategic weapons. And, in fact, both powers have proceeded to develop new generations of weapons. So the image of denial is a very questionable one.

The second image is *ideological* and one-sided — although it comes in two opposite versions. To some persons, especially in the West, the arms race is viewed as the result of the "Soviet drive for world domination" or for "military superiority." Western arms, therefore, are purely "defensive" or "deterrent." The opposite version views the arms race as the result of "capitalist and imperialist forces." The arms of the Soviet Union and other "socialist" countries are simply a "defensive" response of the "peace-loving peoples."

These opposite versions are mirror-images of one another: they may help to explain some public attitudes, as well as propaganda, but their essential resemblance suggests that they do not adequately explain the objective realities.

A third image was suggested by former US Secretary of Defense Robert McNamara: the *"action-reaction phenomenon."* This is essentially a psychological explanation. The emphasis here is on the escalation of mutual anxiety. Each side responds to what it perceives to be hostile intentions or deployments on the other side. As arms accumulate in number and variety, there is a vicious upward spiral of mounting insecurity and over-reaction. This explanation certainly seems to have some validity. If it provided a complete account of the dynamics of the arms race, we could clearly say that the task of public opinion leadership is to reduce fear and anxiety in both policy-makers and the public. But it is increasingly clear that this is only a partial account of the vertical proliferation of weapons. Weapons research and development is often more than a reaction to particular cues: it may be a matter of anticipation or of attempted superiority, or even of pointless momentum.

This suggests a fourth image: the strategic doctrine of the *"worst possible case."* Here the emphasis is on a pattern of virtually limitless weapons development and deployment to meet every conceivable contingency rather than simply reacting to the other side. This is *arms proliferation through infinite anticipation.* There is a preoccupation with what we might call "rational fantasies": with every imaginable scenario far into the future, no matter what the other side actually does, or seems to be doing. One of the clearest statements of this approach was once provided by the US director of defense research and engineering, John Foster:

> In each case [of weapons development] it seems to me the Soviet Union is following the US lead and that the United States is not reacting to Soviet actions. Our current effort to get a MIRV capability on our missiles is not reacting to a Soviet capability so much as it is moving ahead again to make sure that, whatever they do of the possible things that we imagine they might do, we will be prepared.[1]

To the extent that Foster's explanation corresponds with reality, weapons development appears to be largely inaccessible both to public opinion and to the policies of the other side. More serious, this dynamic suggests the propensity of worst-case analysis for self-fulfilling prophecies: the worst cases are often made more likely because they are anticipated on the most unlikely evidence. Nearly four decades ago, Reinhold Niebuhr offered one of his witty paradoxes: "It is the business of military strategists to prepare for all eventualities, and it is the fatal error of such strategists to create the eventualities for which they must prepare."

There is a fifth and final image of the arms race: the *bureaucratic momentum of military technology.* This image suggests that repeated cycles of weapons research, development, production, and deployment have habituated major military powers to the dynamic of institutional drives which appear to be increasingly autonomous. The patterns seem remarkably similar in the Soviet Union and the United States, suggesting again that conventional ideologies do not illuminate the arms race very much. "Generations" of weapons breed new "generations" in both countries. There is a relentless push toward maximization of technology, reinforced by strategists and engineers with a compulsion to innovate and by industrialists managing vast production empires (whether or not they make profits). Then (at least in the US) there are workers and unions with vested interests in defense jobs, and politicians seeking to satisfy the industrialists and workers in their constituencies.

The force of this bureaucratic momentum may have little to do with fear of the "enemy," or with the objective requirements of national security, or even with a healthy economy. It may produce an arms posture which is lacking in both strategic coherence and political relevance.

In another portion of Robert McNamara's San Francisco speech of September 18, 1967, the Secretary of Defense suggested an alternative to his own "action-reaction" image:

> There is a kind of mad momentum intrinsic to the development of all nuclear weaponry. If a system works — and works well — there is a strong pressure from all directions to procure and deploy the weapon out of all proportion to the prudent level required.

Citing that statement Herbert York, who had managed military research and engineering for the Pentagon, observes: "The technological side of the arms race has a life of its own, almost independent of policy and politics." York's explanation of "technological excesses" highlights the following:

1. A combination of patriotic zeal and "religious faith in technology" gratifies "psychic and spiritual needs" and therefore transcends greed and malice: self-esteem is generated by commitment to weapons development as a holy cause and by the stimulus of military technology to their imaginations.

2. Strong personal bonds develop between R and D, procurement, and industrial types.

3. Interservice rivalries and competing congressional committees generate phony intelligence, invent "problems to fit the solution they have spent much of their lives discovering and developing," and produce "gross misapplications of 'worst-case' analysis."[2]

What is striking about York's analysis is the degree to which the arms race dissociates its prime participants from political realities, both domestic and international. Military technology is portrayed as a profoundly alienating force, even while it seems to gratify some individual needs. (In this respect, it resembles the theologies promoted by electronic evangelism.)

York disclaims any attempt to assess overall causes of the arms race or to assign blame for it. His survey of the steps by which it has developed, however, leads him to this conclusion:

> I have found in the majority of those cases that the rate and scale of the individual steps has, in the final analysis, been determined by unilateral actions of the United States. . . . The reasons are that we are richer and more powerful, that our science and technology are more dynamic, that we generate more ideas of all kinds. For these very reasons, we can and must take the lead in cooling the arms race, in putting the genie back into the bottle, in inducing the rest of the world to move in the direction of arms control, disarmament and sanity.[3]

There may be elements of truth in all five of these images of the arms race. The dynamic realities are surely complex and multifaceted. Perhaps the most adequate picture focuses on the image of bureaucratic momentum, with more than a side glance at worst-case planning and action-reaction. Yet the dominant image in these early 1980s — the portrait shared by the Reagan Administration and much of the American public — is ideological. This fix on ideological causation and the evils of the Russians cuts the nerve of American responsibility as Herbert York sees it. The issue of initiative and responsibility in ending the arms race requires us to look at doctrines of linkage, of vertical proliferation, and of connections between nuclear and conventional escalation.

Linkage and the Arms Race

It has become a cliché to assert, with a posture of profundity, that disarmament cannot be achieved in a political vacuum. What is less obvious is the pattern of connections between disarmament and other policy issues. Since the late 1960s various conceptions of "linkage" have been put forth to explain these connections. The aura of mystification surrounding this topic has obscured its caprices and contradictions. Perhaps the most crucial question is whether a doctrine of linkage spurs progress toward disarmament or rationalizes opposition to it.

In one sense, linkage is (or ought to be) an obvious fact of life. It is the recognition of the interdependence of nations and the interconnectedness of issues. Decisions about nuclear weapons and warfare affect, potentially, every nation, every other policy area, and the future of the human species.

In a somewhat more limited sense, linkage is the insistence that arms control and disarmament must be viewed as components of a broad conception of national security. If disarmament advocates too often fail to articulate such a comprehensive vision of security, however, hardliners too often identify security primarily with military force, failing to appreciate the severe limits to the utility of force and the salience of non-military components of security.

A third notion of linkage views disarmament as the prime catalyst to détente in both military and non-military affairs. This idea of catalytic linkage gained enthusiastic advocates in the first Nixon Administration. A week after his inauguration, Nixon held his first press conference and announced:

> What I want to do is to see to it that we have strategic arms talks in a way and at a time that will promote, if possible, progress on outstanding political problems at the same time—for example, on the problem of the Mid-East and on other outstanding problems in which the United States and the Soviet Union, acting together, can serve the cause of peace.

Nuclear accords with the Soviet Union were viewed, for a time, as "the hub of a widening, thickening network of contacts between the two great powers. The wider and denser this connecting web, Nixon and his associates believed, and the more deeply enmeshed the Soviet Union became, the more moderate, and less hostile to American interests would be Soviet policies the world over." This hope was closely connected with commercial expectations of a much greater volume of profitable trade between the superpowers.[4]

It is doubtful, however, that this positive doctrine of catalytic linkage ever served as the single-minded view of Richard Nixon, Secretary of State William Rogers, or NSC Adviser Henry Kissinger. Kissinger, the dominant intellectual force in the policy community, had evolved a rather ambiguous notion of linkage. On the positive side, he did affirm that détente was indivisible: every problem of US-Soviet relations was linked with every other problem between them. But this affirmation had its negative counterpoint: a punitive approach to arms control which sought to make Brezhnev "behave" in Indochina, the Middle East, and Angola as the price of SALT agreements. Soviet Ambassador Anatoly Dobrynin came to regard linkage as "a form of extortion bordering on blackmail."[5] Rogers came into bitter conflict with Kissinger over the true meaning of linkage, stressing a more positive approach to SALT regardless of developments in other policy areas.

The Carter Administration, plagued with chronic disabilities in articulating a coherent foreign policy, vacillated between ingenuousness and belligerence in addressing the question of linkage. The White House wanted the world to believe that an aggressive and well-advertised campaign for human rights on behalf of Soviet dissidents, even on the eve of its first SALT talks with the Soviets in Moscow, need not have any fall-out on SALT. Yet the White House also increasingly charged that Soviet policies in Africa were hurting SALT prospects. Zbigniew Brzezinski complained in February 1978 that both SALT negotiations and ratification were being damaged by events in the Horn of Africa. In a remarkably ambiguous formulation, the NSC Adviser announced: "Linkages may be imposed by unwarranted exploitation of local conflicts for larger international purposes." At a press conference the very next day, Jimmy Carter declared that Soviet intervention in the Horn was jeopardizing the possibility of Senate ratification of SALT. "We don't initiate the linkage," he added. Thus a passive and implicitly punitive doctrine of linkage had taken hold which, combined with an unwillingness to explicate clearly the transcendent importance of nuclear issues, contributed to the delay and eventual demise of SALT II. *Pravda* lost no time in charging that linkage, once again, "smacks of crude blackmail which is impermissible in international relations."[6]

It is the tension and inconstancy between catalytic and punitive views of linkage which have confused the American public and, no doubt, vexed the Soviet Union. One view stresses an activist pursuit of disarmament, while hoping but not waiting for progress in other policies. The other stresses a more reactive, wait-and-see bargaining approach which tends to hold up disarmament until satisfactions are won in other areas. The Nixon-Ford regime ended on this reactive, punitive note. The Carter Administration started out activist, tried for a while to repudiate any notion that SALT was a matter of rewards and punishments, then wound up making so many concessions to the more punitive chauvinists that the credibility of détente was destroyed.

The Reagan Administration made its commitments to punitive linkage clear and unambiguous: the arms race was all the Soviets' fault and they would not be rewarded with a SALT agreement until they behaved themselves all over the world. Thus the most one-sided and least sophisticated ideological image of the arms race made a startling comeback in 1981. It is a projection of all evil onto the enemy in disregard of the enemy's own insecurities and the grossness of the arms race on both sides.

The most authoritative expression of this view was given by Secretary of State Haig in a July 14, 1981, address to the Foreign Policy Association. Haig set forth the principle that arms control would only be sought "bearing in mind the whole context of Soviet conduct worldwide." Then he added:

> Such 'linkage' is not a creation of US policy; it is a fact of life. A policy of pretending there is no linkage promotes reverse linkage. It ends up by saying that in order to preserve arms control, we have to tolerate Soviet aggression. This Administration will never accept such an appalling conclusion.

Recalling that Haig was once Kissinger's deputy in the White House, we may say that Haig personifies the reactive, punitive notions of linkage developed by Kissinger but that the deputy has sloughed off his mentor's sense of ambiguities. But then Kissinger seems to have done so himself.

Two days later, *The New York Times* editorially rebuked Secretary Haig for tying disarmament so rigidly to Afghanistan, the Iran-Iraq war, Cambodia, Chad, Cuba, Angola, and Ethiopia:

> Such loose talk about 'linkage' implies that SALT is not a gain for American security but a concession that the United States can safely withhold from the Soviet Union in wider bargaining. But it has always been the absence of good relations and the

certainty of continued ideological and military rivalry that has made it vital to both countries, and the world, to stabilize the nuclear balance. To argue that a political settlement must first be achieved is a prescription, or a pretext, for an uncontrolled and disastrous arms race.[7]

It is precisely the failure of punitive linkers to put arms control into a prudent context of genuine security that discredits their dogma of linkage. It becomes self-righteous and ideological and loses sight of the security interests the American people have in stopping the arms race. It is, as Curt Gasteyger noted, escapist in seeking refuge from difficult economic and social problems in the more familiar environment of US-Soviet conflict. It insists on linkages which are untenable and it repudiates linkages which are imperative. The real issue is not linkage or no linkage: it is linkage with *what?*

The what that must not be subordinated to any other interest is the very life of Planet Earth. It is not the Soviet threat that must be absolutized but the survival of the human species. It is this transcendent understanding of linkage which must motivate the idea of disarmament. It is to connect the superpower arms race with the global proliferation of nuclear weapons. It is to recognize that the SALT process and nuclear testing are inseparably linked with the Non-Proliferation Treaty—a linkage which seems to have escaped the notice of Henry Kissinger, Alexander Haig, and Ronald Reagan.

It is myopic to argue that this or that political controversy in this or that part of the world must be solved before proceeding to disarmament. It is not that tranquility will make disarmament possible: it is precisely that troubles make disarmament necessary. It is no refutation of disarmament to point to persistent US-Soviet conflicts: those very conflicts demand curbs on the arms race.

President John F. Kennedy objected to the assertion that disarmament should be postponed to times of "fair weather":

A sea wall is not needed when the seas are calm. Sound disarmament agreements, deeply rooted in mankind's mutual interest in survival, must serve as a bulwark against the tidal waves of war and its destructiveness. Let no one, then, say that we cannot arrive at such agreements in troubled times, for it is then that their need is greatest.[8]

Vertical and Horizontal Proliferation

Whatever the causes of the nuclear race between the two super-powers, the roll call of nuclear weapons states is clearly lengthening in the 1980s. The nuclear parade, after Hiroshima, was joined by the USSR in 1949, Britain in 1952, France in 1960, and China in 1964. This limited nuclear club of five members was probably crashed during the past decade by several other countries with both the requisite technology and political motives. While the boundary between nuclear weapons states and non-nuclear weapon states is now fuzzier than ever, the following countries are among the most likely proliferators: India, Pakistan, Israel, Iraq, Libya, South Africa, Argentina, Brazil, Taiwan, and South Korea. More than fifteen additional countries (such as the Federal Republic of Germany, Sweden, Canada, Australia, and Japan) have the requisite technology but will not, foreseeably, have the political motivation to become nuclear weapon states. Six Soviet bloc countries with nuclear reactors are hardly likely to become nuclear-weapon states, given the tight control of the Soviet Union over all such matters within its sphere of influence. However, possible theft of fissionable materials or tactical nuclear weapons by still other governments, political movements, or criminal syndicates is hardly an incredible short-cut to proliferation.

Thomas Schelling, whose nuclear studies have focused more on deterrence than on proliferation, observed in 1975 during the first intimations of the new nuclear crisis: "A reasoned evaluation . . . suggests that we will not be able to regulate nuclear weapons around the world in 1999 any better than we can control the Saturday-night special, heroin, or pornography today."[9] That forecast can hardly be less valid in the 1980s than it was in 1975.

How do we account for this seemingly uncontrollable increase in nuclear promiscuity? Any serious attempt to understand the causes of this horizontal arms race must take account of a variety of factors, including:

1. The availability of nuclear technology and materials;
2. The effectiveness of the international non-proliferation regime;
3. Local and regional conflicts;
4. The behavior of nuclear weapon states.

These factors will be more fully examined in the chapter on nuclear diplomacy. We have already noted that the bilateral preoccupations of deterrence theorists have tended to incapacitate them for coping effectively with nuclear weapons spread, that superpower prerogatives claimed for nuclear weapons provide bad role models, and that counterforce apologists now propose an untimely new round of vertical proliferation.

The term "vertical proliferation" is one bit of nuclear jargon that did not originate in American think tanks. It was originally a polemical term invented by non-nuclear weapon states to put the onus for proliferation on the superpowers instead of on the nuclear morality of lesser powers. However, as the undeniable realities of nuclear escalation by the US and USSR persisted for more than a decade after they signed the Non-Proliferation Treaty, "vertical proliferation" began to pass the lips of American and Soviet diplomats and scholars.

While the superpowers have frequently denied any direct link between their own vertical proliferation and the horizontal proliferation of other countries, they have occasionally argued just the opposite. When the Carter Administration was actively promoting the ratification of the SALT II Treaty, one of its most earnest arguments was that the failure of SALT II would be a very dangerous catalyst to the breakdown of the Non-Proliferation Treaty and the spread of nuclear weapons.

It cannot be doubted that the political motives of most nuclear-prone states derive largely from local and regional rivalries which are not primarily superpower affairs. Whatever their motives, however, their capabilities are clearly subject to superpower influence and the effectiveness of international institutions. The non-nuclear coalition in the United Nations and the Non-Proliferation Treaty has understandably and unceasingly argued that the US and USSR bear the primary responsibility for nuclear weapons spread because of their failure to halt their own arms race, to share energy technology, and to provide adequate support for the International Atomic Energy Agency, the prime enforcement arm of the NPT. In short, vertical proliferation is held to be the basic cause of horizontal proliferation. And horizontal proliferation may be the most likely cause of nuclear war.

William Epstein, a Canadian who served for many years as Director of the Disarmament Division of the UN Secretariat, has written the definitive study of the politics of proliferation, grimly titled *The Last Chance.* He concludes:

> The US and the USSR must accept the burden of changing the world's attitude toward nuclear weapons. Only they can halt and reverse the vertical proliferation of nuclear weapons, which may

well be a necessary condition for preventing horizontal proliferation and nongovernmental proliferation. If they continue to
militarize the world with both nuclear and conventional
weapons, they can hardly expect that other countries . . . will
refrain from acquiring such weapons. They have the great responsibility of establishing the illegitimacy of the nuclear arms
race and the legitimacy of nuclear restraint and arms control.[10]

Nuclear and Conventional Escalation

Closely related to the vertical-horizontal proliferation pattern
is the complex interaction between the nuclear arms race and conventional arms races. It has long been recognized, for example, that
progress in European Mutual and Balanced Force Reduction talks
(MBFR) in Vienna depended on prior progress in the SALT talks.
On the other hand, some NATO leaders have long advocated a
buildup of conventional forces in order to lessen the West's dependence on nuclear weapons.

However, it is the rapid growth of conventional arms exports
to the Third World which has raised the most vexing questions of
nuclear dynamics. In 1981, the Reagan Administration disclosed
that it would relax the Carter Administration's guidelines on arms
sales (guidelines which were largely ineffective at that) in order to
divert Third World temptations to go nuclear.

Here, then, is the hard question: do conventional weapons
buildups diminish or enhance the probabilities of going nuclear?

Let us look at the dynamics of the US conventional military
market as it developed during the 1970s from a less-than-$1 billion
a year level to $14 billion a year. At least ten factors, revealing a
complex mix of political and economic considerations, appear to be
involved. No fewer than four of these must be seen as residues of
the Vietnam War:

1. The Nixon Doctrine, which signified an intention to reduce
US military intervention in Asia (and elsewhere), was accompanied
by the promotion of arms purchases to nations which would
assume more responsibility for their own defense — after buying
American. More negatively, a number of Asian nations (South
Korea, Taiwan, Pakistan, perhaps others) were troubled by the implications of US defeat — loss of face and credibility — in Indochina,
and resolved to acquire more military hardware for themselves.
More recently, a US official asserted: "If we are not going to be the
world's policeman, then nations able to purchase their own police
force are almost certain to go ahead and do so."

2. With the winding down of aerospace industries after the Vietnam War peak of 1968 (and the simultaneous phase-out of the Apollo moon program), the Nixon Administration zealously promoted arms sales to maintain production lines, corporate profits, and defense employment — and, no doubt, to forestall political reprisals from districts experiencing industrial shut-downs. (Aerospace employment, in fact, dropped from 1.5 million in 1968 to less than 1 million in 1971.)

3. The Vietnam War provoked serious problems of inflation and balance of payments. The payments problem became acute in October 1971 when the US registered its first trade deficit in 78 years, whereupon President Nixon renewed his pressure on the Pentagon to promote arms sales.

4. Because the Vietnam War made direct military aid extremely unpopular in Congress and with the general public, the Nixon Administration deliberately emphasized weapons sales as a more tolerable form of arms transfer, particularly because sales were seen as a way of circumventing the congressional appropriations process. Military trade replaced aid as the dominant mode. However, the distinction between aid and trade remains obfuscated by Foreign Military Sales (FMS) Credits from US Treasury funds or government guarantees of private bank loans for purchasing US weapons. The effect of this lending program, amounting to $2.1 billion in FY 1978, is to promote arms sales to those countries which cannot afford to pay cash.

There were still other factors in the early 1970s which were less connected with the Indochina experience:

5. As the armed forces found their research and development costs escalating severely for new forms of high military technology, they were increasingly determined to hold unit costs down by selling large quantities to foreign customers. This determination marked the shift from dumping surplus and obsolete weapons abroad to soliciting foreign capital to help pay for the most sophisticated weapons in the US. Former Secretary of State Henry Kissinger testified to a congressional committee that arms sales "permit our defense industries to achieve significant economies through scale of production — economies that are passed along through lower prices to our armed forces." The Congressional Budget Office estimated that $8 billion in US arms exports would save the Pentagon $560 million in weapons costs. Ironically, therefore, arms sales are rationalized as an important device for reducing the defense budget.

6. The British withdrew from the Persian Gulf area in 1971, providing the Nixon Administration with an important new rationale for boosting arms sales in that strategic region. Such sales were touted as "a systematic US effort to strengthen local self-defense capabilities" in the Gulf area, according to Deputy Assistant Secretary of Defense James H. Noyes in 1973.

7. The greatest single boost to arms sales, largely in that same Persian Gulf area, came with the oil crisis in 1973-74 and OPEC's quadrupling of oil prices. Countries like Iran and Saudi Arabia suddenly had billions to spend on their military ambitions as well as their domestic development; the US and its NATO allies suffered severe new balance of payments problems which could be relieved by selling OPEC powers the arms they wanted. US arms exports to Persian Gulf states were only $861 million in 1972; in 1974 they amounted to $6.5 billion, a more than sevenfold increase in two years. Thus the "recycling of petrodollars" became a powerful engine of the arms traffic. To "bring those dollars back home" was a popular public cry. In the five-year period 1974-78, military sales to Iran totaled $16.3 billion; to Saudi Arabia, $12.3 billion; to Israel, $5 billion. These three countries thus received more than two-thirds of all US arms exports in that period.

8. An important feature of Henry Kissinger's diplomatic style was to sweeten difficult negotiations, such as the shuttle diplomacy in the Middle East or the leasing of military bases in Spain, with promises of fighters, missiles, and nuclear technology. Thus an ironic form of conflict resolution developed: overcome immediate political obstacles by pledging weapons and technology which could make conflict even more violent in the long run. As the *Defense Monitor* puts it: "Like the thoughtful gift of wine or flowers to one's hostess, an agreement to supply arms warms the atmosphere of diplomatic parleys. The willingness to give or sell arms has become a token of friendship, a gesture of American faith and goodwill."

9. The progress of military technology in other countries faced with inflated fuel costs and balance of payments problems confronted the US with greatly intensified competition in the world military market. This competition became both a spur and a justification for the US to become even more zealous in its merchandising. Political and commercial motives were at stake in the argument, "If *we* don't sell them the weapons they want, others will." This advent of a many-sided conventional arms competition has now made US unilateral restraint politically difficult. France, the

United Kingdom, the Federal Republic of Germany, Italy, and Sweden are all important arms suppliers — in addition to the Soviet Union, Czechoslovakia, Poland, and China. Arms exports are also mounting for countries as diverse as Belgium, Spain, Switzerland, Hungary, Israel, and Brazil. Having led the world in the arms trade for many years, some Americans are more determined than ever to remain Number One.

Notwithstanding the Carter Administration's professed concern about arms sales, Undersecretary of State Lucy W. Benson (senior official in charge of arms sales) declared: "No one ever said that we should not be the largest. . . . I have every expectation that we will remain the largest arms exporter for the foreseeable future." However, Soviet sales may have matched, if not exceeded, US sales to developing countries in 1981. Meanwhile, both Britain and France have declined to enter a sales-restricting agreement with the US. Sir Ronald Ellis, chief of weapons sales for the UK Ministry of Defence, acknowledged several years ago: "This country is absolutely dependent on exports, and that increasingly includes overseas arms sales." In fact, Britain has doubled its sales since 1977. The French clearly depend on arms sales to help solve payments problems, provide jobs, and help finance their own advanced combat aircraft. Result: French sales jumped from $500 million in 1973 to $8 billion in 1980. US-Soviet CAT (Conventional Arms Transfer) talks, inaugurated in December 1977 and intended to limit sales to the Third World, have collapsed along with the SALT talks.

10. The conventional arms race became incalculably tangled with nuclear proliferation following the oil crisis, India's test explosion of May 1974, and reports of other nations (such as Israel) acquiring nuclear weapons capabilities. A new "Doves' Dilemma" — whether to step up sales of highly sophisticated conventional weapons in order to reduce temptations to go nuclear — confronted US policy-makers. Joseph S. Nye, the State Department officer who chaired the Carter Administration's National Security Council Group on Non-proliferation, said: "There is no question that our conventional arms sales also play a part in affecting motivations to turn to nuclear weapons." (Oppositely, the sale of aircraft or missiles capable of carrying nuclear weapons increasingly suggests that conventional arms sales might promote nuclear proliferation. Further, the rapid acquisition of conventional arms by one state could prompt a hostile neighbor to take a cheaper, quicker route to deterrence or prestige: going nuclear.) Whatever the causal linkages between them, both nuclear proliferation and the conventional

arms trade became dramatically more critical during the 1970s. Policy-makers continued to assume that conventional arms exports can help to contain nuclear weapons spread.

In the early 1980s that assumption seemed threatened from the opposite direction. The military market could well be stimulating the nuclear arms race.

CHAPTER 5

Nuclear Diplomacy: The Two and the Many

The moon and other celestial bodies shall be used by all States parties to the treaty exclusively for peaceful purposes. The establishment of military bases, installations and fortifications, the testing of any type of weapons and the conduct of military manoeuvres on celestial bodies shall be forbidden. — Article 4, Outer Space Treaty of 1966

As an amateur astronomer, I am relieved that the moon and other celestial bodies have so far been spared the terrors of the arms race. Just how far the writ of Earth runs into the Solar System or beyond is a wondrous question. The Outer Space Treaty, however, does not do Earth itself much good at present. It is the nuclear weapons on our own celestial body that must be the primary object of diplomacy. If they can be controlled, reduced, and eventually banished, we shall hardly have to worry about a nuclear battle on the moon.

In the Third Nuclear Age, it is clear that disarmament policies have not firmly withstood either the vertical or horizontal proliferation of nuclear weapons, nor have they effectively constrained conventional arms races. It may be said, of course, that things would be even worse had it not been for the disarmament agreements of the 1960s and 1970s. But it may also be said that diplomatic styles of coping with nuclear testing, proliferation, and strategic arms have actually tended to escalate the arms race. Paradoxically, both claims may be valid. Their apparent contradiction, however, suggests the need for candid evaluation of nuclear diplomacy to date.

Peripheralism

While the First Nuclear Age of the 1940s and 1950s was marked by repeated exhibitions of dramatic and highly propagandized proposals by both the US and USSR — proposals leading nowhere — the Second Nuclear Age saw the negotiation of a whole series of disarmament treaties. Those treaties, however, did not really restrict the central strategic forces of the superpowers themselves. They staged an exhibition of *peripheralism:* making a show of progress by avoiding the central issues.

The Nuclear Test Ban Treaty of 1963 did eliminate atmospheric testing by three nuclear powers (US, USSR, UK). It also marked, at least temporarily, a détente of sorts—partly because it was the first fruit of the new seriousness about arms control, partly because of enduring traumas from the Cuban missile crisis of the previous October, partly because Pope John XXIII's 1963 encyclical, *Pacem in Terris,* recognized changes and splits within the communist world and shifted the Vatican from confrontation to coexistence, and partly because President Kennedy's "Strategy for Peace" address at American University on June 10, 1963, confessed: "We must re-examine our own attitude" and not "see only a distorted and desperate view of the other side." That address announced, simultaneously with announcements in Moscow and London, that "an early agreement" on a test ban was in prospect. The treaty was initialed six weeks later and signed in Moscow August 5, 1963.

Yet that treaty's preamble, which declared the purpose of "seeking to achieve the discontinuance of all test explosions of nuclear weapons for all times," remains unfulfilled. Actually, there has been much more nuclear testing since 1963 than before. The three nuclear signatories simply resorted to a much more costly program of underground testing—which helps to explain why France and China refused to sign. In fact, the US Joint Chiefs of Staff agreed to support this partial ban only on condition that testing could continue underground and that a stand-by capacity for renewed atmospheric testing would be retained. The 1963 treaty affirmed the United Nations objective which would "put an end to the armaments race and eliminate the incentive to the production and testing of all kinds of weapons"—but the development of new nuclear weapons proceeded unhindered by that rhetoric.

Moreover, the Partial Test Ban disarmed the disarmament movement itself in the United States, Britain, and other countries because that movement had campaigned so largely on the emotional issue of atmospheric fallout. Fears of Strontium 90 and contaminated mothers' milk were not steadfastly directed toward the arms race itself. Indeed, it has only been late in this Third Nuclear Age that the nuclear disarmament movement has resumed anything like its vigor of the late 1950s and early 1960s.

A quarter of a century after Adlai Stevenson raised the test ban issue in his 1956 campaign, nuclear testing continues. The prospects for completing a Comprehensive Test Ban (CTB) in the early 1980s, after several years of renewed negotiations by the three "depositaries" (US, USSR, UK) seemed to promise fulfilment, are doubtful at best. Carnes Lord of Reagan's National Security Council staff has plainly announced that a CTB is "not good arms control." He questioned the adequacy of seismic monitoring and other means of verification, warned of the risks of Soviet "cheating and spoofing," and insisted that nuclear weapons require periodic testing because of "deterioration." Lord was most emphatic in lamenting that the "impact on US weapons programs would be devastating," not least because a CTB might mean "dismantling nuclear weapons labs" which would be very costly to reestablish.[1]

Carnes Lord's fear is, of course, precisely the hope of disarmament advocates all over the world: that a CTB would prove to be the most effective brake on the momentum of military technology. Such a prospect surely explains the continuing resistance of the Pentagon to a total test ban. The professed concerns about verification and "nuclear rot" are more likely matters of camouflage. A long succession of UN expert groups and US scientific associations has expressed high confidence in available technologies of verification.

A less technological and more diplomatic case for a CTB has been offered by Ralph Earle II, President Carter's last Director of the Arms Control and Disarmament Agency and head of the US SALT delegation in 1980. Ambassador Earle, in a March 1981 interview, confided: "I see the Test Ban, frankly, more as a political vehicle. As the NPT Review Conference [last] summer showed, a test ban would be a major political plus in dealing with the rest of the world."[2] However, Reagan's ACDA Director, Eugene Rostow, preferred ratification of the 1974 Threshold Test Ban Treaty which would permit continued testing of weapons up to 150 kilotons, a level below which the US has managed to conduct ninety percent of its underground tests. William Epstein, former UN Director of Disarmament, predicted that ratification of this permissive and "spurious" treaty would cause a CTB to be abandoned or postponed for at least a decade, spur proliferation, and "conceivably provide the excuse for some countries to withdraw from the Non-Proliferation Treaty."[3]

Whatever the fate of CTB diplomacy, peripheralism has characterized all the other treaties of the Second Nuclear Age. The

Antarctic, Outer Space, Seabed, Latin American Nuclear Free Zone, and Non-Proliferation treaties have had no discernible restraint upon the vertical arms race of the superpowers. Many activists worked long and hard to win public support for these treaties, perhaps in the illusion that they would lead to nuclear disarmament.

None of these accords literally requires disarmament — except the Non-Proliferation Treaty's "good faith" pledge of disarmament. Some of them are *non-armament treaties*. For, after all, our diplomats have been preoccupied with banning weapons we don't have, agreeing not to make weapons our government never intended to make, protecting places where nobody lives (such as Antarctica, the Seabed, and the Moon), and preventing *other* countries from getting the kind of weapons we keep producing. Again, the word is *peripheralism*. Or, we might say, the *trivialization of disarmament*.

A more positive case could be made for those treaties if, having emphasized their catalytic potential, it could be shown that they have led to other treaties which have reversed the strategic arms race of the nuclear weapon states. Which brings us to SALT.

Bilateral Disarmament: The Case of SALT II

Surely the most strenuous exercise in disarmament diplomacy has been the Strategic Arms Limitation Talks (SALT). If other agreements have been peripheral, the superpowers have repeatedly proclaimed SALT as the "centerpiece of détente." While the achievements of SALT since November 1969 may seem peripheral or trivial, the Nixon-Ford and Carter Administrations (as well as the Brezhnev Politburo) through the 1970s accorded SALT a lordly status. In fact, it was precisely this mystification of SALT and the high prerogatives associated with it that offended many other countries, both nuclear and non-nuclear, and even dismayed US government officials in other policy areas.

Almost from the beginning, there have been tensions between SALT as a secretive, bilateral monopoly and the more open multilateral forums such as the United Nations, the Geneva-based Committee on Disarmament, and the Non-Proliferation Treaty. It is not only issues of secrecy and participation which have generated the tensions: it has been claims about linkage between vertical and horizontal proliferation, bitter complaints about nuclear double standards, and frustrations over the record of SALT itself.

Conflicting expectations of the SALT process also account for these tensions. Those who expected substantial disarmament in the 1970s were bound to be dismayed by the subordination of arms control to strategic military doctrines and programs. Mason Willrich, former ACDA official, candidly asserted in 1974 that the "codification and stabilization of nuclear deterrence" was the "hoped-for effect of SALT." From the outset, it had been "clear that neither side was contemplating complete nuclear disarmament or the reduction of strategic forces down to levels of minimum deterrence. If anything emerged, it would be a slice of the disarmament apple."[4]

Nevertheless, SALT had also emerged from a welter of multilateral commitments during the 1960s, particularly the 1963 Test Ban and the 1968 Non-Proliferation Treaty. As the SALT process was building its pretentious prerogatives throughout the 1970s, there was an arrogant tendency to forget its connections with these multilateral concerns. Yet the historical linkage was actually celebrated on July 1, 1968, when, on the occasion of signing the Non-Proliferation Treaty, the US and USSR announced their agreement to begin the SALT talks. Unfortunately, the Soviet guns of August 1968 in Czechoslovakia and the US presidential election delayed the actual start of SALT until November 1969 — by which time the Nixon Administration had not only moved ahead with its Safeguard ABM system but also toward full-scale MIRV deployment.

Thus the pristine motive for SALT in the minds of many arms controllers — to forestall ABMs and the MIRVs which were rationalized as a response to ABMs — was frustrated at the very outset. To put the matter even more sharply: SALT I avoided the most critical issue at the precise moment it should have been faced — namely, the threat of a new arms race in offensive nuclear weapons technology, spurred by the hydra-headed MIRVs. Not completed until 1972, SALT I did halt the deployment of extensive defensive systems (which neither side really wanted anyway) under the ABM Treaty. SALT I also concluded an Interim Agreement which set temporary limits on the number of offensive missiles (1,710 for the US, 2,300 for the USSR) — a very asymmetrical and inadequate framework for negotiating nuclear reductions which was repaired, in principle, by SALT II's framework of "equal aggregates." SALT I did nothing to limit the number of warheads or throw-weight or bombers or US forward-based systems in Europe or British or French nuclear weapons.

The failure to stop the multiplication of nuclear warheads through MIRVs is perhaps the most serious blot on the entire record of détente. Nothing in the history of SALT can efface the fact that the superpowers now have many thousands more nuclear warheads than they had in 1969. SALT I gave them a license to do so — which license seriously diminished the legitimacy of the SALT process itself. By the time the SALT II Treaty had been negotiated in 1979, MIRV programs had increased the number of US separately targetable missile warheads from 1,710 to over 8,000 and Soviet warheads from 2,300 to 5,000.

Henry Kissinger's enthusiasm for SALT I was hardly an endorsement of arms limitations as such, much less of disarmament. The great thing about the Interim Agreement, he said, was that it "allowed us to proceed with a crucial technological development" (MIRVs) and it "stopped no offensive program we were contemplating building."[5] A rather romantic pro-Kissinger account of the SALT I negotiations, John Newhouse's *Cold Dawn,* described the process as "probably the most fascinating episodic negotiation since the Congress of Vienna." At a December 3, 1974, press conference, Kissinger himself vented some second thoughts in a rare moment of modesty: "I would say in retrospect that I wish I had thought through the implications of a MIRVed world more thoughtfully in 1969 and 1970 than I did."

Yet the SALT I negotiator, ACDA Director Gerard Smith, had originally advocated a ban on both ABMs and MIRV testing. (Nixon threatened to fire Smith unless he supported ABMs.) Then in March 1970, Nixon's Advisory Committee on Arms Control and Disarmament, chaired by the venerable John McCloy, also recommended a ban on ABMs and MIRV testing. In June, Senator Edward W. Brooke (R. — Mass.) introduced a MIRV moratorium resolution which passed the Senate 72-6 — a position also endorsed by Congressman John Anderson (Ill.), chairman of the House Republican Conference. But Secretary of Defense Melvin Laird, JCS Chairman General Earle Wheeler, Navy Chief Admiral Thomas Moorer, and Pentagon veteran Paul Nitze (then on the SALT delegation) were fervently committed to MIRVs. Kissinger eventually went along with them, explaining that the Soviets would not accept a ban on MIRV technology before doing any MIRV testing themselves. By the time the Nixon Administration's commitment to MIRVs was clear to the Russians, Kissinger was probably right. Because Nixon's Science Adviser, Lee DuBridge, also supported a MIRV moratorium and continued the role of arms control advocacy by his predecessors, Nixon abolished the office of Science Adviser.

It must be remembered, however, that an anti-MIRV fight had been waged by the administration's arms control establishment and by Republican leaders in both houses. In retrospect, it was a disaster for national security and for disarmament that that fight was lost a decade ago.

Nevertheless, some positive things must be said for SALT I, at least provisionally. The very fact of a US-Soviet agreement on limiting strategic nuclear weapons, however minimal its restraints, was perhaps more significant than the restraints themselves. For at least a decade, the superpowers called off the expansion of their ABM systems, although ABM research continued and the anti-ABM technology of MIRVs was unrestrained. A process for continuing negotiations and consultation had been institutionalized and bureaucratized so that, whenever the political will was ready, agreements could be speedily facilitated. Perhaps the most important piece of diplomatic machinery was the Standing Consultative Commission (SCC) established by Article XIII of the ABM Treaty: a bilateral body to review compliance with both that treaty and the Interim Offensive Agreement. The SCC has now had a decade of generally satisfactory experience in hearing grievances concerning alleged violations and in promoting mutual confidence in verification procedures. Legal expiration of the still-honored Interim Agreement in 1977 prior to any SALT II Treaty, along with the Reagan Administration's fresh drive for new ABM systems, could wreck this consultative machinery.

There is a continuing legacy of SALT I which we must now recall in the 1980s: the political payoffs which the Nixon Administration made to secure support for the accords from some senators and the Joint Chiefs of Staff. Defense Secretary Laird promised not only that full-scale MIRV deployment could continue but that Trident submarine, cruise missile, and B-1 bomber development could continue. If the B-1 must be regarded as anachronistic, the Trident program is the most devastating weapons system ever, while cruise missiles are proving to be the most disruptive weapons from the standpoint of arms control stability and verification.

Nixon campaigned in the Watergate year of 1972 largely on the issues of peace and détente, with SALT I and the China trip as his trophies. Nixon's Moscow summit in May, which concluded SALT I, was a well-publicized election year sequel to the Peking journey. Less publicized were the haste and confusion with which administration negotiators finished agreements burdened with ambiguities and asymmetries. SALT negotiator Gerard Smith was excluded from these climactic negotiations which were monopolized by Kissinger. This and further snubs led to Smith's virtually forced resignation as both negotiator and ACDA Director. Some said Smith had been made a sacrificial lamb offered up to placate hardline senators like Henry Jackson. After the election, the negotiating authority itself was stripped from the director's post, at Jackson's insistence.

Most of Smith's top aides were purged. Nixon accommodated Jackson's demands that the SALT delegation itself be purged, with the exception of MIRV protagonist Paul Nitze. (Later it would be Nitze who did most to sound the strategic alarms about Soviet MIRVs, which could have been prevented if SALT I had banned MIRVs.) ACDA's advisory council was deactivated. The ACDA research budget was cut in half; total ACDA funds were reduced from $10 million to $8 million. Public affairs functions were crippled.[6] Thus the price of ostentatious détente may be the gutting of the arms control bureaucracy. A new ACDA director, Fred Iklé, was imported from the RAND corporation: a man whose commitments to weapons development and counterforce dogmas further demoralized the disarmament agency—the same commitments that now are in the service of the Pentagon as Undersecretary for Policy.

As the SALT II talks began in 1972, there was good reason to question whether there was any serious commitment among top Nixon officials to SALT as a process for actually reversing the arms race. Certainly the second round began with very heavy burdens of domestic political costs already incurred by SALT I—costs that would greatly complicate negotiations with the Russians.

Watergate further diminished the will and capacity of the Nixon-Ford Administration to proceed with SALT II, although Ford's 1974 journey to Vladivostok did establish the principle of equality in limits on both strategic launchers (2,400) and MIRVed weapons (1,320). If the very high levels seemed once again to legitimize weapons buildups rather than reductions, even these figures were far from firm because of subsequent US-Soviet differences as to whether they had agreed to limit cruise missiles. The Russians said yes, they had: the Ford Administration said no. Here is Richard Burt's version, published in *Foreign Affairs:*

> The Vladivostok aide memoire said that air-launched missiles with ranges that exceeded 600 kilometers were to be limited in the accord—shortly after the summit, Secretary of State Henry Kissinger told reporters that this referred to air-launched *ballistic* missiles and not to the new generation of precision-

guided, long-range cruise missiles that the United States had under development.[7]

The Soviets understandably felt they had been misled.

During 1975 President Ford and Secretary Kissinger several times "backed away from concessions previously made" (according to Leslie Gelb in an October 16, 1975, report in *The New York Times*). The risks of Soviet agreement were running too high to suit Republican conservatives. Moreover, Kissinger and the Pentagon were at odds over the importance of two weapons which Kissinger regarded as military "hang-ups" holding up the SALT process: the Soviet Backfire bomber (Kissinger discounted claims it was a heavy bomber) and the US cruise missile (Kissinger complained that Pentagon "geniuses think the goddamn thing is a cure for cancer and the common cold").[8] Following a September National Security Council meeting which severely cramped the Secretary of State's room for negotiation, Kissinger was dispatched to New York to give Foreign Minister Andrei Gromyko a new proposal that the US apparently knew would be unacceptable.

Four months later, in January 1976, Kissinger went off to Moscow with still another set of proposals. His mandate for that journey remains a matter of historical controversy, the more so because it nearly brought SALT II to a successful conclusion. These new proposals would have reduced the Vladivostok launcher limit by ten percent (from 2,400 to 2,160) and limited the production rate of Soviet Backfire bombers (which the Soviets have always denied were long-range strategic bombers). But Kissinger offered, in return, to place cruise missile aircraft under the MIRV ceiling and also to limit the range of such missiles to 1,500 kilometers. When the Soviets (perhaps unexpectedly) appeared ready to accept such a compromise, an embarrassed administration withdrew from it.[9] Once again the Soviets felt they had good reason to question whether the US was negotiating in good faith. But the domestic political commitment to cruise missiles was too strong to be negotiated away. Secretary of Defense Donald Rumsfeld and AC-DA Director Fred Iklé were particularly adamant in protecting cruise missiles against any concessions to the USSR. Besides, it was now an election year in which Ford had to face Ronald Reagan (who nearly beat him) — which led to a political decision to shelve any serious intentions to proceed with SALT II. Had the treaty been completed in 1976, the revival of the Cold War might have been prevented.

President Carter's professed seriousness about nuclear disarmament in his inaugural hope that "nuclear weapons could be rid from the face of the earth" and his zeal for non-proliferation seemed to give SALT II a new lease on life. After a somewhat hasty policy review, Carter sent Secretary Vance to Moscow in March 1977 on a new SALT II mission. There was, I believe, a serious contradiction in that mission which, quite aside from Carter's aggressive rhetoric on human rights, was bound to provoke a Soviet rejection. Moreover, Carter's public dramatizing of the Vance mission and its mobilization of public pressure on the Russians tended, as George Kennan put it, to violate everything we have learned about US-Soviet relations in the past two decades. Jan Lodal, director of program analysis for the National Security Council from 1973 to 1975, reported that the Carter-Vance proposals of 1977 would have forced the Soviets to eliminate 400-600 new delivery systems, with the US obliged to eliminate none, or fewer than 100. The USSR would have to forego planned deployments of 400-500 ICBMs with MIRVs, with no corresponding renunciations by the US. Half of Soviet heavy missiles would have to be scrapped; the US had chosen not to build any. US cruise missiles would be produced in unlimited numbers — again the cruise! While the US would halt its MX mobile missile (then only in a very early planning stage), the Soviets would have to give up their SS-16 mobile missile and stop all deployments of SS-17, SS-18, and SS-19 missiles already underway. In sum, said Lodal: "The Carter proposal would bring the Soviet strategic program nearly to a halt, yet leave the US program almost untouched."[10]

It is difficult even now to discern the expectations that went with Vance to Moscow. What was dramatically billed as deep arms cuts substantially below Vladivostok levels seemed like the imposition of unilateral disarmament on the Russians while the US could proceed with Tridents, cruises, Mark 12-As, and so on. If Carter is credited with sincerity and serious expectations, then the proposals seem naive and clumsy in the extreme. If the Vance mission was intended to fail, it simply joins the ancient procession of propagandistic disarmament proposals designed to maneuver adversaries onto a sticky wicket from which they cannot escape without seeming to reject disarmament, peace, and motherhood. Perhaps the most plausible explanation is that the deep-cut objectives were indeed Carter's but the actual proposals were shaped to Henry Jackson's specifications in hopes of enlisting the hardline senator as a SALT II protagonist.[11] If this report is valid, it would hardly be the first time that a diplomatic absurdity had been the outcome of domestic political games. The experts on the SALT team were reportedly dismayed by what they regarded as the incompetence and political incoherence of the March 1977 proposals. (The absurdity would be compounded four years later when the Reagan Administration repeatedly cited the March 1977 episode as proof of Soviet refusal to negotiate deep arms cuts. Public understanding lost again.)

Somehow the SALT process recovered in mid-1977 and developed the three components of the accords now known, at last, as SALT II. Consummation was reported as imminent during the fall of 1977 and the early part of 1978. But in the spring of 1978, a mid-term election year, a political decision was apparently made in the White House to stall the SALT process until Congress adjourned for the election — and with Carter's advisers already spooked by the prospect of another election year, 1980, in which Ronald Reagan would be the enemy.

For nearly two years prior to the actual signing of the SALT II Treaty in Vienna June 18, 1979, this three-tiered framework was a matter of public knowledge:

First, a Basic Agreement (lasting through 1985) fixing eventual and equal US-Soviet limits on strategic launchers at 2,250 and further limits on launchers. For example, 820 is the upper limit of land-based missiles topped with MIRVs. The balance of launchers are sub missiles and air-launched cruise missiles. This agreement also spells out a system of verification procedures.

Second, a short-term Protocol regulating the development of new weapons systems (such as mobile missiles and ground-or-sea-launched cruise missiles) by type and range — with no flight testing or deployment permitted during the life of the Protocol, due to expire at the end of 1981.

Third, a Statement of Principles to serve as guidelines for the actual reduction of arms promised for SALT III.

That bare framework hardly looks like a rousing disarmament manifesto. It omits, however, many of the treaty's most important details, some of which were only crafted in the late stages of negotiations. Nor does it tell the story of the negotiating process itself. This fuller explanation of the strategic and political significance of SALT II was seldom offered to the American public in 1979, when Senate ratification should have taken place, if not long before that.

Instead of explicating the historic meaning of the treaty for US-Soviet relations and properly acknowledging that the Soviets had made all the major concessions during the negotiations, the

Carter Administration became obsessed with demonstrating its own anti-Soviet virility in order to beat back the opposition to SALT II. By its macho posturing to escape the taint of appeasement, the White House only reinforced the most hostile stereotypes of Soviet foreign policy instead of making a credible case for détente. Carter's decision to proceed with MX, of all things, came just a month before the treaty's signing and was widely interpreted as more of a domestic political gesture than a strategic necessity.

While the astonishing record of Soviet concessions has yet to crash the consciousness of the American public—so widespread is the myth of US appeasement vs. Soviet intransigence—those concessions are now well-documented in several accounts of the negotiations.[12] Of greatest strategic significance were Soviet accommodations on "fractionation": numbers of warheads on a single launcher, whether a missile or a bomber. The Pentagon had worried the heavy Soviet SS-18 missiles might be powerful enough to mount as many as 40 warheads each; the treaty limited all ICBMs to only ten warheads. (The collapse of SALT II has provoked nightmares about those SS-18s all over again. Nothing discredits the opponents of SALT II more than this blatant failure to recognize the enormous advantage of these constraints on Soviet warheads.) Moreover, while Pentagon studies had indicated that MX (a "light" missile) would be most efficient with only six or eight warheads and the Soviets sought to fix the limit at six, the administration insisted on ten—which the Soviets eventually accepted. Then, when the USSR proposed that its lighter missiles also be permitted ten warheads, the US insisted that the SS-17 be limited to only the four warheads with which it had been tested and the SS-19 to six—which the Soviets also accepted, albeit grudgingly.

The other major fractionation controversy concerned the number of cruise missiles allowable on a single bomber—a parallel to the MIRVing of ICBMs. Here the US position, based on a big technological advantage, demanded high numbers: a new widebodied jet might be able to carry thirty or forty cruise missiles, more than the twenty that a B-52 could carry. While a limit of twenty was accepted on B-52s, the Soviets finally agreed to an average of twenty-eight cruise missiles per bomber, leaving the US free to develop bombers in the 30-40 missile range, after all. This contrast between holding USSR heavy missiles to ten warheads and allowing US bombers several times as many cruise missiles could hardly have made Soviet generals gleeful.

The Russians had also been worried about US plans to make

air-launched cruise missiles into long-range weapons which could be fired from 1,500 or more miles' distance from Soviet targets, thus compensating for the vulnerability of US bombers and frustrating Soviet air defenses. In fact, the Russians were more continuously concerned over the strategic implications of cruise missiles than about any other weapons discussed in SALT. For two years, they sought to hold ALCMs to short ranges. But the Pentagon, especially after President Carter canceled the B-1 bomber in June 1977, became more firmly attached than ever to long-range ALCMs. On September 30, 1978, seated across the Cabinet table from Carter in the White House, Andrei Gromyko conceded, with a rather exasperated display of magnanimity: "You can fly your air-launched cruise missiles around the world if you like." Once again, the Soviets had yielded ground on a central issue.

There were still other Soviet concessions of major importance:

(a) Reducing the 1974 Vladivostok limit of 2,400 launchers to 2,250 which meant scrapping more than 250 older but powerful missiles capable of devastating all US major urban centers — while the US was not obliged to scrap any weapons;

(b) Acquiescing in persistent US demands for sharing a common data base;

(c) Stipulating that the Backfire bomber would not be upgraded into a long-range bomber and that its production rate would not increase.

If the Carter Administration failed to take adequate account of the political significance of these accommodations by an aging Brezhnev coalition which had been ready for SALT II since 1974 — and which might soon be replaced by a younger Politburo less committed to arms control — the administration did emphasize a crucial point. The treaty established, for the first time, the principle of equal limits, thus reinforcing parity and preparing the way for equal reductions in SALT III.

SALT II was also the most important symbol of the détente of the 1970s. That symbolic value was much more precious than any of the treaty's specifics.

SALT II was perceived by most of the world's governments, including all NATO allies, as the prerequisite to progress on other disarmament matters. For stacked up behind that treaty's ratification were a Comprehensive Test Ban, measures to firm up the Non-Proliferation Treaty, mutual force reductions in Europe, anti-satellite weapons talks, and the CAT talks (Conventional Arms

Transfers). The UN General Assembly in 1978 had voted 127-1 (only Albania voting no) to urge the earliest possible conclusion of SALT II. That vote did not reflect universal enthusiasm for SALT itself: it did testify that the non-fulfillment of SALT II was almost universally viewed as the greatest obstacle to progress on all other disarmament issues.

If the treaty itself guaranteed very little in the way of genuine disarmament, its demise could well prove to be the most somber turning-point since Hiroshima. Both vertical and horizontal proliferation are now badly out of control. Military spending is more extravagant than ever. The onus remains heavily on the American people and their government.

Why, after all, did SALT II fail?

SALT II failed, not because the Soviets were unwilling to come to terms: they did come to terms back in January 1976, and, behind all their shows of might, kept making concessions for three more years. Not because of Afghanistan: SALT II was already dead politically weeks before that brutal and cynical invasion which, as much as anything, may have reflected Soviet disillusionment at last with détente and the whole SALT process, stalled for four years because of domestic political games and gaffes in the US.

SALT II died because neither the Carter Administration, nor the Op-Ed pages, nor the disarmament movement, nor the churches ever mustered an effective counterattack to the well-financed New Chauvinists who began to define the terms of debate in our Soviet, security, and arms control policies about 1977. Instead of facing down these policies on their political merits, the Carter people tried to out-tough their critics on new weapons, more defense spending, playing the China card, hyping the Cuban threat, turning the Arms Control and Disarmament Agency over to a general, conspicuously snubbing the UN Special Session on Disarmament, leaking a new counterforce doctrine, ignoring the second Non-Proliferation Treaty Review Conference, and generally turning up the anti-Soviet rhetoric. In the Senate Foreign Relations Committee hearings on the treaty itself in the summer of 1979, administration advocates repeatedly tried to top their critics in promising increased defense spending instead of emphasizing that ratification could mark a turning point in US-Soviet relations. Most of this posturing was ostensibly done for the sake of SALT II. In time, too much of the public and too many senators would buy these promotional messages, but understandably refuse to buy the SALT itself. It was a classic case of a propaganda boomerang.

The Two and the Many

The severe hiatus between bilateral diplomacy like SALT and multilateral diplomacy remains the central political problem for disarmament in the world arena. That problem is hardly visible to the American public. It has been slighted by our leaders and our media. Even the disarmament movement itself has typically failed to make effective connections between superpower politics and multilateral institutions like the United Nations.

This cleft between the Two and the Many is where the most decisive history of our times is being made. It is the gap between US-Soviet rivalry and the most clamorous human needs in 150 other countries, between ideological fixations and the international common good. It is the chasm between the East-West agenda and the North-South agenda — or, worse, the manipulation of the North-South agenda by the East-West agenda. In nuclear terms, it is the superpowers' increasingly futile effort to control horizontal proliferation as a security issue which they imagine is separable from their own vertical proliferation.

Therefore, the history of SALT must not be regarded as the whole history of disarmament in the past two decades. The security interests, disarmament policies, and grievances of other countries must be brought into focus. Four major multilateral events in the Third Nuclear Age have dramatized a new pattern of global bargaining in nuclear diplomacy — a pattern which parallels multilateral struggles over economics, energy, technology, and information. Those four events are the two review conferences on the Non-Proliferation Treaty in 1975 and 1980 and the UN Special Sessions on Disarmament in 1978 and 1982.

The first of the UN Special Sessions on Disarmament (UNSSOD I) in May and June 1978 may serve as a vivid case study of this new world of multilateral diplomacy. To tell the story of that event is not, however, to slough off the SALT process or domestic politics in the US. In fact, that is just where the story of UNSSOD I must begin.

Multilateral Diplomacy: The Case of UNSSOD I

Day after day after day, the dreary drumfire of belligerent words and deeds rolled out of Jimmy Carter's Washington while the UN Special Session on Disarmament was meeting in New York.

This first world disarmament assembly since Hiroshima was made hostage to a small retinue of image-makers who persuaded a besieged president that, for domestic reasons, he must keep up a relentless fusillade of tough anti-Soviet talk and gestures during May and June, avoiding any taint of weakness. It was suggested that SALT II might fail if it got identified with disarmament, of all things.

Jimmy Carter, whose campaign and inaugural promises had featured nuclear disarmament and reduced military spending, had come to believe in his second year that he could not risk offering any significant policy initiatives toward a new international disarmament program. He was even persuaded that he should personally boycott the Special Session—though he was president of the host country for the largest UN aggregation of summit-level personalities since Nikita Khrushchev banged his shoe 18 years before. As press secretary Jody Powell explained it, the President was "too busy" preparing major addresses for NATO and the US Naval Academy to appear at the United Nations. The fact that the dates for the Special Session had been set before Carter's inauguration—and spread from May 23 to the end of June—did not find any reflection in Powell's announcement.

But James Callaghan came to the UN. Pierre Trudeau came. Giscard d'Estaing came. Helmut Schmidt came. Morarji Desai came. They were all in conspicuously good form, having led their governments through serious preparatory exercises and having committed themselves to imaginative policy proposals. Eighteen other heads of state or government came, most in the expectation that Carter would attend also.

But Jimmy Carter did not show up, even though he had once promised to make "a strong and positive contribution" to the Session and earlier had made numerous and solemn pronouncements on the urgency of disarmament. He had a unique opportunity to exercise international leadership at a crucial juncture of perilous nuclear trends and uncontrolled conventional weapons races—and he simply did not lead.

What Carter did was to send his very good vice president to attack Soviet policies and to justify NATO's increased military budgets at the opening of the general debate on disarmament. As delegations from 149 member states waited in hopes that the US would offer something of substance toward a reversal of the arms race, Walter Mondale was made to say:

> We and our NATO allies are strong, and we will remain strong to provide for the defense of our peoples. . . . The NATO summit meeting next week in Washington will recommit the Western

democracies to a military posture capable of deterring and defending against attacks. We will remain prepared to resist attack across the spectrum of conventional, tactical nuclear, and strategic forces. In the face of the continuing military buildup of Warsaw Pact forces, we will moderately increase the defense budgets of our nations.

Mondale did offer a new slogan: the US could now serve as "the eyes and ears of the world" through a new foreign aid program consisting of the kind of hardware employed in the Sinai disengagement—ground sensors and aerial surveillance cameras. The offer was dismissed by many as one more US show of technical prowess to obfuscate political questions. This proposal was not even mentioned in the list of 30 proposals finally recommended by the Assembly for further study.

It would be difficult to exaggerate the extremity of dismay among UN delegates and staff of every kind of political alignment and nonalignment over the postures assumed by the US government during the six weeks of the Special Session. If the Carter guardians wanted their man to present a hard face to the American public and to the Russians, he was widely viewed at the UN as afraid to face up to US responsibility for the arms race, and as clumsy, vacillating and undependable.

Which is not to say that the Assembly was totally unprepared for such a bad show. After many months of promises that SALT II and test ban accords were "just around the corner"—and general anticipation that these minimal measures would at least help to facilitate an auspicious Special Session—it had become clear by late spring that no such accords were imminent. Curiously, there were repeated assurances at the Session that neither the arms talks nor US-Soviet working relations at the UN had been impaired by all the public displays of acrimony. If Carter's envoys were getting along well with the Russians, his administration's public rhetoric poured so much fuel on the fire of anti-Soviet animosities that Senate ratification of both a test ban and SALT II was almost certainly made much more problematical.

Moreover, the Special Session got under way without the Carter Administration's having submitted any advance policy paper to the Preparatory Committee. The United States was thus the only major country in the world (except China) which neglected to produce such a paper. What that omission really disclosed was a failure from the top to put the administration through a thorough process of developing a comprehensive and coherent disarmament-and-security policy.

Nor had the administration undertaken a major public information program on the Session so that citizens and the press could be engaged in advance. One slim ACDA brochure, delayed for many months, made its appearance only after the Session had convened. The White House waited until just several days before the Session convened to reveal the names of delegation members, thus depriving citizen organizations of advance opportunities to communicate with those members. My own proposal for a Citizens' Commission for the Special Session — a device for recruiting voluntary leadership to augment the meager public affairs resources of the Arms Control and Disarmament Agency — was endorsed and personally put to the President by Hubert Humphrey in the last weeks of his life but languished without acceptance or implementation during the six months before the Session.

These evidences of downgrading the importance of the Special Session help to account for the scant and superficial US media coverage accorded this "largest, most representative meeting ever convened to consider the problem of disarmament" (Kurt Waldheim). Everybody had said beforehand that activated public opinion would be the most important result of an Assembly which could not negotiate or conclude new disarmament treaties — and the role of the US press was seen as crucial in making it a (awful cliché!) "consciousness-raising event."

But, alas, the press tends to wait for the White House to provide the cues. Canadian William Epstein, former UN Director of Disarmament Affairs and a member of his country's delegation to the Session, lamented at the end of it all: "One of the most depressing aspects of the Special Session was the failure of the press and other media to give adequate coverage to what might be the most important conference of this decade." UN correspondents for major newspapers reported continuing resistance from their editors to publishing substantial stories on the Session. It was almost: no President, no news.

The efforts of numerous NGOs (non-governmental organizations) to alert and inform the American public in the preparatory months were impressive in their variety and competence. But the NGOs never reached enough people to begin to compensate for the defaults of the administration and the press. Result: most US citizens never knew that the first world disarmament assembly in 46 years was taking place. Probably the greatest media impact was generated by Paul Newman's interview on NBC's "Today" show. (Newman was a winsomely conscientious and well-informed member of the US delegation who was willing to use his celebrity status to publicize the issues.)

There is still more to be said about the unhelpful deportment of the US government—but the credibility of this report no doubt requires several caveats.

The Special Session scored some positive achievements which could not be forfended by all the bad news. Moreover, the personnel of the US delegation—including James Leonard, Adrian Fisher, Lawrence Weiler, George McGovern, Congressmen Paul Simon and Charles Whalen, Marjorie Benton, Harold Willens, Paul Newman, Richard Creecy—earned much respect and appreciation for their performances under the duress of dismal policy directives.

Several US delegates joined in a deputation to the White House to relay the intensity of many other delegations' concerns over administration conduct. They succeeded in persuading the President to announce a qualified "negative assurance": a US pledge not to attack non-nuclear-weapon states with nuclear weapons, provided such states were parties to the Non-Proliferation Treaty (or were otherwise clearly under nuclear safeguards) and were not allied or associated with a nuclear-weapon state. Both the Soviet Union and the United Kingdom offered similar assurances during the Session.

If Carter didn't show up, neither did Brezhnev nor any other Soviet bloc head of state or government. And, yes, the Soviet Union's own adventurism, weapons buildup, Central European troop deployments, and shabby treatment of dissidents had been major stimulants to tensions with the US and other NATO countries.

Yet Soviet restraint at the Session, in the face of both US and Chinese criticisms, was rather impressive. More seriously, it is sad to observe that the Soviets, so often given to blatant propaganda on disarmament matters, had received so little public notice in the US for numerous accommodations they had made in recent months, such as: (1) relaxing their claims to "peaceful" nuclear explosions so that a Comprehensive Test Ban might be concluded; (2) accepting, for the first time, parity of conventional forces in Europe; (3) agreeing in SALT to reduce the ceiling on strategic delivery vehicles from the 1974 Vladivostok level of 2,400 down to 2,250. Foreign Minister Andrei Gromyko's opening speech used unprecedented

Soviet language in promising readiness to negotiate "substantial reductions" in missiles and bombers following a SALT II agreement. The *Pravda* response to President Carter's Annapolis speech was (save for a few stock Soviet phrases) a remarkably moderate and objective analysis, not only of the problems of détente but of the political situation in the United States. Finally, the USSR even acquiesced in the elimination of all references to the neutron bomb in the Special Session's Final Document — a matter of great wonder in view of the heavy Soviet investment in an anti-neutron bomb campaign over the previous year.

The "dreary drumfire" began shortly before the Special Session with disclosure of the administration's plans for a new "blast bomb" which would be the opposite of the neutron bomb: a "reduced residual radiation" (RRR) weapon with maximum blast and minimum fallout.

Then came Zbigniew Brzezinski's trip to Peking (the very weekend before the Session began) and his "playing the China card": sharing SALT secrets, offering strategically-valuable technology forbidden to the Soviets, declaring mutual strategic interests, encouraging Chinese arms purchases from Western Europe. The anti-Soviet animus of these tactics was among the clumsiest and most dangerous activities of the Carter Administration.

Then came a NATO summit meeting in Washington, colliding with the first full week of the Special Session and presenting the spectacle of Carter's trying to alarm the allies about Soviet conduct in Africa (greeted by Prime Minister Callaghan's twit: "these new American Christopher Columbuses just discovering Africa for the first time") and to multiply NATO military hardware.

Then the Navy's public claim that technological breakthroughs in computerized sonar systems gave the US a new anti-submarine capability of virtually neutralizing the Soviet sub fleet against attacks on US shipping.

And Carter's commencement address at the Naval Academy — an address designed to "clarify" US-Soviet relations but whose sensible paragraphs were drowned out by a shrill ideological chauvinism reminiscent of John Foster Dulles. As Senator and UN Delegate Charles Mathias, Jr. (R—Md.) put it, the Annapolis speech sounded like "an antiphonal chorus between dove and hawk." It was later revealed that the speech reflected conflicting priorities between Secretary Vance and Brzezinski, the former responsible for the language on détente and the latter for the more macho lines.

The drumfire rolled on and on:

(a) A new Pentagon plan for MX mobile missiles based on random deployment;

(b) The first public cruise missile test, ceremonially attended by a gleeful Harold Brown;

(c) A plan for proceeding to produce neutron bomb components;

(d) A resurrection of US chemical warfare;

(e) A re-emphasis on civil defense, suggesting a heightened expectation of the possibilities of war;

(f) Carter's highly publicized attendance at a mock anti-Soviet maneuver in Texas which shot up over $1 million of ammunition for his "education."

It would surely be too much to claim that all these events in May and June were contrived to sabotage the Special Session on Disarmament. But it is hardly more consoling to be assured that they occurred in complete disregard of the UN.

This tale of two cities must now shift from Washington back to New York for a more intimate look at the UN scene from May 23 to June 30. The most spectacular moments—as well as the most tedious ones—came during the three-week general debate when many of the world's political celebrities stood at the rostrum of the Assembly Hall.

There was the president of France, Valery Giscard d'Estaing, leading his nation out of 16 years of isolation from disarmament matters in an eloquent address rich in substance and concept. Giscard promised French participation in a reformed version of the Geneva-based negotiating body, the 31-nation CCD (Conference of the Committee on Disarmament) which his nation had boycotted since 1962 because of the permanent US-Soviet monopoly of the co-chairmanship. Joined by Britain, Canada, Australia, China, Romania, Sweden, and the Non-Aligned States, French pressure led to an agreement, very late in the Session, upon a new Committee on Disarmament (CD) with rotating chairmanship, enlarged and more representative membership (up to 40), and linked more directly to the UN through an executive secretary to be named by the UN Secretary General. The prospect of eventual Chinese participation, as well as that of France, made this agreement on machinery perhaps the most important practical achievement of the Session. (Both France and China subsequently joined the CD.)

Giscard declared: "Disarmament should be with the help of all, under the supervision of all, for the benefit of all." This insistence on universality in the structures and processes of disarmament was also voiced forcefully by Foreign Minister Huang Hua of China and many of the Non-Aligned speakers. Such insistence led to the resurrection of the UN Disarmament Commission, universal in membership but inactive since 1965, to serve as the UN's deliberative body in this field.

Every nation understandably wants a share in disarmament action affecting its own safety and survival — a moral claim too glibly ignored by the nuclear powers. The Final Document's section on "Principles" gives strong emphasis to universality:

> All the peoples of the world have a vital interest in the success of disarmament negotiations. . . . All States have the right to participate in disarmament negotiations. They have the right to participate on an equal footing in those multilateral disarmament negotiations which have a direct bearing on their national security.

These principles were not fully institutionalized in the new machinery but they reflect the impatience and resentment most nations felt over the "hegemony" (favorite Chinese word!) of the superpowers, particularly in nuclear affairs.

Giscard also elaborated a number of French proposals which clearly marked a new bid for leadership in the disarmament field, including: a Satellite Monitoring Agency, a World Institute for Disarmament Studies, a Disarmament and Development Fund, and a reconvening of the Helsinki Conference on Security and Cooperation in Europe to reverse continental force buildups.

Giscard's May 25 address was immediately followed by his press conference, the unfortunate effect of which was to empty the press gallery during the important subsequent address. Ambassador Alfonso Garcia Robles, head of the Mexican delegation and former foreign minister, had emerged in the past decade as the UN's most knowledgeable and masterful leader in disarmament affairs. Father of the Treaty of Tlatelolco creating a Latin American nuclear-free zone, Garcia Robles was the man to whom the Assembly turned during its last week to serve as a "super coordinator" when the working groups proved unable to achieve consensus on major nuclear, conventional, and machinery issues. Together with Ambassador Carlos Ortiz de Rozas of Argentina, chairman of both the Preparatory Committee and the Ad Hoc Committee (of the Whole) during the Session, Garcia Robles won high praise from all sides for patient but determined leadership in wresting every conceivable possibility of useful consensus from the unwieldly Assembly. For seven days and six nights, typically 20 hours at a stretch, Garcia Robles kept the final negotiating marathon going, postponing one public meeting after another, until the Final Document was completed. He has long deserved a Nobel Prize and surely added to his merits.

Garcia Robles's opening-round address scolded the superpowers for making "dead letters" of their 1961 principles of "general and complete disarmament" and Article VI of the Non-Proliferation Treaty. Article VI is the most problematical provision of the NPT, formally obligating the nuclear powers to take significant measures toward nuclear disarmament. This obligation was written into the treaty in 1968 at the insistence of the non-nuclear-weapon states as a precondition of their own nuclear renunciation. Instead of moving toward nuclear disarmament, Garcia Robles protested, the US and USSR have brought a "hitherto unimagined momentum" to the arms race, stockpiling nuclear arsenals now equivalent to one million Hiroshima bombs. He voiced the Third World's appeal to the Session to frame a comprehensive new disarmament strategy in which smaller and poorer states could fully share. The linkage between disarmament and economic development, with world military spending over $400 billion a year in 1978, was a persistent theme in the general debate.

It was the Non-Aligned States, reaffirming a 1961 Belgrade appeal at their Fifth Summit in Sri Lanka in 1976, whose proposal for a Special Session on Disarmament finally was adopted by the General Assembly in December 1976. Throughout the preparatory meetings and the Session itself, the Non-Aligned insisted that nuclear issues be accorded the highest priority. The lack of significant nuclear initiatives from the superpowers at the Special Session found the Non-Aligned indisposed to accommodate superpower positions on nuclear technology and conventional disarmament concerns. These new realities of global bargaining had yet to be fully apprehended by the US and USSR — but they are the realities which must be faced if there is to be an effective international system for coping with the new nuclear crisis.

India emerged as the political pace-setter of the Non-Aligned, beginning with Morarji Desai's June 9 address which combined India's clearest statement of nuclear weapons renunciation with a sharp attack on the military, disarmament and energy policies of the superpowers. Desai justified India's refusal heretofore to sign the Non-Proliferation Treaty on the grounds that the Treaty is "patently discriminatory." Repeating objections stated to President Carter on his visit to India the preceding January, during which Carter urged Desai to support US non-proliferation policy, Desai complained that the NPT "makes an invidious distinction between countries having nuclear weaponry and those devoted to the pursuit of nuclear research and technology entirely for peaceful purposes. Paradoxically, the Treaty gives the former a monopoly of power and confers on them freedom for commercial exploitation of nuclear know-how, while on the latter it places restrictions which may impede peaceful development of nuclear science."

After Desai's departure, India was represented by an eminent and energetic delegation which continued to press the superpowers on nuclear issues. When a meaningful degree of consensus on these issues seemed unlikely at the start of the final week, India introduced two resolutions calling for a moratorium on nuclear testing and a legal convention against the use of nuclear weapons as "a crime against humanity." Invoking his prestige as a veteran of US-Soviet diplomacy, octogenarian Averell Harriman made a rather paternalistic appeal to the non-nuclear-weapon states not to push the superpowers on nuclear issues more properly handled by the SALT and test ban talks. With obvious reluctance, India eventually withdrew its resolutions after reporting that "some reflection" of its position could be found in the Final Document, "thanks to the cooperation of some of the nuclear-weapon states."

Less than 48 hours later, with the Session having adjourned, *The New York Times* reported that US earnestness on a comprehensive test ban had been forsaken in favor of continued low-yield testing demanded by Energy Secretary James Schlesinger and the Joint Chiefs of Staff. It was another bad moment for US credibility.

Earlier, on May 26, Prime Minister Pierre Elliott Trudeau of Canada had proposed to curb the arms race by a "strategy of suffocation," depriving it of "the oxygen on which it feeds." Emphasizing the unrestrained momentum of military technology, Trudeau offered the world's first official proposal of a ban on flight-testing of all new strategic weapons systems. Three other measures of "suffocation" were a comprehensive test ban, a halt in all production of fissionable materials for weapons purposes, and an agreement to limit and then reduce spending on new strategic nuclear weapons systems.

A forceful appeal to link nuclear and conventional threats was made by Chancellor Helmut Schmidt of Germany. Eschewing proposals which focus exclusively on the renunciation of nuclear war, Schmidt declared: "Whoever is the first to take up arms of whatever kind and resorts to or threatens military attack" violates the UN Charter's prohibition of the use or threat of force. "Either it applies totally or not at all," he asserted.

Nigeria, whose Ambassador Adeniji chaired the drafting group on nuclear disarmament, won approval for a modest but very practical proposal: 20 annual UN disarmament fellowships for diplomats from developing countries. In international disarmament work, poorer nations typically confront legions of "experts" trained in the military, industrial and academic establishments of the richer nations. (The Nigerian plan has been implemented by the UN Disarmament Centre and will help to compensate for this lack of parity in disarmament personnel.)

The Final Document is certainly the most complete and substantial statement on the entire range of disarmament topics ever officially approved by the world's governments. Consisting of a Preamble and four principal parts—Introduction, Declaration, Programme of Action, Machinery—it is the closest the nations have come to creating a disarmament charter. It was Mexico that insisted most vigorously in the Preparatory Committee that a single, comprehensive document be adopted by consensus rather than a series of separate resolutions and votes. And it was Mexico's Alfonso Garcia Robles who repeatedly urged the Session to avoid a "dispersion of efforts" and to build a "foundation for a new strategy of disarmament that will permit the words and intentions to become deeds and facts."

The moral authority of Garcia Robles finally proved to be irresistible on this basic point. The Final Document inevitably reflects the world's political and ideological strains and the ambiguities of language required for consensual adoption. The bracketing of dozens of topics of controversy and their de-bracketing through a painstaking search for reconciling phraseology was the *modus operandi* of the Session. Yet the Final Document sets forth a vital framework—at once historical, political, and moral—within which disarmament issues may be better understood by citizens of every country. Particularly instructive are paragraphs which interpret linkages between disarmament and such other universal concerns as security, economic development, environment, and human rights.

The very first paragraph of the Introduction affirms that security "has always been one of the most profound aspirations of humanity. . . . Yet the accumulation of weapons, particularly nuclear weapons, today constitutes much more a threat than a protection for the future of mankind. . . . To meet this historic challenge is in the political and economic interests of all the nations and peoples of the world as well as in the interests of ensuring their genuine security and peaceful future."

These words may not sing easily but they tell the truth all peoples need to hear. After all, neither the UN nor its member states function in a political vacuum. Nongovernmental forces which link peoples with their public institutions have much to do with determining the political climate for disarmament.

It is just here that the Special Session witnessed a development of extraordinary importance: an unprecedented participation of NGOs in UN work on political and security issues. Largely through the efforts of the NGO Committee on Disarmament (at UN Headquarters), chaired by Homer A. Jack of the World Conference on Religion and Peace, NGOs published the Session's indispensable daily paper, *Disarmament Times;* established the Disarmament Information Bureau in a UN Plaza storefront; obtained authorization for an entire day of NGO testimony in the Assembly Hall, with 25 international organizations participating, and for six research institutes to have a half-day at the rostrum; organized coffee houses, citizen assemblies, consultations and other programs. Homer Jack's personal resourcefulness put him continually in the center of groups of delegates, UN staff, and reporters, as well as NGOs, who looked to him for leadership.

During NGO Day on June 12, General Secretary Philip Potter of the World Council of Churches stoutly repudiated the increasing concentration of material and human resources on armaments, often "secretly in the corridors of power and beyond social control." Dr. Potter charged that military technology increasingly "frustrates disarmament negotiations" because it keeps changing "the nature of the problems which have to be faced." Yet he declined simply to condemn governments and politicians, acknowledging that the churches themselves "have often been so allied to the forces of disorder and oppression that they have promoted or connived in wars and in the war psychosis."

A similarly confessional tone was struck by Ciaran McKeown of the Peace People of Northern Ireland, speaking on behalf of the International Fellowship of Reconciliation. Addressing his remarks more to religious and peace groups than to official delegations, McKeown said these groups do not have "the moral right to sit on the mountainside in judgment of governments and militarism."

Their own failures and conflicts have largely prevented the advent of "a green summer of peace." After observing that scientific estimates of probabilities would find that disarmament itself is "highly improbable," Ciaran McKeown envisioned a "great explosion of reconciliation within the human family" whose consequences would be "almost too happy and creative to think about from our present desperate perspective."

It was a singularly quiet and wistful moment in the great Assembly Hall. After three weeks of general debate and its wearisome rhetoric, poetic words could still stir many tired spirits. Just about everyone there seemed to realize afresh that humanity had arrived at a juncture where the "highly improbable" had become absolutely necessary—but would be marvelous when it came.

The Non-Proliferation Treaty

The connections between nuclear deterrence, counterforce, arms race dynamics, SALT, and the UN, on one hand, and the Non-Proliferation Treaty, on the other, have already been touched upon. The NPT is such a comprehensive, complex and, in some respects, imprecise instrument of international law that it is bound to get linked with virtually every nuclear topic. Because the NPT has its own polity formally outside the UN (although the UN has serviced its review conferences), this chapter might well include NPT in a series of multilateral case studies. From my catbird seat as chairman of United States NGOs at the 1975 and 1980 review conferences, I have been tempted to do just that. However, the repetition would soon become obvious: the story of those conferences is essentially the same story we have already told about the UN Special Session of 1978. It is the story of unresolved impasses between the Two and the Many, between the nuclear haves and the nuclear have-nots, between vertical and horizontal proliferation.[13]

If such full-length narratives need not be repeated here, the importance of the treaty itself needs all the emphasis it can get. Whatever its limitations, the Non-Proliferation Treaty provides the most significant political and ethical framework for coping with nuclear questions. A full survey of NPT issues is perhaps the best possible primer for understanding the arms race in its multilateral dimensions. It is pedagogically vital even if it is politically anemic. Three characteristics of the treaty underscore that point:

1. The NPT is an omnibus compact that comprehends virtually every aspect of the new nuclear crisis. As such it offers a cooperative framework for developing a coherent global nuclear policy—a

policy which articulates disarmament, the prevention of nuclear weapons spread, energy development, trade, and nuclear safety. These are problems which simply cannot be handled piecemeal or unilaterally.

2. The NPT is a multilateral covenant of incomparable moral significance. At the heart of the treaty is a balance of obligations affecting the deepest security interests and development needs of parties to the treaty: renunciation of nuclear weapons (by 111 countries to date) in return for commitments by nuclear weapon states (US, USSR, UK) to take effective measures toward nuclear disarmament and also to share freely the fruits of energy technology.

3. The NPT is, in fact, the only legal instrument now in effect which actually requires nuclear disarmament.

These are reasons enough to be resolutely determined to make the treaty a success—and to be deeply distressed when the whole non-proliferation system appears to be losing its legitimacy and its effectiveness. No doubt the blame is widely to be shared. But the nuclear weaponry, energy technology, strategic dogmas, and political myopia of the US national security establishment are hardly the least responsible for the imminent breakdown of this vital system of international cooperation. Years of complacency and sheer neglect of NPT issues in the early 1970s contributed to the perilous nuclear isolationism which continues to characterize US policy itself.

If the very existence of the treaty was unavoidably discriminatory (only the immediate and total renunciation of nuclear weapons by every nation could have averted nuclear discrimination), the nuclear haves were clearly obliged to join the have-nots in early and genuine moves toward renunciation. The treaty envisioned such obvious moves as "the discontinuance of all test explosions of nuclear weapons for all time," the cessation of manufacture of such weapons, and the progressive liquidation of nuclear stockpiles.

Discrimination under the treaty was thus legitimized only in a provisional sense. There was an overriding imperative of equity. This was more than an abstract moral claim. *In a world infused by an increasingly vigorous ethos of egalitarian nationalisms, the satisfaction of legitimate claims to equity is a matter of political realism.* A lack of diplomatic sensitivity to this egalitarian ethos, particularly in such ultimate matters as the peril and promise of nuclear power, can be catastrophic. Lincoln Bloomfield has written that political considerations of prestige and nondiscrimination are fundamental to any universal agreement on non-proliferation: "In an era dominated by demands for identity, respect, equity, and participation, it seems reasonable to ask whether, with the best will in the world, the present NPT system of discrimination, denial, and second-class citizenship will in fact achieve its aim of preventing the further spread of nuclear weapons."[14] NPT's balance of obligations also extends to the sharing of nuclear technology for peaceful purposes (Article IV). There is, however, a double standard concerning inspections: non-nuclear states are obliged to submit to the safeguards system of the International Atomic Energy Agency (Article III), while nuclear weapon states are not subject to such monitoring. The adequacy of IAEA safeguards was severely questioned following Israel's June 1981 attack on Iraq's nuclear reactor — but it has also been questioned because of the very modest levels of US and Soviet financial support.

Forty potential NPT parties remain outside the treaty, thus exposing its very partial character. Non-members include France, China, India, Pakistan, Argentina, Brazil, Israel, South Africa — all nuclear or nuclear-prone states, most of whom have repeatedly protested the treaty's double standards and have hardly received any fresh incentives to join from the dismal proceedings at the two review conferences.

It was the "good faith" commitment to nuclear disarmament under Article VI that proved most contentious in both 1975 and 1980. The wording of Article VI is somewhat problematical:

> Each of the parties to the treaty undertakes to pursue negotiations in good faith on effective measures relating to cessation of the nuclear arms race at an early date and to nuclear disarmament, and on a treaty on general and complete disarmament under strict and effective international control.

It takes licentious literalism in reading that language, along with an ignorance of the historic circumstances which made Article VI the necessary *quid pro quo* for the non-nuclear states, to excuse the superpowers from what was clearly intended to be a solemn legal obligation to nuclear disarmament.

The bargaining over Article VI issues at Geneva in 1975 centered on three draft protocols introduced by Alfonso Garcia Robles, then Mexico's UN ambassador, leader of the non-nuclear coalition, and lightning rod for US and Soviet attacks upon all who dared to criticize the superpowers' interpretations of the treaty. Garcia Robles was joined by 17 other delegations in these protocols on three "good faith" measures: test ban, reduction of nuclear arsenals, and security assurances. The protocols were aimed directly at NPT's balance of obligations. They were ingeniously designed to encourage mutually reinforcing incentives between nuclear and non-nuclear states. Most important were two which linked horizontal and vertical proliferation. One of these provided for a ten-year test ban when the number of treaty accessions reached 100 (there were then 95; now there are 114). The other provided a phased reduction in US and Soviet nuclear arsenals as treaty accessions reached 100 and beyond. Thus, incentives to join the treaty would be coupled with incentives to unwind the strategic arms spiral. Garcia Robles was willing to be flexible on the numbers but he was firm on the principle of reciprocity.

Garcia Robles had a majority of delegations behind his protocols but US and Soviet opposition was fierce and unrelenting. David Klein, acting head of the US delegation (in the absence of Fred Iklé), declared:

> We cannot and will not accept the imposition of rigid and artificial deadlines. Arms control involves technical problems beyond any simple exercise in arithmetic. We believe that the actions of the United States in the past five years have been fully consistent with Article VI. Criticisms of SALT under Article VI greatly and unfairly underestimate the significance of SALT.

Both superpowers fended off further criticisms with promises that the completion of SALT II and a CTB were just ahead. (That, again, was May 1975.)

A mix of moral and technical claims was erected to wall off this trespassing by non-nuclear states on the private property of SALT. The moral claim was that only the US and USSR are fully "responsible" and "mature" in handling nuclear issues. Other claimants to nuclear wisdom were only "mischievous." The Cuban missile crisis of 1962 earned these moral credentials for the superpowers: only they have really "looked into the nuclear abyss." Technical pretenses were similar. Only the US and USSR really knew the complex problems of managing and reducing nuclear arsenals. Technical proposals for safeguards (such as regional, multinational fuel cycle centers) were given highest priority by the US delegations in both 1975 and 1980. Thus were technical preoccupations pushed to the obfuscation of political issues — and the discounting of equity.

These tactics of stonewalling against non-nuclear weapon states may have been cleverly contrived as manipulations of conference diplomacy — but in the larger context of world politics they proved to be clumsy in the extreme.

In the historical background of the unfortunate US performance at Geneva in 1975 were several factors. For one, Henry Kissinger had paid no serious attention to NPT from its official start in 1970 until the shock of India's 1974 explosion. He was preoccupied with SALT and seemed to regard NPT as a peripheral if not settled question. Gerard Smith's duties as SALT negotiator made his concentration on NPT and other issues very problematical during his ACDA directorship which ended in 1972. The old Atomic Energy Commission, which had unwisely been vested with both the promotion and regulation of nuclear energy, had aggressively fostered complacency about "peaceful" nuclear energy until an accumulation of safety and security troubles led to the abolition of AEC in 1974. Fred Iklé's undoubted seriousness about non-proliferation during his ACDA directorship at the time of NPT I was nevertheless a personification of technical obsessions and a disdain for complainants about vertical proliferation.

When the second NPT Review Conference convened in Geneva in August 1980, the superpowers had to face the music for their failures on SALT II and a CTB. The US delegation (as previously noted) also, quite unexpectedly, had to withstand severe castigation for the just-unveiled counterforce doctrines of PD 59. Inga Thorsson of Sweden, who had chaired NPT I and produced a 1975 final document which papered over the Article VI disputes, declared at the start of NPT II:

> Military strategists now seem to have some feeling of nuclear weapons being antiseptic. They are thinkable. And the idea that nuclear war could be fought and won is gaining ground and this is extremely, extremely unfortunate.

Garcia Robles was back, too, with a set of five rather modest proposals on nuclear disarmament which provided the platform for the non-nuclear states — and with a confession about PD 59: "The new strategies for 'limited nuclear war' and 'prolonged nuclear war' are absolutely incomprehensible."

This time there would be no papering over the Article VI disputes. There was no final document — only bitterness and disarray, made worse by an incredibly complacent and self-congratulatory US final statement offered by Ralph Earle II. The line-ups on unresolved questions were as follows:

a) Whether Article VI should be regarded as at least partially fulfilled or as a dead letter (Western and socialist states "welcome progress"; Sweden and Group of 77 denied any real progress);

b) Whether a final document should include data on weapons tests, warheads, and military spending (77 wanted such data; US and others questioned credibility of any such data);

c) Whether to request fidelity to norms of SALT II pending ratification (virtually all delegations urged SALT II ratification in order to press on to other disarmament negotiations, but USSR opposed any formal obligation lest ratification be delayed indefinitely);

d) Whether to call for a nuclear test moratorium, pending completion of a treaty (widely supported, but US, UK, and USSR opposed);

e) Whether to fix a timetable for completion of a CTB (77 asked trilateral talks to end in early 1982 but trilateral powers opposed);

f) Whether to criticize nuclear-weapon states for strategic doctrines promoting proliferation, such as "limited nuclear war" (77 and others supported; US opposed).

NPT II did experience a surprising potential for agreement on technical issues. Nonaligned demands for assured supplies under Article IV collided with Western pressures for full-scope IAEA safeguards under Article III. Yet this conflict was well on the way to documentary resolution as adjournment neared. It was the unresolved disputes over the political issues of nuclear disarmament that spilled over into energy issues and precluded a final consensus on either set of issues. This time the non-nuclear weapon states would not permit technical schemes to obscure the balance of obligations.

The viability of NPT had been threatened in advance by a new coalition of members and non-members which had met the month before in Buenos Aires as the "Non-Aligned Coordinating Countries on the Peaceful Uses of Nuclear Energy." The fact that Argentina, a non-NPT party, hosted the conference was symbolically important. Yet such NPT members as Nigeria, Iraq, Peru, Romania, Yugoslavia, and the Philippines showed up. The Buenos Aires conference was a not-so-subtle signal that many nonaligned countries have become disillusioned with the Non-Proliferation Treaty. Nothing happened at NPT II to inhibit this new shift of nuclear politics to the larger bargaining arena of North-South struggles. Whether the threats of some nations to withdraw from the NPT itself would be carried out remained to be seen.

As NPT II adjourned, the delegate from Morocco spoke for many, if not most, when he caustically announced, "The curtain is finally coming down spectacularly on a comedy act that has been playing for the last four weeks, thanks to the efforts of the three nuclear-weapon states parties to the NPT."

Probably less than one percent of the American public were even aware that the conference had taken place, so wide had become the buffer zone between domestic and world politics—and so great the perils of nuclear isolationism.

A few weeks later, in his campaign debate with Ronald Reagan, President Carter melodramatically reverted to the problem of nuclear proliferation with a show of zeal reminiscent of his 1976 campaign. Carter revealed that his young daughter Amy had advised him to consider nuclear proliferation as the world's most serious problem. This earnestness was juxtaposed to Reagan's earlier (and still inexplicable) campaign comment that proliferation was "none of our business." As President, Reagan issued a statement on July 16, 1981, indicating that he had come to recognize proliferation as "a severe threat to international peace, regional and global stability and the security interests of the United States and other countries." While he pledged to "continue to support adherence" to NPT, his seven policy guidelines were preoccupied with the problems of technology transfer and controls. Reagan's statement made no reference to vertical proliferation, the political issues of nuclear disarmament, or US obligations thereto.

There would not be another NPT Review Conference until 1985—but there would be a Second UN Special Session on Disarmament in 1982 when the Two and the Many would struggle again over the question of responsibility for the nuclear arms race.

CHAPTER 6

The Politics of Disarmament

I used to say when I was working in the White House that we were fighting a four-front war when we tried to do something about arms limitations. We had to deal with the Pentagon, we had to deal with the Congress, we had to deal with the public; and I was never certain which of these groups gave us more problems because we rarely got to deal with the Russians. — Jerome Wiesner, former Science Adviser to President Kennedy in 1970 testimony before the Arms Control Subcommittee of the Senate Foreign Relations Committee

The basic problems of disarmament are political. There are daunting technical problems, to be sure — but it is the political control of technology that matters most. There are difficult diplomatic problems with both the USSR and non-nuclear states — but American presidents have learned that negotiating with the Senate or the Joint Chiefs of Staff is usually more difficult than negotiating with the Russians. There are serious economic problems connected with military spending, technology, and significant arms reductions — but the US government's own studies have repeatedly concluded that the civilian economy can generate enough aggregate demand if political leadership wills to reduce armaments and plans for conversion.

In surveying alternative images of the arms race, we spoke of the disciplines of domestic politics as being more fundamental than the arts of diplomacy. To put it more positively, a well-ordered body politic is increasingly the basic prerequisite of the diplomacy of disarmament. This volume, in seeking to demythologize defense and disarmament and put them into contextual perspectives, has been littered with dozens of indications of linkages with domestic politics. An impressionistic summary of these data may usefully precede a more schematic discussion of the politics of disarmament.

Review of Political Connections

With regard to *presidential leadership,* we have noted how chief executives may propagandize abroad for disarmament ideas they discredit at home; how a president may deflect political reprisals from districts facing shutdowns of aerospace industries by promotion of overseas arms sales; how a presidency exhausted by political scandal may lack the capital to pursue disarmament and may even sound alarms about an artificial security crisis; how a presidency increasingly perceived by the public as weak and vacillating may feel driven to macho posturing for the sake of a SALT treaty but may boomerang by making the opposition more credible than ever; how the multilateral diplomacy of the UN and NPT can be undermined by a president who feels he cannot make a public showing or any policy initiatives.

With regard to *electoral politics,* we have seen how a campaign based on claims of a "missile gap" initiated an unending chain of follies involving ICBMs; how the start of SALT was called off in the election year of 1968; how the election year of 1972 spurred a hurryup SALT I agreement that avoided the crucial issue of MIRVs; how SALT II on the threshold of agreement was called off in the election year of 1976; how SALT II was undermined by advance electioneering for 1980 before being called off again; how a counterforce doctrine was unveiled on the eve of a national convention in 1980.

With regard to *legislative politics,* we have noted how a MIRV moratorium with broad congressional support from the President's own party and with the backing of ACDA can be overwhelmed by a phalanx of Pentagon elites; how the arms trade got promoted as an alternative to military aid because it offered a detour around congressional appropriations hurdles; how competition between congressional committees can stimulate military technology and defense contracts; how a treaty proposal requiring senate consent can be so shaped to meet the specifications of hawkish senators that it becomes totally unrealistic as an offering to the Soviet Union; how a senate hearing on a negotiated treaty can be turned into partisan competition for increased military spending instead of an edifying review of foreign policy.

With regard to *bureaucratic politics,* we have seen how often strategic doctrines emerge as rationalizations after the fact of technological innovation; how decision-making about military programs can appear to be a flea-market of conflicting interests; how the Joint Chiefs of Staff have often tended toward the most primitive stereotypes of adversaries and quick fixes on military force; how extravagant promises to the Joint Chiefs of Staff about new weapons systems have been the price of the 1963 Test Ban and both SALT I and SALT II; how the purge and gutting of ACDA were political pay-offs after SALT I; how strategic doctrines and arms escalation can be generated by interservice rivalries; how the isolation of professional military men from civilian politics can narrow their world-views and their visions of national security.

With regard to *group politics,* we have noted the primary role of civilian think tanks in concocting military dogmas; the domestic hegemony of groups like the Committee on the Present Danger in defining the terms of national security debate; the disarming of the disarmament movement by a limited test ban, peripheral treaties, and Pyrrhic victories; the crucial role of deterrence moderates in resisting counterforce maximalists; the potential aid of Western European groups in helping the American public to understand the Euro-strategic arms race and the continuing imperatives of détente.

If many of these political connections have discouraging implications, there is no non-political escape from them — much as some diplomats, scholars, and clergy would like to escape from politics. The so-called "military-industrial complex" is not a coherent conspiracy behind the political scenes: it is an increasingly visible, audible, and incoherent mishmash.[1] Marshall Shulman, still a professor at Columbia University before becoming Soviet affairs adviser in the Carter Administration, seemed well prepared for the irrationalities of national security policy of which he would publicly complain in 1979. In 1975, he wrote:

> The baffling contrast between the arms controllers' assumptions of rationality and the behavior of the real world led to a shift of emphasis in the early nineteen-seventies toward the political dimensions of the subject. All who had served in government knew from their experiences that there was little correspondence between the rational models of decision-making and the donneybrook world of service rivalries, bureaucratic jostling, and the clash of parochial interests of pressure groups that determine the way nations behave in practice. While the intellectually more interesting conceptual state of the art moved but slightly from the high plateau it had reached, the facts of life that politicians take for granted became the new preoccupation of the arms control community. Belatedly and a shade reluctantly, they turned their attention to domestic politics — to the decision-making process and to the bureaucracies and the political and economic constituencies involved in it.[2]

Shulman had no reason to revise this picture of the existential realities of arms control (and US-Soviet affairs) when his own expertise was increasingly sidetracked and détente was judged a political liability by the White House.

The issues of disarmament must be made more political, not less so. It is the chronic aversion of many citizens to the politics of national security that must be overcome. That tired-but-true cliché about "political will" must be empowered by a body politic which understands and steadfastly supports a disarmament policy that enhances their true security. There is no major area of public policy more troubled by *widespread feelings of powerlessness* than disarmament. We must try to understand the sources of these feelings if the very idea of disarmament is to have a chance. Among those sources are the following:

Sources of Powerlessness

1. Perhaps most people in the world today have come to a mood of political resignation in the face of what often seems to be the *irresistible power of policy-makers*. All areas of life have become politicized in most societies, regardless of ideological differences. Government, military, and economic institutions seem overwhelming. Individuals feel vulnerable, victimized, ineffective. Such feelings among Americans, however, are more than matched by those of other peoples who feel overmatched by the influence of "superpowers," an inequitable world market, and multinational corporations: which add up to the painful conviction that even one's own government is too powerless to cope with external forces.

2. Defense and disarmament issues, in particular, are widely perceived to be overwhelming in their *technical complexity*. Most folks seem to feel that such issues should be left to "the experts"— an attitude which makes it very difficult for disarmament groups to convert issues into political action.

This difficulty is compounded right now by the sheer number of new weapons systems under development in the US.

For several years, a coalition of activists waged a campaign against the B-1 bomber. When President Carter decided to scrap the B-1 bomber, there was euphoria among peaceniks who thought they had won a great victory. But it turned out to be a Pyrrhic victory, for the price of it was a go-ahead to the Pentagon to proceed instead with the cruise missile. And the cruise missile is precisely that new weapon whose technical characteristics made it most difficult to come to an effective new nuclear agreement with the Russians.

Moreover, while the anti-B-1 campaign was being waged, still another weapons system was being developed: in fact, the most devastating weapons system ever, the Trident missile-submarine. To top it all, the B-1 itself is coming back—and still another bomber. So even technically well-informed activists must decide how effectively they can engage public concern in piecemeal attacks on each individual new weapons system dreamed up by the military. If piecemeal resistance to particular weapons is not good enough, what more comprehensive political strategy is required to cope with these multiple and simultaneous new creatures of military technology? We are perilously close to the limits of what a democratic political system can handle.

3. In no area of government policy is there more *official secrecy* than in matters of security and disarmament, thus increasing the gap between decision-makers and citizens. Every kind of significant military information is likely to be called "classified" in the promiscuous abuse of civil liberties. The real security of citizens and of their education and media is curtailed in the very name of "security." Curiously, both the US and USSR have been willing to share strategic data with each other that they will not reveal to their own citizens. There is also a tendency within government itself to impose so much secrecy that important policy-makers are denied information they really require for the proper performance of their duties. For example, the US decision to proceed with the development of MIRV missiles was concealed from the Senate Foreign Relations Committee for three years—yet that decision of the mid-sixties was one of the most momentous foreign relations decisions ever made. Therefore, even important politicians can feel powerless!

How to open up a meaningful *political* process early enough in the cycle of weapons technology so that Congress, the general public, and other nations may share in the most fateful decisions before they become irreversible—that is a very big question.

This very same question arises with regard to the massive escalation of arms sales by the US since 1970. In a 1977 editorial on the billion-dollar AWACS (airborne-warning-and-control system) sale to Iran, *The Washington Post* declared: "The whole AWACS episode suggests that, by the time a deal gets to the stage of congressional review, it is too late to do much about it." Even when the House of Representatives by a three-to-one vote opposed an even bigger $8.5 billion AWACS-related deal with Saudi Arabia in 1981 —the largest arms deal in history—the Reagan White House successfully applied extraordinary pressures to gain Senate approval by a 52-48 vote.

In no area of public policy has the shift from legislative to bureaucratic decision-making been more emphatic than in military and disarmament affairs.

4. Bureaucratic power, technical complexity, and official secrecy would all be more tolerable if citizens were confident that they could trust their own government. The reality, however, is an attitude of profound *cynicism* about government in many countries. Because governments in both "liberal" and "socialist" societies so often seem to violate their own constitutions and laws, deceive their citizens, and abuse human rights, the public's sense of political despair can frustrate effective action by groups committed to peace and social justice. As a college teacher of political science, I have found widespread cynicism among students to be just about the most serious challenge I have had to face. It is a problem which increases my own sense of powerlessness!

5. In most countries, persons committed to disarmament are painfully aware of the *small size and marginal status of the disarmament constituency* itself — if by constituency we really mean an attentive and informed public steadfastly prepared to engage in political action. Credibility and confidence are often hard to come by in the peace movement, especially in the face of the seemingly tough "political realism" which has sustained Cold War attitudes, shaped mass opinion, and often made disarmament advocates seem naive if not ridiculous. Thus is the very cause of disarmament portrayed as impotent.

6. Parallel to this weakness of the disarmament constituency is the *low status and priority of disarmament within the structures of government.* In almost every government, the basic reality is the same: *defense* is a top-level, high-priority, high-prestige, well-financed, well-staffed, well-propagandized operation of senior cabinet rank, while *disarmament* is a low-level, under-budgeted, under-staffed, invisible and anonymous subdivision in the policy hierarchy.

7. Because disarmament is a low priority within most governments, disarmament action groups tend to find themselves in an adversary relationship with the policy community — even to the point of considerable estrangement. Government typically takes a *negative and manipulative attitude toward NGOs,* especially in disarmament. This attitude has also been carried over into the United Nations, of all places, where disarmament has traditionally been

viewed by some governments as an illegitimate activity for citizen groups, who should presumably deal only with economic, social, and other less "political" problems.

8. A final source of feelings of powerlessness is the realization that there has been *no substantial progress* toward genuine disarmament. Any movement is hard to sustain if it is lacking in success stories and even token victories.

Electoral Politics and the Arms Race

Behind the charades of shifting rationalizations for new strategic nuclear weapons may lie something more than the self-aggrandizement of the Pentagon. Presidents, senators, and representatives seldom let their eyes wander from the electoral clock for very long. The habits of politicians tending to self-preservation are at least as well-developed as they are for most other human beings. A new weapons system may be more for political protection than for national security—although incumbents may become so earnestly persuaded of their indispensability to the nation that they can no longer see the difference.

The Johnson Administration's ABM decision of late 1967, on the eve of a predictably tough election year, may fit this pattern of political protection. If the state of anti-missile technology made that decision virtually incredible as an anti-Soviet move, the state of Chinese ICBM technology made it even more incredible as an anti-Chinese weapon. Yet the latter rationale was announced. What might really account for such a decision? James Reston of *The New York Times* offered one very credible explanation which the White House could hardly advertise: the ABM was an "anti-Republican missile." Arms controllers profoundly disturbed at the thought of what ABMs might do (and did do) to provoke a new offensive missile race could hardly be relieved that the real explanation for the new weapon may have been "only political."

The arms race between Democrats and Republicans has too often become more threatening than the arms race between the United States and the Soviet Union. Or, more accurately perhaps, electoral warfare within the US has become a prime factor in escalating the Cold War.

Since the late 1960s, we have seen the game of presidential competition become a relentless, never-ending spectacle which has caused the conduct of our government itself to become more and more non-rational and which, above all, has made our foreign policy hostage to this perpetual electioneering. It is a game which astounds our allies and confounds our adversaries even when we reach agreement at the diplomatic level. It is a game which seems to favor unemployed outsiders who pander to populist sentiments against government and politicians (Nixon, Carter, Reagan). It is a game which is costly beyond calculation. It is a game in which so-called "reforms" like presidential primaries have become perverted so that most people wind up being disfranchised.

Our capricious and unrepresentative primaries in 1980 — thirty-eight of them — were so spread out that people who voted in April, May, and June knew it was too late to affect the decisions of the conventions. Groups concerned about peace, disarmament, and minority issues felt particularly disfranchised.

In the Fall 1980 issue of *Foreign Policy,* Laurence Radway wrote of "The Curse of Free Elections" which narrow the public's conception of our own national interest. This "perpetual campaigning encourages the continuing mobilization of a mass inclined to a hard line in foreign policy." Our primaries tend to generate and manipulate the most irrational popular pressures, especially of a chauvinistic kind. The general public's conception of the national interests of the United States is narrower today than it has been at any time since Pearl Harbor.

The redemption of our nominating systems means seriously working either for some kind of consolidated primaries or for some open caucus plan such as they have in Minnesota. Another systemic task, the reconstruction of our political parties, is closely related to the first. The basic bewildering question has become: how can we hold *any* group accountable for governing this country? That, to my mind, is inescapably a problem of party responsibility of some kind.

We seldom see this issue with any clarity from within our churches. We have this fatuous, ultimately irresponsible image of citizenship which holds that the good citizen does not commit herself to any party — but weighs all the issues and then votes. The net effect of all this is to reinforce the privatization, alienation, and cynicism of too much of the public, all in the name of independent voting or Christian transcendence.

In advance of the 1980 elections the Arms Control Association noted that thirteen senators of both parties who had been strong proponents of arms control were up for re-election. In the elections, six of those thirteen were defeated. Their defeats may have been somehow connected with a common complaint of the staffs of pro-SALT senators in 1979 and 1980: they were getting no mail from the churches.

In a country burdened with dissensus, we badly need vital new coalitions and idea factories in the form of political parties capable of their own indispensable ministry of reconciliation. One of the most perceptive political analysts, David Broder, has made a plea for the renewal of our political system in a book published before the 1980 elections, *Changing of the Guard: Power and Leadership in America.* The next two decades, says Broder, should be "as much a period of institutional rehabilitation and repair as the last two decades were a time of disparagement and destruction of the machinery of our government."

ACDA and Bureaucratic Politics

The tribulations of the US Arms Control and Disarmament Agency, vested by law with primary bureaucratic responsibilities for disarmament, have frequently punctuated the sentences of this book. While ACDA was once too severely portrayed as "a stillborn dove with unflexed wings," the obstacles to a successful politics of disarmament may be brought into clearer view if we focus on that agency and its limitations.

Undoubtedly the most vivid and complete portrait of ACDA in action is Duncan L. Clarke's *Politics of Arms Control: The Role and Effectiveness of the U.S. Arms Control and Disarmament Agency* (1979). Clarke acknowledges that ACDA is neither the only nor the most important actor in the disarmament process, but his book suggests that ACDA be regarded as "the touchstone, the lens through which the process is viewed." His many years of haunting the halls of ACDA and related bureaucracies, which led him through more than 250 formal interviews, provided him with a treasury of data for evaluating ACDA's four major functions: (1) research; (2) management of negotiations; (3) control systems; and (4) public information. Here are some of Clarke's findings (supplemented by other sources and by some observations for which Clarke should not be held accountable):

To be called an "arms controller" within the bureaucracy is commonly to be put down as soft-headed if not treasonable. Henry Kissinger, notwithstanding his own preoccupations with SALT, habitually referred to ACDA officials as "arms controllers" in voice-tones which suggested derision. The realistic-sounding label of "arms control" as a substitute for "disarmament" has never provided much protective coloration. ACDA cadres tend to be regarded as weak and ineffective in comparison with the "tough guy" images which are cultivated elsewhere in the national security bureaucracies, especially in the State Department.

ACDA directors have customarily been selected for their conservative, military, and establishment credentials. William C. Foster had been a lifelong Republican, Deputy Secretary of Defense, and strong protagonist for strategic missiles when he was named the agency's first director—in effect, replacing the ultra-establishment conservative John McCloy who had served for some months as John Kennedy's Disarmament Adviser. Gerard Smith's career as a Republican attorney and national security official commended him to the Nixon Administration—at least, at the start. He was replaced by Fred Iklé, a weapons advocate from the RAND Corporation whose harsh anti-Soviet views put him to the right side of both the CIA and the Pentagon on SALT issues. While Paul Warnke was portrayed by some as liberal and dovish, he had been a prosperous lawyer who had served the Pentagon as General Counsel and later Assistant Secretary of Defense for International Security Affairs. He was replaced by General George Seignious, former staff director of the Joint Chiefs of Staff, chief Pentagon promoter of arms sales, and commandant of The Citadel. Reagan appointed Eugene Rostow, conservative Yale Law School professor and nominal Democrat, who had chaired the Committee on the Present Danger's campaign against SALT II. (And, as a separate appointee, SALT negotiator General Edward Rowny, the former Joint Chiefs of Staff man on the SALT delegation who resigned to campaign against SALT II.)

These are the men who have been named to lead ACDA—no doubt to toughen up the image of those despised "arms controllers." None has been a lifelong professional disarmer; none could rightly be called a disarmament visionary.

Notwithstanding their establishment and even Pentagon resumés, however, no ACDA director with the exception of Paul Warnke has had much direct access to the President. In the agency's first fifteen years (1961-76), none secured a close relationship with the Chief Executive. From the beginning, the Joint Chiefs of Staff have persistently labored to block such a relationship. Even in Warnke's case, there were obstructions. When Warnke, backed by Secretary of State Vance, proposed to President Carter a halt in the production of fissionable materials for weapons purposes as a US initiative prior to the 1978 UN Disarmament Session, Secretary of Defense Harold Brown complained that such a proposal should have been cleared with the Pentagon (not that there was much chance of that!)—and the proposal died. Warnke increasingly found that NSC Adviser Brzezinski sat on policy papers that Warnke wanted to go directly to Carter. Some months after Warnke's resignation in October 1978 (his tenure at ACDA lasted only a year and a half) he observed that Carter had increasingly isolated himself behind advisers who took too narrow a view of national security. The reference was hardly obscure.

The Joint Chiefs of Staff, particularly in ACDA's first years, were concerned about much more than the director's access to the President: they tended to be hostile to the very existence of ACDA. Major General Dale O. Smith, Special Assistant to JCS for Arms Control 1961-63, later testified to the House Foreign Affairs Committee:

> The underlying arms control philosophy governing ACDA is that our nuclear armaments by themselves cause world tensions and thus must be reduced, even unilaterally. The military view is that world tensions are caused by international political differences and that our nuclear armaments provide the deterrent and protection necessary in this unstable environment. Thus the two philosophies are diametrically opposed and a constant under-the-table conflict is in process between ACDA and JCS. . . . ACDA should be abolished forthwith.[3]

General Smith thus subscribed to the "realist" doctrine of the 1950s and 1960s which held that weapons merely reflect political realities. However, that hangover from pre-nuclear history dulled the military's own perceptions of a massive new political reality: the increasingly autonomous momentum of military technology in the strategic nuclear arms race.

There should be no surprise at such a conflict between the JCS and arms controllers: the military establishment's natural drive is to deploy weapons. The real question is whether that conflict is intentionally structured or, on the contrary, forfeited to the Pentagon. Does civilian leadership effectively discipline the military by providing effective countervailing power within bureaucratic and legislative structures? If the Pentagon is permitted, both in public and private, to be an aggressive advocate for more weapons systems, there must be at least an equal opportunity for the vigorous advocacy of arms control and disarmament. That opportunity has seldom, if ever, been facilitated by the institutional line-ups in the national security bureaucracy.

The government's critical need for countervailing power in matters of military technology can be obscured in two opposite ways. One is when the civilian leadership of the Pentagon overrides the JCS and becomes aggressively committed to arms control. That has rarely happened—but it did sporadically mark Robert McNamara's tenure as Secretary of Defense. His support for the Partial Test Ban in the fact of JCS opposition, as well as his own opposition to ABMs, caused much grumbling among the military. Less obvious was the degree to which McNamara's interest in arms control eclipsed ACDA and further isolated Director William Foster from the White House.

The opposite problem occurs when ACDA's own leadership defaults on its advocacy role, either by timidity or by excessive collusion with the Department of Defense. The latter marked Fred Iklé's stint as ACDA Director under Nixon and Ford. Iklé entered office as a publicized protagonist for counterforce, which solidified his ties with DOD Secretary James Schlesinger. While he took an intense interest in technical aspects of non-proliferation (a subject which had been almost totally ignored by the Kissinger regime at NSC), Iklé was an advocate of precisely those weapons systems like cruise missiles which were frustrating the progress of SALT. A State Department official complained: "ACDA is so much in bed with Defense that those who do favor arms control feel awkward going to ACDA . . . Consequently, we don't give ACDA's papers the kind of weight they might otherwise receive."

These variable patterns of ACDA's relations with the Pentagon, all of which dramatize ACDA's peripheral status, may be detailed further by noting the following:

1. ACDA has largely been excluded from weapons decisions and the military budget, at Pentagon insistence, even while having ACDA's own arms control proposals "cleared to death" with the Pentagon and the entire national security bureaucracy. The arms control impact statements (ACIS) mandated by Congress after 1975, were vigorously opposed by both DOD and OMB (Office of Management and Budget) and have yet to be proved potent tools of constraint on military technology. In fact, the Reagan Administration demoted ACIS by subordinating them to a new bureau with an opposite function: an Office of Strategic Assessments apparently charged with monitoring ACDA's own impact on military technology. Was ACDA really becoming a threat to the Pentagon?

2. ACDA has repeatedly been denied access to military information affecting future arms negotiations and defense budgets, while being subjected to humiliatingly stringent security restrictions.

3. ACDA has typically been underbudgeted and understaffed for its research responsibilities on nuclear subjects, especially research in the social sciences.

4. Problems of rapid staff turnover and intramural strife have compromised ACDA's institutional memory, morale, and capacity for long-range planning. These problems reflect not only the second-class status of the agency in the security hierarchy: they reflect the manipulation of personnel appointments to the agency by such extramural powers as the Pentagon and Senator Henry M. Jackson.

5. ACDA, unlike the Pentagon, lacks a basic requirement of bureaucratic clout: a powerful, well-organized constituency. On the one hand, "arms controllers" tend to shy away from identification with the "disarmers" so prominent in the NGOs. On the other hand, ACDA lacks the public information resources to compete effectively with those at the Pentagon. While DOD employs more than twice as many public affairs officers as the total membership of both houses of Congress at a cost of tens of millions of dollars, ACDA's information personnel have only recently increased from three to fourteen, with total public affairs budgets well under a million dollars. A related factor of incalculable public impact is that DOD has almost as many marching bands (160) as ACDA has full-time professionals.

Ideas of disarmament may, and must, be prudent in coping with the most daunting strategic questions. They may, and must, be ingenious in creating diplomatic scenarios which are finely tuned to the real possibilities of world politics. But if the ideas of disarmament lack the practical means of advocacy within the national security bureaucracy, neither their brilliance nor prophecy nor geopolitical wisdom will ever be enough to prevail against the momentum of military technology.

Think Tanks

No study of political influence in defense and disarmament affairs can wisely ignore the ascendancy of think tanks in the past two decades. Indeed, any thorough scrutiny of electoral politics or congressional politics or bureaucratic politics or the media must take account of this historic shift in the genesis of public policy. We have earlier noted the dominant role of civilian scholars in formulating the doctrines of deterrence and counterforce that have rationalized US military technology. Those formulations were cultivated largely in such governmental greenhouses as the RAND Corporation.

Since the mid-1970s or so, the patterns of think tank influence have changed significantly. There has been an aggressive development of private study centers financed by massive infusions of corporate wealth. Some of these centers, like the Committee on the Present Danger, are brand new; others, like the American Enterprise Institute, have recently undergone a metamorphosis from unsophisticated propaganda operations to academic arsenals, with budgets big enough to buy up conservative scholars in any field from political science to theology. The ascendancy of such centers must be measured against other developments of recent years, including the decline of both Congress and political parties as idea factories and the continuing shift of public policy from Capitol Hill to the executive bureaucracies. While Congress retains formidable powers for obstructing and intimidating the White House and the bureaucracies, the decentralization of committee authority and the decline of party discipline on the Hill (particularly among the Democrats) have increasingly forfeited policy initiatives to other power centers. Which is where the think tanks have come marching in.

Public policy in the US today is more and more the product of think tanks, most of which are adjuncts to special interests of some sort or other. These new power centers hire expertise, generate policy dogmas, manipulate data, flood the political and academic markets with their publications and films, scheme with growing success to dominate the Op-Ed pages and TV public affairs programs, deploy platoons of consultants to executive and legislative staffs, dispatch cadres to election campaigns and task forces, and generally do much of the dirty work for single-issue and special interest lobbies. Such think tanks, far from being beholden to established government policies, have been empowered by their independent income to assault progressive government programs and to overthrow foreign policies of détente, disarmament, and human rights. They represent the new look of lobbying in an age of policy complexity with growing demands for expertise — or at least the appearance of expertise. They are well equipped to wrap their studies in moral, ideological and even theological packages.

One of the special functions of some think tanks is to provide a shadow bureaucracy made up of exiles from the out-party. In past periods, the Brookings Institution has been notably hospitable to exiled moderates and liberals from Democratic regimes. The Arms Control Association, established under the roof of the Carnegie Endowment for International Peace in 1971, was largely formed by arms controllers who were refugees from the Kennedy and Johnson administrations. By contrast the American Enterprise Institute, two decades after its founding, catapulted into wealth and power when it became essentially the Nixon-Ford regime in exile after 1976. At a show-and-tell panel on think tanks for a gathering of political scientists in December 1980, an AEI official made two proud claims: (1) that AEI had become an objective, nonpartisan center for distinguished scholars; and (2) that over half its scholars were then serving on transition teams for the incoming Reagan Administration. (The dissonance between these claims struck the audience if not the speaker.)

The arena of policy ideas, especially in Washington, is crucial for the politics of disarmament not only because of the powers which shape and broadcast ideas: it is crucial because it is primarily in that arena that the true weaknesses of dominant dogmas may be exposed. Henry Fairlie's savage British wit sometimes threatens a Washingtonian's pride but the *Post* columnist recently portrayed both the powers and weaknesses of think tanks in living color. Contrasting the political naiveté of New York intellectuals with the intellectual poverty of the political capital, Fairlie took delight in reporting that

> the political world in Washington has only a dim notion of what an idea is. Therefore when it thinks that it has seen an idea — even if one has never seen a camel, after all, one knows that it is an animal with a hump — it tends to be overimpressed by it. Washington is at present suffering from the arrival in its midst of institutes which claim that they are in the business of ideas. Never having had a good university, it is bowled over by the new think tanks. Ben Wattenberg [AEI] is curiously described as a scholar, Jeane Kirkpatrick [Georgetown] is sent by Washington to New York as an ambassador of our new intellectual life. The political capital believes that it now is intellectually alive. But it's no more the one than New York is the other.

It hardly is essential to the argument of this book but it is an irresistible bit of levity in our grisly subject to continue with Fairlie's next paragraph — which truly exposes him as a chauvinist for London as a city-state:

> The most obvious result of the division between the political and cultural capital is the rarity in American public life of the cultivated man of affairs, who is a product of the single capitals. The

imitation of him will be found still farther north; for this is why Harvard had to be invented. But when dispatched to Cambridge, he is doubly isolated, from both the political and cultural worlds. Whenever he returns to Washington, to serve another administration, he seems more deformed.[4]

We have earlier recounted the Carter Administration's melancholy retreat from its commitments to détente and disarmament and the consequences of that retreat for SALT II, the UN Special Session, and the Non-Proliferation Treaty. The White House clearly lost the intellectual initiative in national security policy to groups like the Paul Nitze-Eugene Rostow-led Committee on the Present Danger; the American Security Council, its new front group named the Coalition for Peace through Strength, and its affiliated academic base in the Center for Strategic and International Studies at Georgetown University; and the intellectual circle around *Commentary* magazine's neo-conservative editor Norman Podhoretz, who would rail against "the culture of appeasement" in his book *The Present Danger* (1980). The story of "the Carter surrender" to these pressures is detailed in Richard Barnet's *Real Security* (1981).

Less visible than the activities of the ascendant think tanks is their financing. The extensive influence of one man's largesse, dispensed among dozens of hardline, conservative centers, has been graphically portrayed in the case of Richard Scaife, a Pittsburgher and Mellon heir. In the 1973-80 period, Scaife gave the Georgetown Center for Strategic and International Studies $5.3 million; Stanford University's Hoover Institution $3.5 million; New York University's National Security Program and its affiliated National Strategy Information Center $6 million; the Heritage Foundation $3.8 million; the Institute for Foreign Policy Analysis (Cambridge) $1.9 million; the Institute for Contemporary Policy Studies (San Francisco) $1.8 million; Committee on the Present Danger $360,000. That's only a very partial list of Scaife's donations. A survey of eight different anti-SALT studies in 1979 disclosed that all eight had come from groups substantially supported by Scaife. What had seemed like a "paper avalanche" of facts and figures at seminars, briefings, press conferences, and committee hearings had been generated by a network tied together by common funding.[5]

For the most part, the politics of defense and disarmament does not begin on Capitol Hill. It begins in the executive and military bureaucracies and the think tanks which serve them. Too often, when a new weapons system or doctrine or military posture or arms control measure is put before Congress, it has become irreversible politically. Two or three or five years before, there may have been a much better opportunity to have some impact on the concepts and priorities which shaped the political decision. That requires of disarmament advocates a continuing presence in the policy community's bureaucratic and research centers, not simply in its legislative process. This is not to argue that disarmament lobbies should lower their flags on Capitol Hill. It is to urge a much better early warning system if the idea and the politics of disarmament are ever to have a chance to prevail.

The Arms Control Association, the Center for Defense Information, the Institute for Policy Studies, and the Churches' Center for Theology and Public Policy have important roles to play in the think tank arena, but their resources are modest in comparison with those tanks founded upon hardline ideological bases.

There is small likelihood that big money will soon flow toward study centers seriously committed to the exploration of scenarios for genuine disarmament. Wherever dominant strategic dogmas and the politics of national security are threatened with exposure, neither government nor corporate nor foundation funding can be counted upon. Yet the think tank arena has become the inescapable new frontier for the idea of disarmament.

It was with a mixture of skepticism and hope that I testified before the US Commission on Proposals for the National Academy of Peace and Conflict Resolution in July 1980. After suggesting that a non-political, "pure technique" style of conflict studies might be appropriate only to domestic conflicts or Third World boundary disputes, my testimony stated:

> I believe it is imperative for such an Academy to give highest priority to the most massive and most threatening of all international conflicts: the arms race, economic hostilities, and the increasingly bitter scramble for scarce resources. The new political reality in our world is a global bargaining arena which no nation can control and in which conflict resolution must be practiced on a broader scale than ever. The Academy should not be preoccupied with piecemeal approaches to peace.
>
> Surely nothing should be more central to the studies of the Academy than innovative approaches to national security, defense and disarmament. Confronted as we are by authoritative forecasts of nuclear war by the next decade, we must design the most promising preventive strategies our minds can conceive.

With all the research that goes into military hardware, whether in the name of "security" or "arms control," we do not begin to have adequate studies of models for reversing the arms race. Such studies will require the most serious intellectual effort at critical analyses of such strategic dogmas as "deterrence" and "counterforce," as well as of that complex institutional thicket in which military technology so strongly influences political behavior. For the problems of conflict resolution for the super-powers are not simply out there in some international void between boundaries: they are profoundly implicated in our domestic institutions and values.

In this context, the roles of public opinion, bureaucratic-legislative-and-electoral politics, and non-governmental organizations are vital subjects in the study of peacemaking.

I am well aware that some of these subjects range beyond the scope of "conflict resolution" as some have conceived it. They may also seem so controversial as to threaten the political acceptability of the Academy proposal. But I believe it would be better to have no government-sponsored Academy of Peace and Conflict Resolution at all than to have one which conveys simplistic and misleading notions as to the true requirements of peace.

The Media

Any fair assessment of the print and broadcast media must acknowledge that they often meet very high standards of investigative journalism and interpretation in defense and disarmament matters. The picture, however, is distinctly mixed. If *New York Times* military correspondent Drew Middleton and columnist William Safire provide an unrelieved diet of anti-Soviet alarmism, Leslie Gelb and others have offered sensitive and sophisticated interpretations of Soviet and disarmament issues. If the Op-Ed page of *The Washington Post* has for some years now provided a steady flow of regressive chauvinism from columnists George Will, Rowland Evans and Robert Novak, that same paper has served the public very well through Soviet and military affairs reporters Don Oberdorfer, Walter Pincus, and Robert Kaiser. Each of the three commercial TV networks in the US has recently broadcast a high quality series on the arms race, with a CBS five-part series on national defense in June 1981 a particularly outstanding educational venture. In short, there is no good reason for disarmament advocates to be totally cynical or paranoid about The Media, lest they sound like Spiro Agnew.

Yet there are serious limitations in media coverage of disarma-

ment. Just a few minutes before broadcasting a half-hour CBS interview on SALT II in 1978, I was appalled to witness a studio
preview of the five-minute graphic introduction that CBS had prepared. The graphics seriously distorted the military balance between the US and the USSR by highlighting only those numbers in
which the Soviets had an apparent edge, such as numbers of
launchers and throw-weight. If numbers really matter in nuclear
comparisons, the more fundamental fact that the US had
thousands more nuclear warheads than the USSR was not even
mentioned — nor were the strategic advantages of diversity (the
vaunted US triad of ICBMs, submarines, and bombers) or such
qualitative criteria as readiness, reliability, and accuracy indicated.
In short, the broadcast began with a bad tilt to the right. It was not
possible, on the spot, to fix responsibility for such a distortion between the CBS reporters and technicians.

It seems likely that nobody in the media was a more effective
purveyor of mythology on SALT II in the 1977-80 period than
George Will, syndicated columnist for *The Washington Post* and
Newsweek. Writing column after column in opposition to the
treaty — and writing with a formidable combination of literary ele-
gance and a veneer of technical virtuosity — Will harshly portrayed
President Carter, Secretary Vance, and Paul Warnke as appeasers;
gave unending aid to SALT opponents like Senator Henry Jackson;
and made the most speculative and dubious claims about Soviet
military spending, strategic advantage, and negotiating behavior.
Yet he typically wrote in such pontifical style that he could hardly
be suspected of either speculation or dubiety. Some Carter Administration officials were appalled that George Will's relentless
assaults seemed to have intimidated the White House much more
than the Russians had and seldom received an effective reply, either
from the administration or from other columnists in the *Post*. Perhaps more serious was the fact that hundreds of newspapers across
the country which carried Will's columns were simply not disposed
or equipped to feature alternative views.

The most serious shortcoming of US mass media in disarmament affairs is the skimpy and capricious coverage of international
institutions, such as the United Nations, the Committee on Disarmament, and the Non-Proliferation Treaty review conferences.
If those bodies are long on rhetoric and repetitious resolutions and
short on decisive action, that is largely because the nuclear weapon
states have viewed them as "damage limitation" sites rather than
vital centers for mutual security. It is just those bodies, however,

which best reveal the global problems of security and disarmament, the special perspectives of other countries, and the prospects for common programs of action. Those are reasons enough for sustained media interpretation.

Beyond these media that reach millions are the specialty journals on defense and disarmament that reach thousands. Some voice industrial interests, like *Aviation Week and Space Technology*. There are numerous armed forces organs, as well as strategic journals such as *Survival* (published by the International Institute for Strategic Studies) and *International Security* (Harvard). Generally more sympathetic to disarmament are the *Bulletin of the Atomic Scientists, Arms Control Today,* and the *Defense Monitor*—all creatures of Washington-based associations. The UN Disarmament Centre publishes a largely documentary journal, *Disarmament,* while the UN NGOs publish a newspaper, *Disarmament Times*. (The latter shifts from monthly to daily or several-days-a-week publication during UN special sessions and NPT review conferences.) All of these journals serve primarily to inform and, in some cases, to activate very limited publics. Perhaps more influential than any of these are the arms control articles that appear quite regularly in quarterly rivals *Foreign Affairs* and *Foreign Policy*. There has never been a time when there were more information and commentary available to the public on disarmament subjects than there are at present. The motivation of a much larger public, as well as more adequate communication among special publics, remains a prerequisite to an influential disarmament constituency.

Political Economy and the Arms Race

Somehow the politics of disarmament, like "them dry bones," has got to get electoral politics connected to legislative politics and bureaucratic politics and think tank politics and media politics and multilateral politics—and now to economic politics. For there is a massive connectedness between politics and economics in the New Industrial State (to use Galbraith's term). Military technology is increasingly the prime engine of that connectedness.

Neither the limits of this book nor the limits of its author will permit more than cursory treatment of economic aspects of disarmament. However, policy struggles over national security in the 1980s are more than debates over Soviet conduct and strategic doctrine: they are perforce struggles over the priorities and performance of the American economy. They must also become more intentional controversies over the shape of the world economy. The idea of disarmament must therefore engage ideas about inflation, the budget, economic growth, productivity, employment, foreign trade, and Third World development.

These difficult issues, however, should not be overly mystified by pretenses of economic expertise which discourage many citizens from political action upon them. The economics profession itself has been humbled by its inability to account for the most important economic happenings of the past fifteen years. Neither classical, Keynesian, nor Marxist theory seems capable of telling the whole story or confidently prescribing solutions for the mix of inflation, unemployment, and stagnant productivity—at least, not until the supply-side zealots of the Reagan Administration came along. At this writing their nostrums have yet to be fully tested. What to call them is also problematical. They speak the language of laissez-faire but, as Marcus Raskin has suggested, Ronald Reagan came in "riding the Trojan horse of military Keynesianism." The American economy for years has been marked by a kind of "military socialism" or "Pentagon capitalism" in which military budgets have normally exceeded the after-tax profits of all private corporations. Moreover, there has been very little competition for most defense contracts and military industry has enjoyed enormous subsidies making it a very special welfare-state. Thousands of retired military officers become corporate officials with prime military contractors. In short, these are issues which hardly belong to economists alone. They must be made more political than they are.

From the very beginnings of the Reagan Administration, inflation and the Federal Budget became prime arenas for the politics of disarmament.

Inflation is indisputably a wasteful, debilitating malady for millions of our people and most of our institutions. Don Fraser, mayor of Minneapolis and former member of Congress, has said that a lack of seriousness about inflation on the part of liberals is their most grievous failure politically.

But to be serious about the *consequences* of inflation is not necessarily to understand its *causes*.

I believe that, for the past fifteen years, the military factor has been the most massive and most persistent force in the upward spiral of inflation. It is by magnifying this very factor, while presuming that our productivity crisis is somehow an entirely separate "economic" issue, that the Reagan regime seems bent on generating even more economic chaos.

Even if we should assume that government spending is the

prime cause of inflation (which some analysts very much doubt), we must recognize that, year after year, military spending is the largest item in Congressional appropriations. Its share of spending is now rising steeply—at the expense of almost everything else.

If we worry that government waste is a big contributor to inflation, we should know that the costs of multibillion-dollar weapons systems tend to multiply several times over—pushed 'way up by wasteful management, heavy cost overruns, and lack of restraining competition. A relentless temptation too seldom resisted by the Pentagon itself is "gold plating"—loading new weapons with needlessly complex gadgets, then repeatedly ordering design changes to take account of still more recent refinements in gadgetry. Results: economies on interchangeable parts are forfeited and production itself is disorderly and protracted and extravagant. What "gold plating" does to the whole process of military technology is to provide a persistent source of instant obsolescence. The General Accounting Office (GAO) regularly reports billions of dollars in military waste. Former Secretary of Defense Harold Brown confessed that waste within the military establishment was the toughest problem he had to face—and that he hardly succeeded in solving it.

If we accept the classic definition of inflation—too much money chasing too few goods—we must know that military industry increases the money supply for its employees but does not produce goods and services the people can buy. This is the essence of economic sterility: to pump up consumer demand but fail to supply the products. In 1980, *The Wall Street Journal* concluded that military spending is "the worst kind of government outlay, since it eats up materials and other resources that otherwise could be used to produce consumer goods." Such a view from Wall Street must surely confound some Marxists who suppose that capitalism is indissolubly linked with militarism.

If we really look to the roots of our productivity crisis as a source of inflation—in this American economy which not so long ago was the world's pace-setter in industrial productivity—*if* we take the full measure of our obsolete and inefficient plants with their inflated costs which now make competition with other industrial nations so tough in so many product lines, we shall see how much this crisis has been caused by grossly overcommitting our research-and-development personnel and funds to military technology, at the expense of our civilian economy.

Looking ahead, US military spending could well take up more

than 8 percent of the GNP by 1986 (the administration forecasts 7.1 percent) — a percentage matching the highest levels of the Vietnam War. That comparison is sobering because it reminds us that Lyndon Johnson's failure to raise taxes led to heavy deficits and serious inflation. Whether the Reagan Administration's political victory in significantly reducing taxes while rocketing military spending will avoid even larger deficits and inflation in the next several years is a mystery yet to be unfolded.

There is yet a more ultimate scenario waiting in the wings. Troubled by doubts about the adequacy of US industry to meet a protracted future conflict with the Soviet Union, Secretary of Defense Caspar Weinberger in the summer of 1981 mentally began to take a great leap forward that could "dwarf" the military spending already projected. Weinberger

> asked the armed services to indicate what kind of an industrial base would be needed to double or triple defense spending in an emergency, or to devote half the country's GNP (currently almost $3 trillion) to defense in a single year.[6]

Stephen Rosenfeld commented on this great leap:

> We are coming into the presence of a new way of thinking about defense, the idea — unfamiliar since World War II — of a national security commitment so unending and all-consuming as to subdue other economic and social priorities as though we were at war. . . . In this atmosphere, the new ideas on industrial mobilization have progressed from think tanks to Pentagon paper.[7]

The reported source of this new planning for industrial mobilization was Undersecretary of Defense Fred Iklé, former ACDA Director. Iklé wants the US to prepare for a long conventional war. Such preparation would require abandoning environmental constraints, building huge weapons stockpiles, developing standby emergency factories, and readying strict economic controls. These notions were circulated by the San Francisco-based Institute for Contemporary Studies, a think tank favored by Richard M. Scaife to the amount of nearly $2 million.

There is a vicious Doomsday circle at work in such projections. Those who did most to destroy détente in the late 1970s are now insisting that we get ready for war. Why, after all, such an upsurge in military spending? No better answer has been offered than that of Senator Paul Tsongas of Massachusetts:

> Because we have witnessed the death of SALT II and the eclipse
> of arms control. The psychology of the arms race has replaced
> the realism of arms limitation . . . But massive arms spending
> takes away critical capital and technical expertise needed to ad-
> dress America's energy and economic infrastructure needs. And
> if our economy and energy needs are not met, then where are we
> in terms of real national security?

The political point here is prior to the economic one. It was the loss
of a battle for treaty ratification – and the way in which that battle
was fought – which loosed the floodgates of military spending.
Those protagonists for new nuclear weapons who minimize their
costs in relation to conventional arms would do well to recognize
that a failure of nuclear arms control can unleash military extrava-
gance of all kinds. They would also do well to acknowledge that, if
strategic costs have been proportionately modest in recent years,
that is because many weapons systems have been slowly making
their way through the research and development stage. As those
systems move more or less simultaneously into production and deployment – Tridents, cruise missiles, MX, several new types of
bombers, perhaps new ABMs – nuclear weapons costs will hardly
seem modest any more.

The political economy of the arms race is more than a dispute
about the causes of inflation or other theoretical matters: it is the
discovery that the battle over the Federal Budget can become *the*
political arena for virtually every realm of public policy. The Office
of Management and Budget (OMB) has seldom if ever been
equipped with the mandate or the personnel to impose adequate
constraints on military spending. For the first six months of the
Reagan Administration, OMB under David Stockman played an
unprecedented activist role – not, however, as a constraining force
on DOD but as the vanguard of Pentagon aggrandizement while
serving as the scourge of social, health, educational, cultural, and
international development programs. Only when the White House
belatedly realized that its budget deficit was looming much larger
than anticipated did Stockman wage a token battle against Weinberger, leading to a one percent cut in military spending over a
three-year period. Other programs were cut still more severely.

Had Jimmy Carter been re-elected, he would have pushed the
US up from $158 billion in military spending in 1981 to $300 billion
a year by 1986. Then along came Ronald Reagan pushing for still

another $169 billion on top of Carter's projected increases by 1986. After the budget battle of 1981, projected military spending by 1986 amounted to $1.5 trillion — barring the early implementation of Weinberger's "great leap forward" or Iklé's "new industrial base."

The foreign policy implications of these decisions extend far beyond the US-Soviet conflict. Foreign trade could suffer serious reverses if the US continues to mortgage its technology and industrial capacity to the military. Such industrial priorities are bound to frustrate consumer demand and keep interest rates exceedingly high — and high US interest rates are hurting European economies at this writing, with the still further consequence of constraining European development assistance to the Third World. Indirectly, the US is thus aggravating its already ignominious role in economic development: the US currently ranks 16th of 17 industrial countries in ODA (official development aid as a percentage of GNP). There must be a valid doctrine of "linkage" in here somewhere!

For reasons more basic than foreign aid, US relations with the Third World are rapidly becoming a disaster area threatening the security of both. The US government is increasingly isolated in multilateral institutions. That is true not only with regard to disarmament issues we have traced through the UN and the Non-Proliferation Treaty. In the issues of trade and monetary relations, Law of the Sea, food policy, health codes, and technology transfer — all involving North-South and rich-poor conflicts — the US has more and more found itself alone, playing a solitary obstructionist role. The meanness of that role in almost every multilateral forum of the past decade has been played out in poor US preparation, resistance to change, blaming the Third World for all Third World problems, and stalemating international policies.

These troubles have been almost invisible to the American public because our national security bureaucracy has been absorbed in the nuclear arms race, our chief executives have discounted their political importance, and our media have stuck to the White House schedule. Yet the other end of these troubles is much more visible to the Third World. There is an asymmetry in international communications: those who have preponderant power and wealth, even power over communications media, typically cannot perceive the consequences of their own influence. Others, more likely to be the objects of that influence, often enjoy what José Miguez Bonino calls "the epistemological privilege of the poor." They *know* some things the rich and powerful will never know.

Willy Brandt's introduction to the 1980 report of the Independent Commission on International Development, which he chaired, graphically connects North-South issues with military spending as follows:

1. The military expenditure of only half a day would suffice to finance the whole malaria eradication programme of the World Health Organization. Even less would be needed to conquer river-blindness, which is still the scourge of millions.

2. A modern tank costs about $1 million. That amount could improve storage facilities for 100,000 tons of rice and thus save 4,000 tons or more annually. The same sum could provide 1,000 classrooms for 30,000 children—just one tank's worth.

3. For the price of one jet fighter ($20 million) one could set up about 40,000 village pharmacies.

4. One-half of one percent of one year's world military expenditure would pay for all the farm equipment needed to increase food production to the level of self-sufficiency in the world's food-deficit countries by 1990.

So: the Brandt Commission unequivocally views disarmament as essential to survival and security—and as a precondition of economic development. The dogmas of security and economics in the US government right now don't quite point in that direction.

CHAPTER 7

Scenarios of Disarmament

We ought not to be satisfied when people tell us that politics is the art of the possible. Politics should be the art to make possible tomorrow what seems impossible today.
—UN General Assembly President Edvard Hambro in a 1971 address to the American Society of International Law

What of the future? How much of a future will there be? What are we to do?

In this penultimate chapter, we must project the idea of disarmament into scenarios of action. These scenarios have one basic requirement: to roll back the probabilities of nuclear war. The motives are obvious even if the means are not. *Survival,* not only of this generation but of a healthy prospect for future generations. *Security*—authentic security—in a world safeguarded from the twin tyrannies of totalitarian weapons and totalitarian states. *Economic welfare,* made possible by the transformation of technology from destruction to development. *Freedom*—enjoying at last the fullness of human rights and civil liberties because peoples have been delivered from the repressions and brutalities of uncontrolled militarism.

If these motives really activate us, our government should play peace games even more seriously than it has been playing war games. Yet the very idea of peacemaking—of visioning peace, planning for it, working for it—has become strangely suspect and terribly threatening. We have become so thoroughly nurtured in narrow and even false dogmas of security that we rush quickly to stifle any alternative. We may admit that we don't exactly like nuclear weapons—but how hard it now is to imagine getting along without them! We are both the victims and the perpetrators of phony realism.

This absolutely vital imperative of futuring for peace has been choked by the reactive clutches of deterrence. As George and Smoke noted, deterrence has stifled the long-term imagining of a world community. Counterforce is compromising the human future even more severely, spurring the bureaucratic momentum of military technology not only to senseless redundancies but to the compounding of fear in both superpowers.

Nothing documents this obstruction of futuring more concretely than a comparison of military planning with planning for arms control and disarmament within the national security bureaucracies. Strategic weapons have long lead-times and long lifetimes stretching over decades. It typically takes ten to fifteen years to move a weapons system from research and development to production and deployment. The deployments of bombers and missiles may then endure twenty or thirty more years, if not longer, requiring all the costs of maintenance and readiness — and standing as virtually unchallengeable givens which become the despair of disarmament negotiations. Military budgets and force postures thus proceed by five-and ten-year plans, a pattern of public policy which is regarded as socialist if not Bolshevist in any other area.

By contrast, disarmament planning tends to be riveted to immediate platforms. ACDA has neither the mandate nor the personnel to do much long-range planning. Even in the Warnke heydays, ACDA was so taken up with SALT II (and with housekeeping other talks dependent on the fate of SALT II) that the agency had little opportunity seriously to contemplate "next steps," let alone the next decade. This planning imbalance between defense and disarmament is one of the most pernicious faults in the very making of US foreign policy. It is a fault which largely explains the threatening gap between military technology and the verification technology deemed essential to arms control.

Other impediments to disarmament scenarios include the glut of technical complexities which has been permitted to choke the SALT process and other negotiations; cynicism about disarmament itself, often based on a misreading of history; the debilitating sense of powerlessness, even among disarmament advocates; and, warping all the rest, primitive stereotypes of the Soviet Union.

The idea of disarmament must therefore do more than prescribe alternative policies for the government, as important as that surely is. It must point to catalytic strategies, support structures, attitude changes, and mobilized constituencies. This chapter will take up each of these topics in turn.

Policy Alternatives

By way of saying some good things about deterrence moderates who are arms controllers, we have earlier noted a certain triangularity in the national security debate: a shape which requires disarmers to make common cause with arms controllers on some issues. Now we must admit that the debate is even more complicated than that. In fact, we may specify seven scenarios for disarmament, all with variations, all with distinctive visions of the future:

1. *Nuclear superiority.* The claim here is that the US has fallen behind in the arms race, the Soviets are driving for superiority, and the US must undertake a crash program to recover its own strategic superiority. This is the goal of the American Security Council and its affiliated Coalition for Peace Through Strength which lobbied aggressively against SALT II. That means full speed ahead with MX, Tridents, all types of cruise missiles, B-1, Stealth Bomber, a Big Navy. It means counterforce. It means no disarmament. It means arms control only when the US has re-established its superiority and can then force the Soviets to negotiate on American terms. This is a view which no US administration has espoused since the Massive Retaliation days of the 1950s — until the policies of the Reagan Administration disclosed its revival in high places.

2. *Catch-up.* This is the agenda of the Committee on the Present Danger and closely resembles the nuclear superiority model in its counterforce push for new weapons. However, there is a professed commitment to parity rather than superiority. There is much more attention to arms control. But the claim is that the US has fallen behind the Soviet Union. There is much alarm about ICBM vulnerability, the Euro-strategic balance, and Soviet intervention in the Third. World. Arms control must wait until parity has been restored and the Soviets stop provoking linkage. SALT II was rejected as a one-sided treaty freezing the US into a position of permanent inferiority. While this view has been most conspicuously associated with Paul Nitze and Eugene Rostow, it gained ground in the last two years of the Carter Administration, particularly with NSC Adviser Brzezinski and DOD Secretary Brown — even though they professed continued support for SALT II. If there is a strategic debate within the Reagan Administration, it appears to be between catch-up and nuclear superiority.

3. *Controlled escalation.* This was the view which dominated the Nixon-Ford-Kissinger approach to arms control when officials spoke of "rules for the arms race." This was also the dominant view of the Carter Administration while it actively campaigned for SALT II and before it became fully committed to MX, NATO "modernization," and PD 59. The claim was that parity was real in the form

of "essential equivalence" but that the arms race would continue to escalate. It seemed to be a very mechanical model, more the product of engineers than of politicians. The function of SALT II, therefore, was to regulate escalation. Arms control had to preserve options for ALCMs, GLCMs, and MX. Military budgets would continue to increase by at least 3 percent in real terms. (The rhetoric of reduced defense budgets and nuclear disarmament of 1977 and early 1978 had been abandoned.)

4. *Modest de-escalation.* Various proposals have been advanced for steps in the direction of a nuclear moratorium or a nuclear freeze, either on a joint US-Soviet basis or as an "independent national initiative." (That latter term is the virile equivalent of "unilateral initiative.") The claim is that parity is here to stay, escalation is pointless, and some new catalyst is needed to unwind the spiral. On the more token side, there have been proposals to halt all production of fissionable materials for weapons purposes, or stop nuclear testing—or flight testing—for some finite period. More comprehensive but presupposing Soviet agreement is the "Mutual Nuclear-Weapon Freeze" campaign launched in 1980. That campaign's platform calls for "a mutual freeze on the testing, production, and deployment of nuclear weapons and of missiles and new aircraft designed primarily to deliver nuclear weapons." All such steps are supported with the assurance that they would do nothing to impair national security.

5. *Minimal deterrence.* Without abandoning the notion that some nuclear weapons are essential to national security, this view proposes a drastic reduction of military forces, leaving a lean model of defense and deterrence. The claim is that 5,000 or 1,000 or even 200 residual strategic warheads could provide as much effective deterrence as 10,000—a claim once contemplated by Robert McNamara and Jimmy Carter. The Boston Study Group's recommendations in *The Price of Defense* (1979) aimed at $50 billion annual reductions in military spending by phasing out all ICBMs, mothballing ten of thirteen aircraft carriers, trimming the Navy to two hundred ships, eliminating amphibious attack forces, withdrawing from Asian bases, reducing US troops in Europe by 40,000, and halting all work on cruise missiles, Tridents, and MX—thus endorsing a nuclear freeze. SALT II was also endorsed as a very minimal step toward a minimal deterrent.

George Kennan's 1981 plan called for

an immediate across-the-boards reduction by 50 percent of the nuclear arsenals now being maintained by the superpowers—a reduction affecting in equal measure all forms of the weapon, strategic, medium range, and tactical, as well as their means of delivery—all this to be implemented at once and without further wrangling by the experts, and to be subject to such national means of verification as now lie at the disposal of the two powers.

The unveiling of that plan by the 77-year-old Kennan at the Einstein memorial luncheon in Washington was perhaps the most poignant moment of disarmament advocacy since John Kennedy's "Strategy for Peace" address of 1963—thanks to Kennan's directness and startling eloquence. (The full text of Kennan's address, "Like Lemmings Heading for the Sea," is published in the Appendix.)

6. *GCD.* The term "general and complete disarmament" may be used with either utopian or strategic connotations. While it endures in UN rhetoric, it has fallen on hard times in American usage since the McCloy-Zorin Agreement of 1961. In its historical, strategic sense it is somewhat less eschatological than it may sound, referring to a phased program of arms reductions down to police force levels "under strict and effective international controls." Some scheme of UN peacekeeping is involved. Grenville Clark and Louis B. Sohn elaborated such proposals in *World Peace Through World Law* (1958, revised 1964 and 1973), suggesting the attractions of GCD to world federalists. Robert Johansen of the Institute for World Order has proposed a 25-year program in five-year phases: (1) consciousness-raising and a nuclear freeze; (2) 10 percent annual reductions in military spending, no new weapons testing or deployment; (3) minimal deterrent, continue 10 percent reductions; (4) dismantle remaining nuclear weapons, 20 percent reductions; and (5) all military production and spending cease, new global security organization established.[1] Compatible with such GCD proposals but focusing more on domestic than international institutions are Gene Sharp's ideas of "transarmament" to a "post-military society" based on nonviolent civilian defense.[2]

7. *Nuclear abolitionism.* There are radical activist movements which are frankly cynical of electoral and legislative politics, the SALT process, and UN diplomacy. Their preferred model is an anti-establishment populism committed to mass rallies, direct action, the rhetoric of revolution, and the drama of civil disobedience. A current coalition based on such a model is the Mobilization for Survival which combines opposition to all nuclear weapons

with opposition to nuclear energy. The Berrigan brothers, David Dellinger, Sidney Lens, and other veterans of the radical wing of the 1960s anti-war movement have been conspicuous personalities in this new anti-nuclear movement.

These seven alternative future orientations are not altogether mutually exclusive. Some persons and groups, not illogically, identify with two or more of these scenarios. Indeed, an adequate policy scenario should probably comprehend several of them in sequence: perhaps from modest de-escalation to minimal deterrence and, eventually, GCD. A nuclear freeze is certainly compatible with all of these. (It is hardly compatible, however, with nuclear superiority, catch-up, or controlled escalation.) Moreover, such a spectrum suggests a strange bedfellow phenomenon in which some nuclear abolitionists and GCD prophets have found themselves linked with counterforce promoters in opposition to centrist policies like SALT II.

My own short-term agenda for some years has been to complete SALT II in order to facilitate deep cuts through SALT III; conclude a Comprehensive Test Ban; firm up the Non-Proliferation Treaty by mitigating its invidious discriminations and by promoting alternative energy assistance; forswear all new counterforce weapons (Trident, MX, cruise missiles, Euro-strategic missiles); halt fissionable materials production; scale down defense spending; curb arms exports; renounce interventionary strike forces. These were not an original or random list: they were conceived as interrelated components of a feasible disarmament program for the 1970s and early 1980s. For instance, a CTB and deep nuclear cuts could be viewed as the most important steps toward redeeming the Non-Proliferation Treaty — and, since proliferation seemed the most likely scenario for nuclear war, that redemption has been a priority second to none. Similarly, the forswearing of new weapons systems could mean significant reductions in military budgets.

But that "short-term" agenda has increasingly been stretched into a long-term if not impossible scenario by political changes in the US since 1978. My "realism" of a season ago now seems passé. Such a judgment does not instruct me, however, as to whether the way of the future must be more conservative or more radical.

What matters much more than the details of any policy blueprint is the strategic sensibility with which it is pursued. If the general direction of nuclear disarmament is clearly articulated, a great deal of pragmatism and flexibility about how to get there is in order.

Catalytic Strategies

What are the most effective instruments of progress in disarmament? Intimidating arms buildups, stable deterrence, token reductions, deep reductions, a global security plan, or a popular revolution? Is the choice finally between bilateral diplomacy and multilateral diplomacy? Or have arms treaties themselves become a dead end? Or, again, are national initiatives required to create a political climate in which negotiations can produce effective treaties?

If the answers to these questions are not self-evident — and they are not — the astonishing thing is that the questions themselves are so seldom asked.

Whatever may be said for mutual deterrence or for parity as a prerequisite to successful disarmament negotiations, deterrence in practice has proved to be a source of diplomatic impotence. Whatever the possession of nuclear weapons may have done to deter adversaries, it has been a deadly inhibitor of the possessors themselves. The technology of mass destruction tends to make governments reactive rather than empowering them to take political initiatives. This is the paradox of power in the nuclear age: to have The Bomb may be a prestigious and terrifying thing in the eyes of others but it tends to immobilize the will to do anything creative.

One of the tragedies of international conflict is that national leaders often trap themselves in a vicious circle of escalating hostilities in which they cannot envision any redemptive circle of de-escalation. Preoccupation with the scenarios of war preempts the imagination required for the scenarios of peacemaking. They may feel trapped because they are convinced of the absolute righteousness of their own cause and conduct; therefore, the next move toward peace must come from the enemy. They may discover how useless and dangerous nuclear threats have become in almost all situations: what, then, can they do with all their arsenals of annihilation? They may be strait-jacketed by the notion that no initiative toward peace is possible without a jointly negotiated and agreed treaty: to reduce arms unilaterally is to show weakness or naiveté or loss of nerve and is to invite attack. Thus do hardliners actually surrender to the momentum of the arms race with its increasing insecurity, irrationality, and loss of autonomy. The very determination to appear powerful and threatening may cripple the actual power to *act*. Two decades ago, Erich Fromm said we are becoming "a world of impotent men directed by virile machines" in both the US and USSR.

Action must begin somewhere if the vicious circle is to be broken. This is the crucial question for disarmament: what are the dynamics of the power to act? How can that power be generated? How can it be made effective? What is the catalytic strategy which offers the best promise of multiplying its influence for peacemaking?

This is, above all, a question of human interaction and not of technology. Deterrence strategists have engaged in infinite exercises of mutual mind-reading — but typically with crude if not subhuman "psycho-logics." Catalytic strategies require the sophisticated insights of humanistic psychologists. Fortunately, such psychologists as Charles Osgood and Erich Fromm have devoted substantial study to the problems of nuclear diplomacy.

Osgood has provided the definitive scenario of conflict resolution between nuclear adversaries in *An Alternative to War or Surrender* (1962) and other writings. He grounds the reality of unilateral initiatives in the reciprocal action of the arms race itself: each side decides to develop a weapon or increase its stockpile without making that action contingent on any agreement with its adversary. Yet that decision becomes a stimulus to the adversary to catch up and get ahead. Osgood argues that the arms race thus provides a model for its own reversal: graduated reciprocation in tension reduction (GRIT/R), with emphasis on the motivating power of unilateral initiatives.

Osgood's testimony to the effective power of unilateral action gains confirmation from our previous analysis of nuclear dynamics. Two former directors of research and engineering for the Pentagon — one an advocate, the other a critic — emphasized the unilateralism of the arms race on the US side. For John Foster, the US must keep "moving ahead" instead of just "reacting to Soviet actions." For Herbert York, that is just what the US has been doing all along: the arms race has largely "been determined by the unilateral actions of the United States." So the obvious question is: if unilateral initiatives can escalate the arms race, why can't they empower the de-escalation of the arms race?

Osgood's concerns are with effective power, balance, reciprocity, and genuine security. Unilateralism of this kind is not a one-sided exercise. In fact, Osgood stresses the importance of firmness, warnings against encroachments, and even retaining nuclear deterrents to the last stages of disarmament — in contrast with those whose scenarios envision nuclear disarmament prior to conventional disarmament.

Addressing himself to the question of guidelines for unilateral initiatives capable of inducing reciprocation, Osgood specifies the following:

1) Unilateral acts must be perceived by an opponent as reducing his external threat.
2) Unilateral acts must be accompanied by explicit invitations to reciprocation.
3) Unilateral acts must be executed without being dependent on the opponent's promise to reciprocate.
4) Unilateral acts must be planned in sequences and continued over considerable periods regardless of reciprocation by an opponent.
5) Unilateral acts must be announced in advance and widely publicized as part of a consistent policy.[3]

Osgood is not opposed to bilateral or multilateral treaties as such. His concern is to empower governments to reverse the arms race and create an atmosphere in which more permanent solutions to the problems of survival and security may be undertaken cooperatively. He provides not only an alternative to both war and surrender: he rescues us from an either/or choice between unilateral and mutual disarmament, suggesting that both are necessary. Osgood testifies that the greatest resistance to his approach has come from those who are burdened with a "bogy-man conception" of the Soviet enemy. His reply: initiatives are still required to test the intentions of the Soviets and to validate our own perceptions. Inaction compounds our ignorance and forfeits the favor of world opinion.

Others who have urged that the dynamics of disarmament require more than formal treaties, slowly and tediously agreed upon, are Thomas Schelling (*The Strategy of Conflict,* 1962) and Stanley Hoffmann (*The State of War,* 1965), both of Harvard. Schelling introduced the concept of "tacit bargaining" between adversaries who may not be engaged in negotiations at all — but who make independent choices having the effect of an agreement that provides advantages for both sides. Hoffmann noted that modern treaty-making, given the pace of technological innovations and the manipulative style of diplomacy in matters of disarmament, may increasingly be displaced by "reciprocal interaction, i.e., arms control through unilateral measures" which show serious self-restraint. Here we may say that "tacit bargains" or "reciprocal interactions," like Osgood's initiatives, may help prepare the political environment for better and stronger treaties.

George Kennan, too, addressed the catalytic question of how to break out of the vicious circle of the arms race. While he regretted the collapse of SALT II, which he and his Committee on East-West Accord supported, Kennan saw little to be gained by maintaining the style of the SALT process to date. He had "no illusion that negotiations on the SALT pattern—negotiations, that is, in which each side is obsessed with the chimera of relative advantage and strives only to retain a maximum of the weaponry for itself while putting its opponents to the maximum disadvantage"—could ever break out of the circle. Such negotiations "are not a way of escape from the weapons race; they are an integral part of it."

It was as an alternative to such protracted, self-indulgent negotiations that Kennan made his 50 percent reduction proposals, insisting on immediate implementation. For him the catalyst must be a "bold and sweeping departure—a departure that would cut surgically through the exaggerated anxieties, the self-engendered nightmares, and the sophisticated mathematics of destruction, in which we all have been entangled over these recent years, and would permit us to move, with courage and decision, to the heart of the problem."

There is no abstract principle for determining whether such a "bold and sweeping departure" or a more modest initiative will best serve the need for catalytic intervention to reverse the arms spiral at any particular time. Twenty years ago, Amitai Etzioni persuasively advocated a strategy of "gradualism" in *The Hard Way to Peace:* step-by-step reduction of tensions beginning with modest concessions and negotiating balanced and carefully phased reductions. Prior to the 1978 UN Special Session on Disarmament, with neither SALT II nor a CTB an early prospect, I argued that "any one or combination of the following modest steps (either as a US or joint initiative) would make the Special Session a momentous event" without risking US security in any meaningful sense:

(a) Cessation of the production of fissionable materials for weapons purposes;
(b) Cessation of flight tests of all vehicles for delivering nuclear weapons;
(c) A three-to-five year moratorium on the development and production of all new nuclear weapons systems;
(d) A clear renunciation of the use or threat of nuclear weapons against States that have no nuclear weapons on their territories; and

(3) A slight percentage reduction of military spending with funds transferred to economic development.[4]

None of these steps would have required any actual disarmament: no weapons would have been dismantled thereby. Yet any one of them might well have been a vital catalyst not only to US-Soviet détente but to multilateral negotiations. Three of them would have somewhat inhibited the pace of military technology. Despite urgings from the State Department and ACDA that some such step would strengthen the US position at the UN, the White House declined to offer any initiative at all. There was much confusion around President Carter as to what constituted real strength and what constituted weakness.

Of course, there must be an assessment of risks in contemplating any initiative. But those risks are hardly confined to unilateral initiatives. They accompany any bilateral process or multilateral policy. More to the point: the risks of the arms race itself and its further escalation have become infinitely more ominous than any token reductions, any nuclear freeze, or even any Kennan plan. Both the freeze proposal and the Kennan "departure," after all, require reciprocity from the Soviet Union. The risk, if any, lies in Soviet rejection or preconditions: measuring its concessions in SALT II and its yielding to US demands on CTB and MBFR, the Brezhnev regime may have exhausted most of its power to accommodate, at least temporarily.

Among the risks of disarmament that really matter are the following:

1. A sudden unilateral act of drastic disarmament, with no provision for reciprocity, might provoke a massive public reaction amounting to a coup and might boomerang toward arms escalation. Domestic political support is essential.

2. The Soviet Union (or some other country) might miscalculate the meaning of a disarmament initiative, either viewing it as a hostile propaganda maneuver or exploiting it as a sign of weakness. Osgood's guidelines help to minimize this risk.

3. Nuclear disarmament by the US, without adequate consultation with allies and provision for alternative security relationships, might provoke countries now "under the nuclear umbrella" to go nuclear themselves. Ironically, either vertical proliferation or unilateral disarmament can stimulate horizontal proliferation.

In short, whatever the preferred futures of disarmament advocates, there is no legitimate escape from the imperative of prudence in thinking through a catalytic strategy to reverse the arms race. Because there are risks and boomerangs on every side, a strategy of flexible response is at least as appropriate to disarmament as it is to defense.

There is a mixture of the politics of hope and the politics of caution, of vision and pragmatism, of initiative and prudence at the center of any disarmament scenario that deserves to be acted out. This mixture was extraordinarily well prescribed by a man who found himself at the lonely summit of multilateral diplomacy nearly three decades ago: Dag Hammarskjöld. We need to rediscover the fact that Hammarskjöld regularly addressed the prospects for disarmament in his annual reports and press conferences and personally intervened in Security Council sessions in a most timely way. At a 1958 press conference following his intervention in a Security Council debate on nuclear testing, the Secretary-General was asked whether he had not risked offending one of the Big Powers by speaking as he had. He replied that he was well aware how important it was for him to maintain the trust of the Big Powers and how slow and complicated the disarmament process could be, then added:

> But there is a point in the development of disarmament when every time an initiative is taken in good faith and its possible consequences, its possible values, are not fully explored, I have the feeling that we have missed the bus. And we should not be too sure that the road will remain open for buses in all the future. That sense of urgency, that sense of responsibility, in the face of every new opening, from wherever it comes and whatever its immediate limited substance, was what prompted me.[5]

Hammarskjöld was continually prepared to reinforce any promising initiative because he had a lively sense of the risks of failing to do so. He believed the political momentum of the disarmament process was more crucial than the technical features of particular proposals — an openness to diversity too often lacking in arms controllers and disarmers.

Two years later, in the introduction to his annual report, Hammarskjöld insisted that pragmatic and ultimate scenarios must be reconciled through long-range planning and not condemned to contradiction.

> It is certainly not productive to approach the disarmament problem solely on a pragmatic basis, without integration of the steps

taken into a plan ultimately aiming at full disarmament. Likewise, however, it seems unrealistic to approach the total problem oblivious of the fact that all political experience and all previous negotiation show that the road to progress lies in the direction of efforts to contain and reduce the area of disagreement by mobilizing such common interests as may exist and as may override any other special interests tending in the opposite direction.[6]

The date of that report was 31 August, 1960.

Support Structures

Most disarmament scenarios include some picture of an international structure which will facilitate arms limitation and may ultimately provide an alternative security system. For mutual deterrence advocates, the maintenance of a somewhat mystified, transpolitical structure of "stable deterrence" is central to all security planning. They are not all agreed, however, as to whether such a structure regulates an inevitably escalatory race, postulates a freeze, or facilitates drastic reductions. GCD proponents look to a rational evolution toward a nuclear-free world and perhaps a postmilitary society ordered by a global security system. Revolutionaries seek to overthrow dominant political and economic institutions, whether violently or nonviolently — but are seldom agreed or articulate as to what the New Society will look like, either domestically or internationally.

Meanwhile, an intricate complex of disarmament structures has been evolving in the international system. At a sub-global level, those structures include the SALT process and its Standing Consultative Commission, the MBFR and post-Helsinki forums in Europe, and the Latin American Nuclear Free Zone. The most comprehensive and representative institutions are to be found in the United Nations and its affiliated structures like the Committee on Disarmament (Geneva), the International Atomic Energy Agency (Vienna), and the Non-Proliferation Treaty. It was the reconstruction of the CD, the resurrection of the UN Disarmament Commission, and the enhancement of the research and information programs of the UN Disarmament Centre, all at the 1978 Special Session, which set the stage for a more auspicious future if member governments will to act. Since 1978, numerous special committees and expert groups have been reviewing proposals for feasible treaties, new research institutes, a UN satellite system, a disarmament and development fund, and even a World Disarmament Campaign. In a word, the machinery is all around but the power has yet to be turned on.

The key to empowerment of any or all of these existing international structures is not to be found in changing their organization charts: it is to be found within domestic political systems. That surely means some changes within Soviet and French and Israeli and Pakistani and Brazilian systems. But the primacy of American responsibility must not be denied.

Whatever the future of the beleaguered US Arms Control and Disarmament Agency, the vicissitudes of that single agency in an era of bureaucratized policy-making have clearly exposed the lack of parity between defense and disarmament. The rallying point for disarmament advocates can hardly be to make ACDA's budget equal the Pentagon's: the US does not need 3,000,000 arms control bureaucrats or a trillion dollars worth of disarmament technology. What it does need is bureaucratic parity in research, long-range planning, access to the White House, participation in weapons and budget decisions, personnel status, and public information programs. The budget of ACDA or any successor agency must be measured by its adequacy in sustaining these minimal functions. The cost of one jet fighter plane ($20 million) now seems to be a level of funding above which the annual budget of ACDA must not be allowed to rise! Beyond budgeting, the leadership of ACDA must be able and willing to play an advocacy and even adversary role on behalf of disarmament. Here, too, the organization charts matter much less than the existential power relationships.

There is, of course, a much larger constellation of power relationships within the American political system which must be ordered if disarmament is to have a chance. Among the necessary components would seem to be the following:

1. A political administration seriously committed to arms control and disarmament;

2. A Department of Defense which is either supportive of arms limitations or restrained from imposing a veto on every serious disarmament proposal;

3. A supportive majority in Congress, whether through a vital majority party or bipartisanship;

4. Strong academic support from think tanks and universities;

5. A high media priority on full and fair reporting of defense and disarmament issues;

6. A sustained public constituency, including leaders from industry, finance, labor, and religion.

In any long-range futuring, the last of these is surely most important — that is, if democratic politics still have a chance to operate within a warfare state.

Attitude Changes

Like Ezekiel's vision of dry bones coming together and waiting for the breath of life, there must be a pattern of interconnected elements in any long-term program for policy change. If a vision of disarmament requires a catalytic strategy, and a catalytic strategy requires support structures, a full scenario must spotlight attitude changes which will breathe life into support structures. Disarmament policy changes, linked as they must be with the spinal cords of security, extend in as many directions as any field of public policy. Attitudes toward national security itself are basic to such changes.

We have seen how genuine security can be frustrated by the new paradoxes of power in the Third Nuclear Age — how the very power to act can be crippled by the technology that is supposed to make us secure. A security policy preoccupied with threats (deterrence), supplemented if not repealed by a policy based on presumptions of limiting and winning nuclear wars (counterforce), more and more propels the nation and the whole world toward the Ultimate Insecurity. Security now requires, as never before, a clear-eyed, humane perception of adversaries lest the clumsiest moves be made and the most perilous self-fulfilling prophecies be launched. Security increasingly demands equitable participation from heretofore "weak" nations now in new positions to bargain, to withhold, to threaten, and even to draw us to our own doom. Security is more than ever composed of economic and social imperatives frustrated by the arms race. Security imposes a strenuous new challenge to the democratic body politic: to let politics be politics and not the machine tool of military technology. Security drives us to a recovery of our very nationhood, our common purposes and our general welfare which can never be well served by regressive chauvinism or repressive bureaucracies ostensibly committed to our national security.

Richard Barnet's conception of "real security" for Americans devotes major attention to these subjective and even spiritual requirements:

> Nostalgia for lost power that can never be recovered is no basis for security; the mindless accumulation of weaponry is sapping the spirit of the people. The power that can make us secure is not the power to bend other nations to our will, but the power to

> remake an America that is once again committed to the values
> for which the nation was founded — justice, opportunity, and
> the liberation of the human spirit. . . . The real danger in a dark
> and turbulent time is that we scare ourselves into impotence, and
> perhaps oblivion, because we have forgotten why we became a
> nation.[7]

It is only such a positive and fully rounded attitude toward national security that can provide an adequate framework for attitudes toward disarmament itself. Prospects for disarmament are continually deflowered by public skepticism and even ravaged by professional cynicism — all in the name of "national security." This is where the "realists" have so often done their worst damage: promoting skepticism and cynicism.

Here again we may draw on the greater wisdom of Dag Hammarskjöld. On May 19, 1955, at a press conference in UN Headquarters, a reporter noted that many of his journalistic colleagues and even UN personnel took "a very cynical attitude regarding the possibilities of disarmament." There was a tendency to view disarmament as "a road show put on by the diplomats because the customers expect it." The prevalent assumption was that "political problems must be solved first and then disarmament will take care of itself." What was the Secretary General's own attitude? Hammarskjöld replied that such cynicism was "irresponsible." He insisted:

> There have been no precedents or experiences which entitle us
> not to try again. It is quite true that there is an interplay between
> political factors . . . on the one side, and disarmament on the
> other. But, when people say, in those simple terms, that if the
> political situation improves, disarmament will follow and that,
> for that reason, it does not make sense to discuss disarmament,
> they overlook one essential factor: that the very study of disarmament may be the vehicle for progress towards greater international political understanding. . . . Disarmament is never the
> result only of the political situation; it is also partly instrumental
> in creating the political situation.[8]

Hammarskjöld's attitude toward disarmament was more than a matter of infinite patience and openness toward every possibility of progress: it was a well-grounded dialectical understanding of historical processes. This was a richer understanding of history than the "realists" had offered because it could appreciate the catalytic influence of one seemingly powerless political action upon another seemingly all-powerful political force. It should be remembered that Hammarskjöld's own diplomatic style abounded in imaginative techniques of "powerlessness": the rather mystical notion of a "UN presence," "fire brigades" of smaller powers to keep Big Powers out of Third World conflicts, "face-saving" exercises in invisible diplomacy, "fallback positions" reconciling major powers in deliberately vague and ambiguous language, *ad hoc* expedients of all kinds, even "hobby diplomacy" making use of photography and poetry and music to touch the humanity of adversaries when threats and propaganda and coercive measures would have failed. It may be doubted whether any other official personality in this century has done as much as Dag Hammarskjöld did to confound conventional stereotypes about power and security. His legacy is a treasury of antidotes to political cynicism. It is even more an implicit testimony to what could be done with disarmament and security studies if they were adequately and imaginatively established.

Something like Hammarskjöld's sensitivities to the seeming contradictions of history would help us better understand why progress in disarmament has often followed or even accompanied discouraging political events. This is again to discount "realist" scenarios about political solutions having to precede disarmament. It is once more to challenge negative and punitive ideas of linkage. It is to point to the positive outcomes which may flow from doing what John Kennedy urged: negotiating even and especially in the most troubled times rather than regarding disarmament only as a fair weather exercise.

The record is rather remarkable. The Partial Test Ban of 1963 was preceded by anything but fair weather: the Bay of Pigs, the stormy summit in Vienna, the Berlin Wall, the Cuban missile crisis. The Non-Proliferation Treaty was completed in 1967-68 in the midst of the worst international and domestic turbulence over Vietnam. The SALT I process began in 1969: Alexander Dubcek's "socialism with a human face" had just been blown away and the US was still more than three years away from disengagement in Vietnam. SALT I finished and SALT II started up in 1972: that was the year of Nixon's China trip, Watergate, and the Christmas bombing of North Vietnam. Neither the Russians nor the Chinese seemed inhibited by linkage—nor were Presidents Kennedy, Johnson, or Nixon prevented by severe political stresses from undertaking these new disarmament commitments. The big exception in those years was the postponement of SALT I after the Soviet invasion of Czechoslovakia on the eve of the chaotic Democratic Convention of 1968: a costly invasion not only for the Czechs. The Democrats' détente was undone, Nixon was elected by a mere half-million votes out of nearly 75 million cast, and the MIRV Age was on.

Even more imperative than changing general attitudes on the meaning of security and the prospects for disarmament is the transformation of attitudes toward the Soviet Union. Such a transformation may, in fact, be a prerequisite to meaningful reorientations to disarmament and security. But it is also bound to be a very difficult and even intimidating task in the 1980s. It will be difficult because powerful institutions, both governmental and private, have enormous vested interests in sustaining the most relentlessly hostile anti-Soviet attitudes. It will also be difficult, however, because the Soviets themselves are difficult and intimidating in so many ways. What is required is not conversion from hostility to romance: it is a more mixed and ambiguous understanding of Soviet conduct. That is very hard for many Americans to achieve, not only because of anti-Soviet propaganda but because our international emotions have never been easily fine-tuned to ambivalence about any major nation, whether ally or adversary. Indeed, American affections have been notoriously fickle and simplistic with regard to the British, the Chinese, the Japanese, and the Germans.

It will not do to deny Soviet repression and economic shortcomings at home and in Eastern Europe, or ignore Soviet brutality in Afghanistan, or overlook Soviet adventurism in Africa, or excuse Soviet refusal to share in major development programs in the Third World, or pretend that the Soviet Union has not been involved in ambitious heavy missile programs and enormous troop and tank deployments: these are facts which explain the disaffection between Soviet leaders and most of the world. But they are not the only facts, nor are they all self-explanatory.

What is most problematical is that millions of Americans, including many governmental officials, also believe many things which are not facts but myths. It is these mostly false beliefs which have such mischievous power to frustrate disarmament. The aggressive merchandising of an elaborate if unsubtle mythology of US-Soviet relations did much to kill SALT II in 1977-80. Among these myths were the following:

1. "Soviet power is growing all over the world." (Not true. Weapons buildups cannot offset Soviet political losses in Yugoslavia, China, Albania, Egypt, Sudan, Somalia, Guinea, and many other countries. The Soviet predicaments in Afghanistan and Ethiopia reveal weaknesses more than strengths.)

2. "US military power declined during the 1970s." (Hardly. That decade saw separately targetable US strategic nuclear warheads multiply five times over, even while development proceeded on Tridents, cruise missiles, MX, Mark 12-A warheads, and other weapons sytems.)

3. "The Soviets are rigid and intransigent in disarmament negotiations, while the US is forever appeasing them." (The reverse is more nearly true. SALT II was repeatedly obstructed by US delays and ploys, while the USSR kept making the major concessions.)

4. "Afghanistan killed SALT II." (SALT II was actually dead politically weeks before Afghanistan. The invasion simply pounded the nail into the coffin.)

5. "Arms negotiations are only a reward for good Soviet behavior." (Surely it is in our own interest to prevent nuclear war, reverse the arms race, and reduce defense spending.)

6. "There's a missile gap in Europe." (See Chapter 3!)

7. "A crash program to build up US arsenals will slow down the Soviet buildup." (Historically, the US has been the pacesetter in military technology, with the Soviets, like Avis, always spurred to catch up — and eventually succeeding, more or less.)

8. "The superpowers can control the nuclear options of other countries." (If they ever could, they can't anymore. The Non-Proliferation Treaty is rapidly losing legitimacy and efficacy. There's a long list of nuclear powers and nuclear-prone countries outside the Treaty.)

9. "The Soviet Union never lives up to its treaty obligations." (False. Soviet compliance with the 1963 Test Ban, SALT I, and even unratified SALT II has been notably good.)

10. "We don't have to trust the Soviets." (Presupposes that our verification technology can solve all our arms control problems, thus postponing indefinitely the political requirements of détente. Ultimately, the US and USSR must begin the slow and difficult process of trusting each other, at least not to destroy each other.)

The conclusion to be drawn from this demythology exercise is not that the Kremlin is basically pacifist or benevolent. It is that the Soviets, through most of the Brezhnev era, were deeply serious about arms limitations. Their record of accommodation and compliance has been at least as impressive as the US record. Whether that somewhat unrequited record will make the Soviets more uncompromising from now on is unclear: that would be an understandable mood if not a wise one. They surely continue to have their own historic reasons for wanting to avoid a nuclear holocaust and relieve the domestic costs of the arms race, both economic and political. Their overextended commitments on all sides must have instructed them on the limits of their power and resources. They may also begin to perceive what most of the world sees: both super-powers have been steadily losing their power and not necessarily to each other. As their capacity to annihilate has grown, their political influence has dissipated. But the Soviets' hard-won sense of parity can hardly be bullied into submission by US threats of escalation.

Still another challenge to attitude change is to raise the question as to whether it is US-Soviet *differences* that matter most. Or is it that our *similarities* are so threatening, not only to each other but to the whole world? Much of the world is troubled by our affinities as nuclear superpowers, isolationists yet interventionists, material-ists, technocrats, centralized and bureaucratized states, and mes-sianic rivals utterly convinced of our own historic destiny and in-vincibility. In the Cold War of the 1950s British historian Herbert Butterfield wrote:

> The greatest menace to our civilization today is the conflict be-tween giant organized systems of self-righteousness — each sys-tem only too delighted to find that the other is wicked — each only too glad that the sins give it the pretext for still deeper hatred and animosity. The effect of the whole situation is bar-barizing, since both sides take the wickedness of the other as the pretext for insults, atrocities, and loathing; and each side feels that its own severities are not vicious at all, but simply punitive acts and laudable measures of judgment.[9]

These harsher images of both Soviets and Americans are too true to life to be ignored. They are lamentably truer in the early 1980s than they have been since the 1950s. They hardly suggest, however, the quick friendliness, lively humor, cultural apprecia-tion, political courage, earnest compassion, profound spirituality, and passion for peace which some citizens of both nations find in each other's company. My own experience of Russian company, both within the USSR and elsewhere, has been a heady mixture of exasperation and exhilaration.

Attitude Changers: the NGOs

Who will take the leadership in this field of dry bones? Who will seize the initiative for changing the attitudes that will give new life to the structures, so that the structures will vitalize the strate-gies, and the strategies will catalyze the policies? Who will finally say: *we* must change public attitudes toward security, disarmament, and our enemies?

There have been rare moments when attitudes have been changed because presidents have dared to say they must be changed. Occasionally, a Lincoln will point to the inadequacies of the dogmas of the past. Occasionally, a John Kennedy will do much to create a better climate for peaceful diplomacy by confessing that "we must re-examine our own attitude"—even toward the Russians. More frequent in recent years, however, has been the use of muted language to conceal a more hostile policy. Richard Nixon in 1969 spoke moderately of "nuclear sufficiency" rather than "nuclear superiority." That was when, to arms controllers who had coined the term, "sufficiency" clearly meant no new strategic weapons—more particularly, no ABMs and no MIRVs—but Nixon soon proceeded with both. Public resistance isn't always the problem that bothers presidents most. Jimmy Carter's presidency began with 70 percent public support for SALT II but he still managed to lose the battle. Ultimately, there is no substitute for courageous and competent leadership.

The very vehicle of leadership, however, must be a public mythology of shared values and attitudes. Those do not simply spring from the heads of presidents. They are nurtured primarily by non-governmental institutions: schools, colleges, media, associations, churches, synagogues. These are the myth-making centers of a free society where attitudes toward security and disarmament must be remade. It is in and through their capacities for attitude generation that the defenses of peace must be built.

The hard fact is that disarmament is a very low priority in almost all educational, religious and citizen organizations not specifically formed to campaign for disarmament. The idea of disarmament has a very dim future unless we wage an internal political struggle in all such institutions to lift disarmament up to the top of their agenda, program, budget, and media. If we do not wage and win such political struggles within non-governmental bodies, we can hardly expect to change governmental policies.

The positive point is: if the colleges and churches of America firmly committed their educational resources to the struggle for disarmament, the political battle would be more than half won. Education for disarmament is much more than a matter of imparting data: it is helping persons develop paradigms of humane meaning within which to keep learning and from which to keep acting. It is exactly the senselessness of much of the subject matter of national security which demands the attention of the humanities as well as the sciences. Theological seminaries should become the new arsenals of sensibility about the arms race.

Paradigms of empowerment for disarmament require some very special institutions to sustain them, including autonomous think tanks and intelligence systems, an independent media base, self-studies by local communities, multilateral connections with many countries, and action networks. If we may say, as we must, that technical issues must be controlled by political purposes, that cannot mean technical questions are trivial. More NGO competence in defense and disarmament is a requisite to credibility — as it should be. Disparagement of "the experts" too often is a cheap grace game on the part of those who don't really care enough to recruit knowledgeable professionals or even to do their own homework.

This study has pointed repeatedly to the need for transnational perspectives on disarmament. There have never been greater opportunities for NGO participation in disarmament activities related to the United Nations. The seeming impotence of the UN is not the last word. If the UN system can increasingly become a facilitator of transnational education and communication on disarmament, the political equations may begin to change at last. If more American citizens were to grasp the compelling political and moral issues between the Two and the Many, between the superpowers and the non-nuclear states, US policy changes might just become possible.

Educational and religious exchanges between the US and USSR are indispensable safeguards against ignorance and hostility. The churches of America have never made a serious effort to muster their own professional resources for understanding the Soviet Union. Denominational and ecumenical programs have been preoccupied with countries in which they have made the heaviest missionary investment — China, India, Southern Africa, Latin America. But missionary education has never had much to do with the Soviet Union. If the churches had a Soviet affairs program, as they have always had their China programs, they might be much better equipped to cope with the political issues of arms control and disarmament. They might have keener sensitivities to the historical and cultural matrix of Soviet policies and anxieties — and a stronger platform from which to criticize Soviet conduct when it makes disarmament more difficult.

Non-governmental organizations are inescapably the prime attitude changers in the realm of disarmament — at least potentially.

But the NGOs are too often at war with each other, working at cross-purposes and dissipating scarce resources. Proliferation and even hostilities among NGO "peacemakers" sometimes amount to a scandal. Of course, diversity and pluralism are the necessary marks of freedom. But a strong political will for disarmament requires a broad popular base which can hardly be built if leadership is short-circuited by self-righteous messianism and organizational chauvinism. Who can doubt that the norm of NGO activity must clearly be the nurture of effective political action which helps to redeem governmental policy? The politics of disarmament requires a capacity for coalition and consensus.

That capacity is more than the manipulation of techniques. It is a capacity for the largest and most inclusive scenarios. It is a special genius for the recovery of nationhood. It is the power to dream and share dreams with a whole society and a whole world.

A dream must be wrapped up in the most precious myths of the American heritage. Martin Luther King, Jr. understood all this very well. When he dared to dream, he had the power both to liberate and to reconcile. A dream of peace in the spirit of Dr. King might go something like this:

> I have a dream that one day, this America, providentially made up of all kindreds and tribes and tongues, will remember that its destiny is harmony among all peoples.
>
> I have a dream that, before too long, this America will recover our heritage of compassion for tyrannized and suffering persons, anywhere in the world.
>
> I have a dream that some day soon, the ingenuity and imagination we Americans have always prized in our most creative citizens will be turned from the works of war to the inventions of peace.
>
> I have a dream that this country's vast talents in organization and cooperation, in mobilization and teamwork, may be turned outward toward a world which must organize the institutions of global cooperation because we know, at last, that threats of mutual terror cannot save Planet Earth from annihilation.
>
> I have a dream that the vision which inspired earlier generations of Americans to work with enormous energy and devotion for the uniting of the nations, by covenant and by charter, will come alive again and lift us out of our sour and sulky isolationism.
>
> I have a dream that the wisdom of our founding mothers and fathers, who knew very well that large standing military

establishments are the enemy of freedom more than its friend, will be rediscovered by this generation of Americans.

And I have a dream that the rights and freedoms which we have always celebrated for ourselves shall happily light up the face of every child in China and Russia, in South Africa and Zimbabwe, in Israel and Arabia, in Vietnam and Cambodia, in Pakistan and India, in Korea North and South, in Germany East and West, in Chile and in Cuba — and in South Bronx and San Antonio — and even Washington, D.C.

CHAPTER 8

A Theology of Peacemaking

Our main concern must be to see that man, whose own folly once drove him from the Garden of Eden, does not now commit the blasphemous act of destroying, whether in fear or in anger or in greed, the great and lovely world in which, even in his fallen state, he has been permitted by the grace of God to live. — George F. Kennan in *The Atlantic Monthly,* May 1959

How, now, shall we do theology? After the long gauntlet of technology, strategy, diplomacy, politics, and scenarios through which the idea of disarmament has been made to run, is further punishment really necessary? Is there only a residual role for theology, if that? Is theology's business only to exhort the world to peace as a platitudinous imperative, while leaving all the details to the experts? Are the political choices as to how best to roll back the probabilities of nuclear war so clear as to make theology itself a superfluity? Or so unclear as to make theology only a further complication, a most unwelcome foul-up factor in the face of the complexities and ambiguities already oppressing politicians and diplomats? Or is the predicament of theology hopeless because the predicament of humanity itself is hopeless?

An affirmative and therefore apocalyptic answer to that last question was provided a generation ago by a president of the World Council of Churches, Bishop Otto Dibelius of Berlin, who had given up all hope:

The Church no longer has the power to guide the happenings of the world. There is not the slightest doubt in my mind that the 'bomb' will be used and the world will destroy itself. Perhaps the only task of the Christian in this age is to prepare mankind to die, to stand by to administer extreme unction to expiring humanity.

Yet humanity still lives — though huge portions of humanity have been wasted by war and poverty. Years and even decades have gone by since that blinding moment on the desert at Alamogordo when there flashed through Robert Oppenheimer's mind the words of God in the *Bhagavad-Gita:*

> I am become death, the shatterer of worlds;
> Waiting that hour that ripens to their doom.

By some incalculable combination of fear and luck, wit and grace, the hour of ultimate doom has not yet arrived. We cannot be sure but it is just possible that the future is still somewhat open to us and that there are other options besides extreme unction worth considering. That shred of hope suggests we should review those other questions about how to do theology.

Doing Theology and Doing Peace

Here are three preliminary answers to those troubled questions:

1. The case for Christian theology has been badly compromised by theologians themselves. They could not resist fascination with nuclear and strategic issues in the First Nuclear Age. As the preface observed, however, they have been strangely disengaged from a host of new issues which have emerged in the Second and Third Nuclear Ages: issues which have to do with (1) the autonomy of technology; (2) the bureaucratization of policy; (3) the dangerous anachronisms of strategic doctrine; (4) the domestic manipulation of nuclear diplomacy; (5) military dislocations of economy; (6) non-military threats to planetary survival; (7) initiative and responsibility in reversing a many-sided arms race; (8) global bargaining systems; (9) nuclear equity and the rights of non-nuclear states; and (10) the meaning of ecumenism with regard to the church's multinational mission for security. While some theologians have continued to speak to war and peace and even disarmament questions — typically in hit-and-run fashion — it is the lack of serious engagement between basic theology and the overpowering dynamics of the arms race in these latter days which must be acknowledged. It is just for that reason that this study has been obliged to proceed in an essentially inductive, empirical, and pre-doctrinal style. There has been no adequate theological framework within which to pursue such a study.

This lament is more than a complaint about the professional priorities of theologians for the past two decades: it is a recollection of their deficiencies even in the First Nuclear Age. The most authoritative and publicized theological statement on nuclear weapons was the 1950 report of the Dun Commission, named by the Federal Council of Churches to study "The Christian Conscience and Weapons of Mass Destruction." Members of the Commission included Angus Dun, Reinhold Niebuhr, Paul Tillich, John C. Bennett, Walter Horton, Albert T. Mollegen, James H. Nichols, and George F. Thomas. While the report rejected preventive war, vengeful conduct in war, and the public hysteria fomented by McCarthyism, its main message was a Cold War call to arms. It appealed for a buildup of military and moral strength, asking Christians

> to support the policies of armament and preparedness and of taxation and consumption restraints required for the maintenance of adequate strength in the free world. Whether or not we can avoid atomic devastation of the world in which we and our children dwell can well depend on the readiness of Americans to have fewer washing machines and television sets and automobiles for the sake of an all-out girding for the responsibilities laid upon us.

The identification of peace with the power of "the free world" was combined with pessimism about the feasibility of any nuclear disarmament agreement.

More striking today than these political judgments by the Dun Report are: (1) its refusal to draw a moral distinction between nuclear and conventional weapons; (2) its justification of nuclear deterrence; and (3) its justification of the actual use of nuclear weapons. When all due allowance is made for the historical setting of the report—Stalinism, Korean War, Chinese revolution, McCarthyism—we may still wonder why such an eminent collection of theologians failed so seriously, both to transcend the foreign policy blunders of their time and to produce a constructive theology of peace and security of enduring worth. At that, two commission members refused to sign: Georgia Harkness because the report caricatured pacifism, Robert L. Calhoun because of the report's "deep-going confusion" between Christian conscience and acquiescence in "military necessity."

At the conclusion of its International Public Hearing on Nuclear Weapons and Disarmament in Amsterdam in November 1981, a 17-member World Council of Churches panel confessed that Christian theology itself had "yet to be liberated from traditional structures of thinking" which obscured the most pressing questions faced by the panel. There was conspicuous dissatisfaction with the appeal of some witnesses to "just war" and "Christian realist" positions, while traditional pacifism claimed few if any new converts. Even appeals to nuclear pacifism were deficient in theological imperatives.

Perhaps the sharpest point is this: traditional differences among Christians in matters of war and peace have actually been defined in terms of their varied orientations toward war alone. Their distinctive and positive orientations toward the imperatives of peacemaking have been underdeveloped if not altogether neglected. Peace is not the same subject as war. To decide whether or how to wage war, either as a national policy or a conscientious individual choice, may have little if anything to do with a strategy for peacemaking. Disarmament can never be adequately articulated theologically in terms of war doctrines: it must be conceived in terms of peacemaking doctrines. That embarrassingly obvious imperative has yet to be taken seriously by most theologians.

2. Another response to our troubled queries about the role of theology is to deny that we have really put off all theology to the end of this book. The very subject matter of defense and disarmament is saturated with mystification and the need to demystify; with myths and the need to demythologize; with dogmatics and the need for alternative perceptions of truth. We have been doing theology all along. It is just because national security cannot be reduced to a technical science of military mathematics that theology has a vital if still-underdeveloped function in addressing the meaning of security and the human foundations upon which security must be established.

Nuclear deterrence, after all, is a quasi-theology. It has a dogmatic character and an elaborate theoretical superstructure. It is prone to absolute claims about the deepest springs of human motivation and conduct — although, like too many churchly theologies, nuclear deterrence lacks a fully rounded view of human experience. While it may or may not name the name of God, deterrence deals in the most ultimate weapons and the most ultimate threats. Deterrence is thus a penultimate eschatology.

It must also be said that deterrence in its purest forms is a *theology of war-avoidance* that is a serious challenge to faith. The very dominance of deterrence among American Christians for three decades points to the lack of alternative theologies of war-avoidance. The fact of the matter is not that deterrence has triumphed over strong and worthy opponents; it is that few Christian thinkers have ever thought very hard or systematically about how to avoid war—except through the manipulation of terror or the fabrication of international machinery. War-avoidance is a very different topic from what Christians have traditionally argued about in their most zealous discussions of war and peace: it is simply not the same question as to whether to fight a war or how to fight a war. It is the question as to how war itself may best be prevented. That had better be made into something far more than a question of techniques and tactics. It should become a fundamental theological question for the mission and ministry of the church.

3. What, after all, are the true priorities of Christian theology? If peace is ranked down low among those many issues which all good Christians perhaps ought to think about from time to time—recognizing, of course, that a few folks might have some far-out opinions about it so we'd better not talk about it too often—a theology of peacemaking will be a sometime and trivial thing, at best. If, in the present state of Christian theology, we suppose that right attitudes toward peace and security are basically a matter of "applied theology," we will hardly know how limited is the supply to be applied.

The first requisite of a faithful Christian theology, for our time and for all time, is to learn again and again how little we know about our faith itself unless and until we *do* the things that make for peace. It is because too much bad theology has trivialized peace that fresh engagement in the struggle for peace is now required to redeem theology itself. Peacemaking is more to be applied to theology just now than theology is to be applied to peacemaking. Only as the churches relocate peacemaking from the humiliating periphery of their concerns to the most exalted center of their worship and their work will they really know what it means to be in Christ.

Karl Barth in 1959 remarked that the churches' inability to take a clear and unequivocal stand against nuclear war and nuclear weapons was their greatest *theological* failure since their failure to stand firmly against the emergence of Nazism in Germany. That comparison is appropriate because it points to the totalitarianism of both Nazism and nuclear weapons. Yet it may seem to underestimate the capacity of the latter to terminate human history. If religious faith be defined as ultimate concern (as it was for Tillich), or as the commitment to beliefs and practices concerning the ultimate problems of human existence (as it is by many sociologists of religion), the ultimacy of nuclear perils is profoundly religious in its very nature. Yet the churches have not made them seem so. They have not told the truth.

To Tell the Truth

If theology is not true to itself — which means that it does not tell the truth even though it claims to be God's Word — it becomes a tool of oppression and violence. There is a largely unheralded connection between peace and truth which must be made firm if all the other themes in a theology of peace are to hold together. Barth's concern about the nuclear arms race was clearly connected with his vision of theology's basic task: helping members of the Christian community

> face squarely the question of the proper relation of their human speech to the Word of God. . . . Theology must give them practice in the right relation to the quest for truth, demonstrating and exemplifying to them the understanding, thought, and discourse proper to it.[1]

The Biblical quest for truth is not for the correct abstractions which define the attributes of God: it is for the liberating Way and Truth and Life which will set people truly free. It unmasks the legalisms and ritualisms which violate spiritual truth. It requires plain speech in penetrating all false claims of security. From the depths of compassion for the people, it exposes every fatuous claim of peace when there is no peace — and when death and destruction are imminent.

The nuclear arms race has become this generation's severest test of truth. It is zealously promoted with false words, deceptive jargon, pretentious dogmatics, hateful propaganda, and arbitrary bars on access to the truth. No realm of public policy is more corrupted by untruthful speech than national security. Walter Millis exposed "the vocabulary of dispassionate terror" which has emerged from some think-tankers: Doomsday Machine, overkill, megadeath, tolerable death rate, thermal effects, unacceptable damage, assured destruction capability, even D.O.E. (Death of Earth).

Demythologizing has become the indispensable theological tool of peacemaking: it is the operation empowering the people of God to understand the stratagems by which inhuman speech violates the Word of God. Those stratagems include a relentless outpouring of myths about weapons, strategy, security, enemies, history, and human nature—from government bureaucracies and adjunct think tanks and co-opted media and electronic theologians.

It is demythologizing which empowers theology with an essentially political method. This is not the whole of theology—for we must live by myths which more and more tell the truth. But neither the regeneration of pristine biblical myths nor the remythologizing of faith in the service of peace can flourish if the ground has yet to be cleared of thickets of lies. It is just here that theology requires an alliance with political science—a seemingly illegitimate liaison compared with the company theology has kept with psychology and sociology. If the style of political science itself is made unabashedly humane instead of being technicized into triviality and irrelevance, there is plenty of room and need for a new *political science of religion* to tell the truths which tend to be overlooked by the psychology of religion and the sociology of religion. This new possibility was implicit in the late Hans Morgenthau's conception of political science. It involved that discipline's "moral commitment" to

> telling the truth about the political world. . . . telling society
> things it does not want to hear. The truth of political science is
> the truth about power, its manifestations, its configurations, its
> limitations, its implications, its laws. Yet, on the other hand,
> one of the main purposes of society is to conceal these truths
> from its members. That concealment, that elaborate and subtle
> and purposeful misunderstanding of the nature of political man
> and of political society, is one of the cornerstones upon which
> all societies are founded.[2]

Morgenthau's wit and wisdom both shine through those words. They testify, as the Quakers have always told us, that speaking truth to power is the very first step in peacemaking. The Quakers themselves haven't always embellished that concept theologically, nor have they always perceived with sympathy the full pressures of government responsibility.

Hans Küng's essay on *Truthfulness* observes that, precisely because this century has been full of lies, there is a "new passion for truthfulness." Lies are not the sins of totalitarian systems only. George Orwell's futuristic *1984* portrays a Ministry of Truth whose "task of counterfeiting history is basically no more than an extrapolation of past experience. But even in our democracies we have brought 'the manipulation of truth' in politics, news media, and propaganda to a high degree of perfection."[3] The prime factor in the manipulation of truth in American politics has long been the aggrandizement of military technology.

For André Dumas, the lie is biblically portrayed as "the first and most poisonous source of injustice." Its essential violence is that it destroys communication, trust, and confidence — and eventually generates hostility and death.

> It is first of all the lie (and not pride, or hate, much less sensuality) that the Bible sees as the work of the crafty serpent, who will later become the divider, the accuser, the murderer, the tempter, Satan, the devil. He utters lies and makes them so attractive that they sound like the truth.[4]

For Dumas, truth telling is much more than a matter of personal legalism: it is absolutely essential to the very life and health of the whole community. It is fundamental to faithful political theology. It is an indispensable basis for genuine security. In a phrase not geared specifically to national security debate, Dumas notes Immanuel Kant's concern about the violence that results from the perversion of words: "All Kant's moral and religious philosophy centres on this inexplicable degeneration of words, made to bring clarity and trust, but put over in such a way that they encourage the pollution of life and separation of men."[5]

Returning to Küng, we note another passage which marks a turning point in his theology of truthfulness: a point best left unmentioned until the passage itself is read. What is he really driving at? Whom is he talking about?

> Within the dominant machinery of bureaucracy truth is the result of political struggle, of the power game of different pressure groups; secrecy is demanded in things that concern everyone; scholarship consequently must serve the system; people speak differently in private from what they do in public, they speak differently from what they write; through fear of commitment they take refuge in esoteric spheres of study, far from the storms, and for the rest adapt themselves tacitly to the party line. Thus people escape from the real difficulties of life, the most urgent decisions are postponed.[6]

Küng is not depicting here the pressures within military bureaucracy or the power of industrial interests or the unreal world of systems analysts in their think tanks. He is describing the Church as he has known it. He is trying to account for the Church's own lies.

Küng devotes a whole chapter to the "Historical Background of the Disregard for Truthfulness" in the Church. Three factors are most explanatory: (1) a "sweeping disregard of truthfulness in moral theology" so that truthfulness was neither a theological virtue nor a moral virtue but always subsumed under some other virtue; (2) the "unhistorical thinking of theology in general"; and (3) a "faulty image of the Church" itself: a siege mentality combined with an "ecclesiology of glory" instead of an "ecclesiology of the Cross."[7] Küng did not ask the question — but who can doubt that an ecclesiology of the Cross is more fit for a theology of peacemaking than an ecclesiology of glory?

It is the churches' growing consciousness of their own need of repentance which may save them from self-righteousness in attacking politicans and diplomats, generals and scholars for their lies. Repentance for chauvinistic theologies which trivialize peacemaking. Repentance for the siege mentalities which have returned to most ecclesiastical bureaucracies in the past dozen years. Repentance for an almost total neglect of disarmament in the missional priorities of most mainline churches in America ever since Hiroshima. Truthfulness requires repentance for the sake of reconcilation.

But neither repentance nor reconciliation by Christians will banish all the lies which are the vanguard of Armageddon. Peace remains a sacrificial struggle, a bearing of the cross, a constant series of defeats which may or may not be vindicated this side of history. Half a century ago, the Viennese poet Stefan Zweig wrote a play whose principal character, Jeremiah, burst forth with these words:

> Peace is not a thing of weakness.
> It calls for heroism and action.
> Day by day you must wrest it from the mouths of liars. You must stand alone against the multitude; for clamor is always on the side of the many, and the liar has ever the first word.
> The meek must be strong.

Peacemaking doubtless requires a theology of power, which is where the "realists" have always begun. But peacemaking requires, even more, a theology of truthfulness which may yet become power. Who knows?

Theological Peripheralism

How shall we account for these parallels between strategic and religious doctrines, between national security bureaucracies and ecclesiastical bureaucracies, in keeping the idea of disarmament marginalized and trivialized? Why is the record of diplomatic peripheralism in disarmament virtually matched by the record of theological peripheralism in disarmament?

At a very basic level, the fact is that government and churches represent the same people. Representative church leadership, especially in the mainline bodies, typically has an affinity with dominant political leadership. Even where denominational heads are personally engaged in peace issues, bureaucratic constraints powerfully inhibit their influence. The parochial and proprietary interests of the churches tend to peripheralize disarmament whether or not there is any conscious support for the military bureaucracies.

Then we must put the question at an even deeper level of ecclesiology and of theological foundations. How clearly do doctrines on the very nature and mission of the Church speak to the central imperatives of peacemaking? Is peacemaking firmly established in the sacraments? Is it even permitted to share in the definition of evangelism? Is it recognized anywhere in the preparation and ordination of clergy? In the consecration of bishops? In the ministry of the laity? What kind of ecclesial status do the churches of America give to their peacemakers? If exalted status is conferred on peacemaking in church rhetoric and resolutions, is that status incarnated in the very life of congregations, missions, seminaries, bureaucracies? How seriously do our less fettered Christian theologians interpret Jesus Christ as the Prince of Peace, invoking as he did special blessings upon peacemakers whose high status merited the closest filial connections with God?

Let us note five different sources of theological difficulty which tend to sanction the peripheralism of disarmament.

1. There is an enduring *theology of charity* in the dominant mission and world service programs of the American churches. While nominal leaders have learned the language of justice and liberation, the operational theology remains fixated on benevolence and relief. This is a theology which can inspire generous support of overseas projects and muster massive donations in the aftermath of disaster. But it has yet to be transformed into a truly preventive theology which cares enough about potential disasters and suffering to become politically engaged. It is this stifling political inhibition which disconnects compassion from any vital commission to disarmament and war-avoidance. While an intramural struggle has recently been somewhat successful in linking philanthropy with economic development, the linkage between militarism and devel-

opment is much more problematical for the churches, thus increasing liberation theology's impatience with "developmentalism." Perhaps he United Nations studies connecting disarmament and Third World development could provide a platform on which to build a new mission theology.

2. *Pacifism* has tended to be more a theology of personal conscience than of world politics. The issues of individual choice concerning military service in wartime or the draft in Cold War-time have sometimes obscured the issues of national and international security, however security may be defined. Moreover, if pacifists can hardly be regarded as allies of the military establishment, they are recurringly tempted to trim the importance of military policy questions by addressing them on the individualistic agenda aroused by the draft. Yet these individualistic and domesticated tendencies are compensated for by the relentless monitoring of military spending by Friends' lobbies, the steadfast presence of Quaker centers in UN disarmament circles in both New York and Geneva, and the extensive service and exchange programs of the peace churches.

3. The classical alternative to pacifism in Christian tradition, the *just war* doctrine, has never seriously generated a war-avoidance or disarmament doctrine. As fruits of academic moral theology, just war ideas have primarily specified criteria for rulers to decide whether, when, and how to wage war—not how to prevent it. The ethics of war is not the same subject as the ethics of peace. That rather wide distinction has yet to occur to some adherents to the just war tradition who persist in trotting it out somewhat inappropriately whenever the very different subject of disarmament arises. Nevertheless, their scholastic criteria might some day be usefully transmuted into norms for deciding on the risks and reciprocities of a disarmament program. In the meantime, the limitations of the traditional theology are suggested by a breakdown of consensus since Hiroshima. Some invoke it to rationalize nuclear deterrence; some invoke it on behalf of nuclear pacifism; some have abandoned the concept altogether.

4. *"Christian realism,"* as expounded by Reinhold Niebuhr and many others, went beyond the just war doctrine's disposition to legitimize war and neglect the imperatives of war-avoidance: it appealed to mythic dogmas concerning the givens in human nature and history in order to emphasize the insolubility of international conflict. Niebuhr had a monumentally tragic vision largely bereft of any creative theory of change and increasingly reactive and polemical toward the "illusions" of any peace proposals. He not

only discounted pacifists: he scorned disarmament, the UN, collective security, world community, international law, and peace research.

Disarmament for Niebuhr, as for other "realists," was most unlikely in a time of tensions, the end of which he could not see: it depended on power relations and prior political solutions. Much as he emphasized transcendence theologically, he could not readily imagine how to transcend immediate political pressures, which he was often too quick to absolutize. Niebuhr's political theology was so haunted by fears of utopia that he largely abandoned all work of futuring to others. Yet it is just that work of futuring—that imaginative opening to better historical possibilities in the face of enemies, cynics, scoffers, and even liars—that is the minimal requirement of peacemaking. That is the Hammarskjöld legacy to theology. A theology of peace must be a theology of hope. The ambiguities of history are not the last word, though they must be soberly reckoned. The question for the politics of disarmament, again and again, is: how shall we try to tilt the ambiguities?[8]

Niebuhr was certainly not lacking in compassion and pastoral sensitivities—but he became less and less concerned about issues of justice and equity outside the bipolar US-Soviet context. His sanctification of the balance of power became a warrant for the nuclear balance of terror. Sloughing off his early pacifism and radicalism by the 1940s, he had become by 1950 preeminently the theologian of coercion, containment, deterrence, stalemate, and US imperial responsibility. He was the dominant personality on the Dun Commission. His invocations had more to do with how to endure the Cold War than how to end it. By 1960, he was a believer in the "missile gap" myth and imagined that the Soviets had the political lead in the Middle East, Asia and Africa. He seriously overestimated the power of Nasser imperialism as a force for Arab unity and Soviet hegemony—in consequence of which he urged: "It is even more important that the United States, as the strongest of the democratic nations, acknowledge the imperial dimensions of its power and accept the responsibilities which are the concomitants of its power."[9] This new American imperialism, frank in its admiration of British colonial "wisdom," was somewhat out of step with the decolonization process in Africa and Asia—which helps to explain why "Christian realism" soon retreated before the vanguards of liberation theology.

5. While Niebuhr invoked the Genesis myth of the Fall in his tragic vision of human sinfulness and political limits, *liberation*

theologians like Gustavo Gutiérrez celebrated the Exodus myth of deliverance in their revolutionary vision of conscientization and empowerment.[10] The new theologians of the late 1960s and after in Latin America preached a political and Incarnational gospel of Christ as Liberator. They were not bashful about futuring. They intentionally resurrected utopianism. Their context was the *praxis* of the class struggle against neocolonialism. Their model of world politics was not a balance of power but an imbalance of dominance-and-dependence shaped largely by economic forces like multinational corporations. They were preparing to overthrow the imperial power which Niebuhr seemed to promote as an anti-Soviet necessity.

These striking differences between an aging realism and a youthful liberation theology were ironic because the Latin thinkers, in many respects, resembled the semi-Marxist Niebuhr of the early 1930s. More important for this study, however, is the fact that neither realists nor liberationists put peace and disarmament at the top of their agenda. Both had prior commitments to the expansion of power and the waging of conflict, violently if necessary. Justice would justify the postponement of peace for the sake of defeating communist tyranny, in the one case, or capitalist oppression, in the other. Like some black theologians after 1965, both realists and liberationists had their own heavy agendas of power and justice which tended to push reconciliation aside. In the unending rounds of Christian polemics, peace has become a loser to both charity and justice.

The liberationists were unlike realists in another radical respect, however. Their political theologies were not intended, like Niebuhr's, to serve the policy planning staffs of their governments. Their style required a solidarity with the poor, in local base communities, rather than liaison with national security elites. Foreign policy prescriptions for diplomats or intergovernmental establishments like the United Nations do not claim much priority in the poorest of Latin barrios or black ghettos. A World Disarmament Campaign might have great difficulty penetrating such communities, even if they should somehow become prime beneficiaries. Yet, as Dennis McCann points out, base communities in Latin America increasingly are confronted by ideologies of national security and the reality of military oppression which promote economic growth while frustrating social change. Political persecution, in which the US may be implicated economically and militarily, thus draws liberation theologians into security and disarmament issues at an indigenous level, even if it seems like a great distance from negotiators in New York or Geneva.

Whatever the marginal status of disarmament in the polemics of Latin or black theologians, it will not do to reproach them for the theological peripheralism of the mainline churches of North America. Nor can white theologians in the US escape their own responsibilities for a theology of peace by parroting the preoccupations of liberationists. They must do in a new way what Niebuhr did a generation ago: engage foreign policy and opinion elites in the arena of national security. And they must do so, losing touch with neither the transcendent mysteries nor the slums of six continents. If there is a more fateful arena for the reconstruction of theology itself than this realm of nuclear dogmatics and disarmament, I cannot imagine what it is.

Theological Centralism: The Incarnation

After all this bad news, is there really any Good News? Is there any music in us? Do we have any songs to sing? Is there Annunciation as well as denunciation in a theology of peace? How shall we shift peacemaking form the periphery to the center of Christian theology? What is the center of Christian theology? Is it not the Incarnation?

> God was in Christ reconciling the world to himself,
>   not counting their trespasses against them,
>   and entrusting to us the message of reconciliation.
> So we are ambassadors for Christ.   (2 Cor. 5:19-20)

Christ, conflict, a whole world becoming reconciled, trust, ambassadors: these are the realities that matter most.

The message of reconciliation is fundamental to peacemaking at any time. But there are frankly some political reasons for featuring the Incarnation right now — as there should be at any time. Our particular reasons have mostly to do with "humanism" having become a bad word once again. Every generation confronts the Christian faith with a new legion of self-styled true believers who try to exorcise "humanism" from the faith itself as well as from our schools, our arts and our politics. They come from the Moral Majority, from the ranks of bishops, from the devotees of new cults, from many directions. But a truly faithful Christian theology in every generation will come forth with a fresh celebration of the ineradicable humanism at the core of the Incarnation. It is the fullness and the glory of God-given humanity in Jesus Christ that we must speak and sing about: a humanity which draws us together across every boundary of politics and nationality and color and sex and faith itself because it lifts us up into the love of God. It is that revelatory vision which must ultimately generate the motive power and style of peacemaking.

Christian humanism in this century has been nourished by thinkers as diverse as Jacques Maritain and Nicholas Berdyaev, Dietrich Bonhoeffer and Donald Baillie, the later Karl Barth and Roger Shinn, Teilhard de Chardin and Nels Ferré.

It was Donald Baillie's beautiful book, *God Was in Christ,* which helped me as a student to take the Incarnation seriously as the central focus of understanding God's action in human history. Yet that understanding can never be complete. The mystery of Divine Humanity forever deepens. William Temple in *Christus Veritas* had said that if anyone claims he "understands the relation of Deity to humanity in Christ he only makes it clear that he does not understand at all what is meant by an Incarnation."[11] The mysterious Incarnation is not just one theme among many theological themes: it is the vital center of all Christian thought. If we cannot connect its meaning with the world struggle for disarmament and peace, we show a profound misconception of both peace and the Incarnation itself. So get ready for Geyer's Dogmatics!

A theological centralism focused on the Incarnation suggests that basic Christian thought need not be constructed on a deductive, hierarchical, or linear model. Theology can be a much more circular exercise in which the centripetal power at the Center keeps drawing all doctrines into itself where they are ultimately vitalized and reconciled. There has been no more dehumanizing or dedivinizing feature in the long history of Christian dogmatics than the tendency to present theology piecemeal: to list and consider all the doctrines separately as if they all had a life of their own. Of course, they do not. It is just this lack of life in so many fossilized doctrines which petrifies spirituality and nullifies peacemaking. The Incarnation draws them together at the Center and empowers them both.

We may take a kind of provisional attitude toward all other doctrines of the Christian faith unless and until they get centralized in the Incarnation. Trinity, revelation, providence, miracle, immortality, Church, sacraments, Kingdom: all must be tested and refined at the Center where God does the heavy work of reconciliation. We can then be almost pragmatic about any doctrinal point of departure for a theology of peacemaking: any or all of them may help us if they lead us to the Center which is the only place peacemaking really belongs. After all, the Center is the only place Christ belongs.

The Incarnation is God becoming very physical. It is the infusion of world-creating Love into visible, fleshly realities. It is the Creator sharing bodily in the conflicts and temptations, joys and treacheries of which his free creatures are capable. It is to risk death for the sake of new life.

In Christ we know that this synthesis of spirit and matter is to be experienced in radically personal terms. But it is a synthesis in which the ultimacy of Love forever overcomes the limitations of physical existence. In Teilhard de Chardin's cosmic vision, the Incarnation is "a renovation, a restoration of all the Forces and Powers of the Universe: the Christ is the instrument, the Center, the Goal of the Whole Creation, animate and material: by him was everything created, sanctified, made alive."[12]

So: to be in Christ is to share in his creative work of redeeming and transforming the material stuff of life. It is, as Teilhard says, to search passionately for Jesus, "hidden in the forces which are raising up the Earth." It bids us: "Plunge into Matter!" And it is costly for us: "To create, to organize the energies of nature, is an inner torment which wrenches whoever undertakes it from that life of security and tranquility which is the real stronghold of egoism."[13] Some have regarded Teilhard's evolutionary vision as excessively optimistic and even magical, as more of a romantic paleontology than a credible theology. But the cosmic proportions and historical dynamism of that vision, grounded in a strong physical sense of Earth and in spiritual torment, all centered in Christ, hardly exaggerate the ultimate dimensions of peacemaking.

Technology is Theology

This plunging into matter is thus not only an individual bodything: it is to participate radically and critically in the human institutions which determine (or may terminate) our material existence.

Technology has become the ever-more-powerful engine of our material existence in most societies in recent decades: its institutional patterns dominate styles of life, work, communication, transportation, knowledge, health, leisure, government — and especially schemes for national security and international aggrandizement. So thoroughly are all our institutions in North America and Europe, including even the churches, committed to relentlessly accelerating modes of technology that our very beliefs and values are increasingly expressed in technological symbols. Moreover, the aspirations and planning of most developing countries are expressed largely in the same symbols. As Ernst Jünger in Nazi Germany (with wicked enthusiasm) put it: "Technology is the metaphysics of the twentieth century." We might say: Technology is the theology of our generation.

What this ascendancy of technical values and commitments has done is to subvert, or invert, Incarnational truth. Our obsessions are not with the Center and Goal of Creation, with the Love which would redeem and reorder all our material existence: they have become fixated upon the stuff to be redeemed. We have become tools of our tools.

This addiction to hyper-technicized values and institutions in every realm of existence is the grossest form of materialism at higher and higher levels of "sophistication." We are increasingly bereft of our own moral and spiritual autonomy. Love is trivialized and sentimentalized as our human relations are increasingly subjected to managerial engineering, commercial manipulation, and bureaucratization.

Thus we are imbued with a trained incapacity to cope critically with the most demonic of all the grossest forms of materialism: the idolatry of military technology in the name of "national security." A relentless drive to produce "generation" upon "generation" of more advanced weapons has not only escalated the life-threatening and life-destroying forces of military establishments to totalitarian levels: it has perverted economic and energy priorities in both developed and developing nations, generated a vicious weapons-petroleum complex, and subverted civil liberties and educational institutions. Will this "generation" of weapons forfeit future generations of human beings?

It is this increasing dissociation between military technology and human realities that makes the arms race the most demonic force ever to contend with the Christ who is struggling to renew the forces of the whole Creation by his transforming love. Military technology becomes more and more the purveyor of *militarism*. In earlier times, "militarist" was an epithet too often and uncharitably launched by pacifists against non-pacifists, especially military personnel. In our time, the most raucous militarists may be civilians. They may be bureaucratic managers or academic mercenaries of demagogic politicians or newspaper columnists.

More often than peace movements recognize, some military officers are their hidden allies in the struggle for peace. Militarism is not synonymous with military policy, which may, or may not, promote real security, political stability, or social and economic development. The World Council of Churches' Consultation on Militarism at Glion in 1977 was radical enough in its theological and ethical critiques. But that Consultation also insisted that Christians be sensitive to the variety of cultures, economic and political systems in which armed forces serve, noting that some positive values do derive from armed forces in some societies. As a sometime lecturer at military institutions and a firm friend of military officers in several countries, I know how much the cause of disarmament itself can gain from the avoidance of stereotypes and scapegoats.

These caveats, however, must not blind Christian theologians to the uncontrolled dynamism of the arms race. Whatever "militarism' may have meant to earlier generations, it now means this: *Militarism is a system of ideology and power which exalts armed forces and armaments themselves at the expense of all other human interests, tending to dominate all social institutions as well as relationships among societies.* While some theologians have tried to comprehend the data of nuclear physics, they now need to be much better informed by the dynamic perspectives of political and military sociology. A theology of peacemaking needs to be utterly serious about what is happening to human society right now and must not be fixated on horrifying calculations of megadeaths in the holocaust to come.

Militarism as an ideology is the antithesis of the idea of disarmament. Militarism is ultimately based on fantasies which are totally dissociated from the struggle for human development. That is why militarism is the world's number one mental health problem. Harold and Margaret Sprout of Princeton University have written of "the dehumanizing effect which seems to come from prolonged concentration on the apparatus of destruction unlimited." This is an effect which can isolate policy-makers at the highest level from realistic assessments of the wider human environment.

Militarism is ultimately anti-humanist not because people get killed in war but because it is a theology which sanctifies the war system. Many who have killed and would kill again cannot fairly be called militarists. It is the grossness of militarism as an idolatry that must be confronted by Incarnationists. For militarism takes a primitive view of human nature and absolutizes aggressiveness.

Militarism tyrannizes politics, sabotages diplomacy, plunders the economy, corrupts science, subverts education, scorns the laws and morals of warfare itself in the name of "military necessity" — and does all these things as a functional theology, even to the point of manipulating established religions. Where the Christian community has not been firmly fortified by the doctrines of a transcendent humanism, it has been precisely the sector of national life most vulnerable to militarism.

In 1915, in the midst of the First World War, the great German sociologist Max Weber wrote an essay reflecting on the tragic and inescapably religious aspects of "modern" war. He observed that the threats and violence of "modern" hostilities imposed a profound sense of sacrifice, pathos, and community — all under the transcendent justification of a uniquely "consecrated meaning of death." While Weber's intimations of militarism as a functional theology remain suggestive, these particular celebrations of national unity and sacrifice seem anachronistic in the Third Nuclear Age. The "consecrated meaning of death" has yielded to such awful apprehensions of annihilation that our theologies are almost driven to repress them. In the military sector itself, these apprehensions have little of the romance of seven decades ago but they are even more absolutist in their ideology of total threats and total violence — and their absurd quantifications of both.

Herman Kahn's *Thinking About the Unthinkable* contains some remarkable invocations to positive thinking about thermonuclear war, such as:

> Those who predict metropolitan area-wide firestorms are in all probability wrong. . . . The usual calculation, which simply extrapolates how much thermal energy is produced from a ground burst weapon, and then makes a simple geometric calculation assuming perfect transmission, is undoubtedly wrong. A high altitude burst does not produce much thermal radiation, but soft X-rays which in turn may heat up the atmosphere — which in turn may radiate heat onto the earth. . . . Many present 'estimates' of death toll and damage caused by large thermonuclear weapons due to fire and firestorm are exaggerated.[14]

The Ultimate Realities

What doctrine of Creation or Redemption or the End-time can tolerate such nuclear dogmatics? What doctrine of Humanity can sanction the consolation that a nuclear war might produce "only" 20 million American deaths, not 100 million, and that even "the destruction of the 50 or so major metropolitan areas" would not really present the US with "any critical difficulty"? What Christian eschatology can vindicate the scenario offered by a Pentagon official to the House Armed Services Committee reporting that, while continuing the war after 300 million deaths would be "very difficult," the analysts had "faced that issue, and we have systems that we believe would survive. For example, certain elements of our Navy almost certainly would survive. . . . "? Something has surely happened to Weber's "consecrated meaning of death."

The Incarnation means that God meets us in the fullness of human realities. Jesus Christ not only discloses the mysterious power of transcendent glory. He reveals humanity itself in a new light. The proper service of Christians to the world is to unveil the world itself in its true shapes and powers. It is the refusal to surrender the claim of being "realistic" to those whose militarism has alienated them from vital contact with the world that God has made and is making yet.

Nuclear technology has lifted us dizzily to a fateful partnership with the Creator which our moral and spiritual credentials have not earned: we can crucify the Christ-possibility in every human life. Deep within us lie the very powers of darkness, the principalities and powers with whom Christ is now contending until the End of All Things.

The initiative is now more with us than ever. Whatever love may mean as the vital dynamic of Christly action, it surely means the power to take the initiative in the most hostile and most threatening conflict situations. It means discerning the signs of the times as John XXIII did in *Pacem in Terris*. It means a repentant remembrance of all those open moments the churches themselves have neglected at each and every step of the arms race since Hiroshima. It means that we must keep breaking into history in new ways, whether that means alternative scenarios, tilting the ambiguities, or simply standing firm and strong against the currents of folly. It means forever seeking to express God's first-loving initiative in Jesus Christ, even and especially to our enemies.

A theology of peacemaking for this time before the End-time must be as wide and round as the world itself. It must glory in the fullness of humanity. It must humanize technology. It must demythologize security. It must know about sin and death but it must keep on the initiative.

A truly world-wide theology of peace will be nourished by the visions of peace in many cultures and many faiths. Dag Hammarskjöld put the Cross at the center of his own mystical view of the Incarnation, yet the Incarnation for him was not a doctrine of religious exclusiveness. It was the opening to the whole world. While Hammarskjöld only rarely testified to his own faith, he stood before the 1954 Assembly of the World Council of Churches in Evanston and spoke freely as a Christian man:

> For the Christian faith the Cross is that place at the center of the world's history . . . where all men and all nations without exception stand revealed as enemies of God . . . and yet where all men stand revealed as beloved of God, precious in God's sight. So understood, the Cross, although it is the unique fact on which the Christian churches should base their hope, should not separate those of Christian faith from others, but should instead be that element in their lives which enables them to stretch out their hands to people of other creeds [and] which we hope one day to see reflected in a world of nations truly united.

It was in that widest ecumenical context that I struggled through to a definition of peace at the Second World Conference on Religion and Peace at Louvain in 1974. I particularly appreciated the wisdom of some Eastern Christians and participants from other Eastern religions concerning two things: the depths of spirituality required for peaceable relationships and the profound kinship among all forms of life. Before leaving Louvain, I said:

> Peace is experiencing the harmony of life:
>   the harmony of a whole self with the Source
>   of all life;
>   the harmony of a compassionate community of justice,
>   free from violence and exploitation;
>   the harmony of humanity with nature.

That is a conception of peace which can surely be grounded in the Incarnation but which is open to the whole world.

Such a conception not only permits a doctrine of security: it demands it. In the prophets we should know that security is a legitimate human aspiration and a divine promise to the oppressed. But security itself must be founded upon justice and peace, all wrapped up together in *shalom*. The security of nations is indivisible. It takes material needs seriously but is not primarily a material or technical matter. It is no guarantee of permanent political or social institutions. It will not overlook the forces of evil and the lust for power in any enemies and will muster all the resistance to evil that makes sense — but it will first of all repent for the evil and the lust for power that make us the threatening enemies of others. It will require a transmutation of our view of power itself — and, I believe, a new idea of disarmament.

All this proclaims a word that too many Christians never want to hear: a theology of peace must be grounded in a theology of politics. After all, *peacemaking is political,* whatever else it is. Even Christians passionately engaged in the peace movement itself often seem to prefer short-circuiting politics in every possible way.

The man who married Dietrich Bonhoeffer's twin sister has written a memoir of Bonhoeffer to serve as an introduction to a new edition of *The Cost of Discipleship.* In that memoir, Gerhard Leibholz said:

> In the earlier stages of his career, Bonhoeffer accepted the traditional Lutheran view that there was a sharp distinction between politics and religion. Gradually, however, he revised his opinion, not because . . . he refused to give Caesar his due, but because he came to recognize that the political authority in Germany had become entirely corrupt and immoral and that a false faith is capable of terrible and monstrous things.[15]

Our own theology of politics must not exempt any of us from being politicians for peace. It must not take for granted that God will intervene unilaterally to save our country or humanity itself from self-destruction, as Billy Graham and some others have tried to promise us. God's gift of freedom is so radical and so real — even in the face of a Holocaust — that there is no fail-safe system this side of history. There is no such escape from political responsibility. Yet to be political is to fulfill our own humanness. God made us all political creatures.

Now for some joyful noise again. Good Christian humanists must never forget the radiance of our gospel and the fact that we have numberless songs to sing about what it means to be fully human. So get ready for the music!

Seven Songs for Christian Humanists
1. ALL HUMAN EXPERIENCE TAKES PLACE WITHIN A WORLD ENDOWED WITH MORAL PURPOSE AND MORAL LAW.

There is no ultimate anarchy in our world. The principles of the good life are not arbitrary or capricious. They are grounded in *justice as lovingkindness* toward every human being. That's the way Creation is. Praise God!

2. HUMANITY IS MORE THAN HUMAN. It is the embodiment of the Holy One, the Loving One who gives life, and gives it again.

Why does this fact of being human entitle anyone, any one at all, any one in any country or of any color or party or movement or religious tribe or social status, to special treatment, to sacred rights?

For the Christian, it is because we must no longer look at anyone from a purely human point of view. That is just the word that precedes Paul's Annunciation that "God was in Christ reconciling the world." Every birth is a miracle. Everyone is a Christ, an image of God, an incarnation of divine love and purpose. If you visit a thief or a rapist or a terrorist in prison, you visit Christ too. Everyone has a capacity for transcendence: for love, creativity, imagination, wisdom.

The Russian theologian, Nicholas Berdyaev, testified:

> The entire world is nothing in comparison with human personality, with the unique person of a man, with his unique fate. . . . When a person enters the world, a unique and unrepeatable personality, then the world process is broken into and compelled to change its course.[16]

The empirical significance of grasping this unique preciousness of every life is also eloquently stated by historian Herbert Butterfield:

> The present generation is perhaps in danger of underestimating the subtlety and complexity of the historical process, and particularly the play of personality and the role of contingency in human events. Every moment in history presents unique combinations of circumstances, and some small and apparently irrelevant occurrence may assume unexpected importance because it happens to be pivotal. Because great things may turn on a tiny pivot, the resolution of an individual human being sometimes acquires a magnified importance in the world.[17]

How glibly we often talk about "the dignity of the individual" without really vivifying the drama of history as Berdyaev and Butterfield do! Given the apparent momentum of military technology, the idea of disarmament can only be vindicated by such a personalized drama of history.

3. HUMAN FULFILLMENT IS AT ONCE RADICALLY PERSONAL AND RADICALLY SOCIAL.

Prophetic theology ultimately repudiates both individual*ism* and collectiv*ism*. Both are dehumanizing abstractions. Individuals have rights, as God's creatures, but their individuality can only be fulfilled in community.

Nations and peoples have rights, too—rights grounded in God's promises of liberation, peace, and security.

The Lord promises an oppressed people, Israel, through the mouth of Ezekiel:

> I will make with you a covenant of peace . . .
>> so that you may dwell securely in the wilderness . . .
> and you shall know that I am the Lord,
>> when I break the bars of your yoke,
>> and deliver you from the hand of those who enslaved you.
> You shall be no more a prey to the nations . . .
> You shall dwell securely, and none shall make you afraid.
>
> (Ez. 34:25-28)

There is nothing new about justice or rights for peoples as well as individuals. There are social rights at the heart of humanity. Black theology, liberation theology should have scored this point with us, if none other. It is hardly a Bolshevik fabrication! True security is part of God's promise of liberation.

4. HUMAN FREEDOM IS WHOLISTIC.

There is a unity of spirit-and-mind-and-body in biblical portraits of personhood.

The promise of abundant life in Christ is the promise of a full and rich development of personhood in all of its varied potential. The denial of that promise in one area of life is bound to affect the other areas.

Charles Malik, the Lebanese diplomat who played a major part in drafting the UN Declaration of Human Rights, emphasized this need for wholeness which he had grasped as a lay theologian. The effort to obtain that UN Declaration, he said, was essentially a struggle "to recapture and reaffirm the full integrity of man." No piecemeal approach, no mere listing of principles, no big separation between legal rights and economic opportunities could really do justice to that effort.

For Christians, no insight is more precious than the recognition that religious liberty is inseparably linked to all other human rights. Religious liberty is virtually meaningless if it is not secured by rights of life, health, assembly, association, free speech, free press, education, and property — to name just a few. A human right, to be meaningful, must be vindicated with a substantial opportunity to practice that right. It must be capable of Incarnation. The social and material facts of life must not thwart such opportunity. Religious liberty itself ultimately requires a whole view of humanity.

The right to life itself, not only as an individual matter but as the most fundamental issue of survival for the whole human family now and for all potential generations, is increasingly threatened with nullification by nuclear technology. Thus every other human right is at the mercy of the arms race. Peacemakers must not allow the slogan "right to life" to be monopolized by single-issue dogmatists. The right to live in a peaceable human community, free from violence and the terror of genocide, must be proclaimed in every pulpit and sung by every choir. The main theme of the 1983 Assembly of the World Council of Churches in Vancouver — "Jesus Christ, the Life of the World" — must be affirmed with absolutely literal seriousness by every Christian congregation. For the very life of the world is indeed what the idea of disarmament is all about. Ecumenism, which literally means the struggle of the whole inhabited Earth to live together in one household, is ultimately synonymous with peacemaking.

5. THE CHRISTIAN RIGHTLY HAS A DELIBERATE, WILLFUL BIAS TOWARD THE POOR, THE POWERLESS, AND THE OPPRESSED.

The prophets' special concern is consistently for those whose humanity has been most often abused. There is no abstract, mechanical notion of equality; equity requires constant affirmative action toward those whose human rights have been denied. We are to bear good news to the poor, release captives, give sight to the blind, liberate the oppressed, proclaim the arrival of a new order of love and justice. We are to be unashamed partisans of the victims of history: it is for them that we must beat our bombers into plowshares and our missiles into pruning hooks. Those nations which have freely chosen to renounce weapons of mass destruction, to make themselves powerless according to the nuclear dogmatics by which the superpowers have sworn, for which they the powerless have been subjected to further humiliations, must no longer be denied the equity and reciprocity they are due. Their Annunciation must now become our renunciation.

A theology of peace must indeed be a theology of conversion — but not just of the solitary soul. It must be conversion of the tools of death into tools of life.

6. THE INCARNATION IS UNIVERSAL.

No society, no religion has a monopoly of concern for the preciousness of human life. That clearly is one of the messages of the Good Samaritan: the recognition of basic human need is not limited to *our* society or *our* religion.

Sometimes this message is obscured by a cultural if not racist arrogance among some Western (even Christian) leaders who like to say that the very notion of human rights is essentially an Anglo-American monopoly. The negative counterpart is the claim that Latins, or Slavs, or Arabs, or Africans, or Asians (or all of the above) lack the high culture required for a proper appreciation of human rights and democratic institutions.

The most moving testimony to the inspiration of human rights I have heard recently came from a Korean, Kim Kwan Suk, general secretary of the Korean Council of Churches, who had spent six months in prison for his dissent against the repressive policies of the Park Chung Hee government — and whose son was sent to prison because he read a statement on human rights in his college chapel. Kim Kwan Suk said:

> People want to be free. People want the security of knowing that their basic rights as human beings cannot be stolen from them, either by their own government or some other power. . . . May the time soon come . . . when we can openly discuss matters of importance to us; when we can read objective facts in our newspapers and have free access to news from outside; when we can have confidence in the courts and believe in the possibility of getting a fair trial and a judgment which reflects the evidence; when teachers can teach according to their best knowledge without fear of dismissal; and when ministers can preach the Word of God freely and openly, fearing only His judgment.

There is another factor to be counted in any effort to compare Western and Eastern claims to be *humane*. The wars and holocausts, the depressions and tyrannies which have been the burden of Western history, even in this century, should provide painful enough cautions against cultural pride in our respect for human life. Our continuing dependence upon weapons capable of annihilating the human species is hardly evidence of our moral superiority over any other people.

The universality of human rights is more than a Western invention, then: it is testimony to human capacities for both justice and injustice in every society. Prophetic theology bids us to recognize the humanity of every enemy who confronts us. After all, Christ is over there on the other side of the border, too. No person, no people, no nation can be an absolute enemy for us.

In March 1979 American and Soviet church leaders, meeting in Geneva, tried to draft the very first joint theological statement ever to represent these two adversary peoples. It was hard going. There were barriers of language and of theological style, of radically different national histories, politics, ideologies, and church situations. Yet it was very late in the Third Nuclear Age and both sides clearly wanted to speak together to the perils of the arms race. The discussions halted at a dreary moment when it seemed the political chasm was too wide to cross. Then Alexey Bichkov, General Secretary of the Union of Evangelical Baptists of the USSR, told a story. On a visit to the States, he had once seen the very funny movie, "The Russians Are Coming! The Russians Are Coming!" He infected the meeting with laughter—then turned very serious: "You will remember that, at the end of the movie, the Russians and Americans got together in the act of rescuing a child. In this Year of the Child, 1979, if we can't get together for the sake of the world's children, we really don't have any hope, do we?" It turned into a moment of reconciliation. There followed some accommodations on both sides, then the final draft of "Choose Life" which would circle the globe and be published even in *Izvestia* so that millions of Soviet citizens could read a Christian document in their government's official newspaper.[18] Looking together toward the end of the Second Millenium, Americans and Russians had asked: "How shall we meet that day!? In what state shall we present our planet to the Creator: shall it be a blooming garden or a lifeless, burnt out, devastated land!?"

7. NOT ONLY IS HUMANITY POSITIVELY GROUNDED IN MORAL LAW: THERE IS DIVINE JUDGMENT UPON NATIONS FOR THEIR INHUMANITIES.

The complacency, hypocrisy, brutality, and exploitiveness of nations are common objects of prophetic warnings in the Scriptures. The sixth chapter of Amos is a severe rebuke to those whose security is materialistic and indulgent:

> Woe to those ensconced so snugly in Zion
>   and to those who feel so safe on the mountain of Samaria . . .
> You think to defer the day of misfortune,
>   but you hasten the reign of violence.
>
> (Amos 6:1, 3 *Jerusalem Bible*)

The best American theologian of the 19th century, Abraham Lincoln, had this tragic sense of judgment for those on both sides of a war who read the same Bible and prayed to the same God. It's all there in that heavy line about slavery in his Second Inaugural: "all the wealth piled up the bond-man's two hundred and fifty years of unrequited toil." Millions were somehow going to pay for that terrible abuse of human sanctity. And we are still paying, heavily.

This same sense of judgment, but judgment from the very heart of a loving Creator, is beautifully expressed in my favorite lines from Martin Luther King, Jr. — lines which showed he had the heart of an astronomer:

> The ultimate weakness of violence is that it is a descending spiral, begetting the very thing it seeks to destroy. Instead of diminishing evil, it multiplies it. . . . Returning violence for violence multiplies violence, adding deeper darkness to a night already devoid of stars. Darkness cannot drive out darkness; only light can do that. Hate cannot drive out hate; only love can do that.

These, then, are seven songs for a Christian humanist theology of peace.

There is so much treasure, so much power, so much love at the very core of our faith that we must never again allow peacemaking to be pushed aside to the periphery of Christian concern — which is what too many of us have done for too long. Disarmament, of course, isn't everything. But without it there won't be anything.

Our Christian challenge is to face up to the message of a Jewish composer, Leonard Bernstein, whose choral "Mass" dedicated the Kennedy Center for the Performing Arts in Washington in September 1971 — a work which wondrously mixes music, theater, liturgy, and — yes! — even politics.

Here are some lines from Paul Hume's review of "Mass," just as it was published in *The Washington Post,* September 9, 1971:

> The central action of 'Mass' surrounds its celebrant from the moment he strikes the first chord on his guitar and gathers around him a swarm of eager, happy choir boys, to the awful,

shuddering climax of the 'Agnus Dei' when he is attacked and tormented by those he thought were his people, so that he hurls the consecrated sacraments of bread and wine to the floor and, in the words of the score, goes 'berserk.' It is a terrifying moment that produces a physical shudder in many who have seen it.

Only after this wrenching collapse can the ultimate, healing reconciliation gradually evolve. . . .

'Mass' throws a spotlight on the terrible pressures that bear down on priests today. At the opening, the Celebrant is happy with his choir boys and young parishioners. But each time he takes another step toward carrying out his supreme priestly function of preparing and celebrating the mass, the sense of separation (and opposition) from his congregation increases.

The nature of their final, crushing thrust is clear in Bernstein's score when, in the 'Agnus Dei,' his directions to the singers and dancers bristle with words like: menacing, wild, attack, savage, barbaric, nasty, relentless, stamp. The Celebrant is forced to retreat from his altar until, just as he completes the consecration, the threats carry him over the edge of reason.

The sting in their attack is that it comes as they advance toward him singing, 'Dona nobis pacem!' It is the cry of the world to its teachers of religion, 'Give us peace!' and the world runs out of patience and won't wait any longer when offered sacraments but no peace.[19]

Choose Life

Joint statement of the representatives of the churches of the USSR and the USA meeting in Geneva in a Consultation on Disarmament, on March 27-29, 1979.

I call heaven and earth to witness against you this day, that I have set before you life and death, blessing and curse. Therefore, choose life, that you and your descendants may live.

(Deuteronomy 30:19)

We make this appeal as servants of Christ gathered from among the churches of the USA and the USSR. We have been drawn together across the differences of language and culture by our common Christian calling to foster life in the midst of a race towards death. We affirm our unity in confessing Christ as Lord and Saviour.

Gathered in Geneva during the season of Lent we have been especially conscious of the sufferings of our Lord who offered Himself that we might have life and have it abundantly (John 10:10). From our faith in Christ, the All Powerful, the Conqueror of Death, we have drawn strength to choose life in spite of the spreading power of death.

Our three day session was marked by acts of worship and included presentation and discussion of theological and technical papers as well as dialogue on issues of peace and disarmament. During this time we heard and considered reports from Ambassador Victor Israelian, USSR, and Ambassador Adrian Fisher, USA, the heads of our two delegations in the Committee on Disarmament in Geneva.

We have been encouraged by the engagement of our two governments in an unprecedented range of disarmament negotiations; by the strengthening of the more significant measures taken by the United Nations for disarmament; by the renewed vitality of non-governmental organizations in the disarmament field; and by the indications that the peoples of the world are calling for disarmament. But our ambassadors' presentations and other information set before us have also filled us with profound anxiety for the future of our own and all peoples.

The Arms Race

We are convinced that the arms race cannot be won; it can only be lost. All of us have long been aware of the nuclear terror. Many people have accepted it as an inescapable part of our contemporary world. Numerous voices in the church have been raised against it in both our countries.

Our experience in this consultation now compels us to cry out against it with one voice. The existence of forces having the capacity to devastate our planet not once or twice, but many times, is absurd and cannot be tolerated. It must be confronted and overcome in the name of the Christ who lives and reigns forever.

We express profound concern about the danger of a precarious balancing of humanity on the brink of nuclear catastrophe. We know that still more terrible weapons are being developed which can only lead to greater fear and suspicion and thus to a still more feverish arms race. Against this we say with one voice—NO! In the name of God—NO!

We are opposed to the arms race not only because of the danger that we will all lose it in the future, but also because we are in fact losing the race now. Already in 1978, the nations of the world were spending more than one billion dollars per day—400 billion per year—on armaments, a sum which is increasing every day. We were informed that the World Health Organization required a mere 83 million dollars, to wipe out smallpox. What could be done with the other thousands of millions!? Could the hungry be fed!? Could the sick be made whole!?

Nor can the cost be measured in money alone. The gifts of God given to his people for the service of the new creation in Christ are everywhere diverted to the destruction of peace and order. Peoples are forced by economic and political pressure to offer up their lives in the manufacture of death. Nations already ravaged are wounded again as their irreplaceable natural resources are consumed in the arms race rather than being employed in the development of just, sustainable and participatory societies for their own people. Widespread moral devastation, cynicism and hopelessness are the only rewards.

Theological Reflections

To address the danger of these fantasies of destruction being acted out in our history on a global scale, we have sought to renew our vision. We have listened again to the ancient words of the prophet Isaiah:

> *He shall judge between the nations, and shall decide for many peoples; and they shall beat their swords into plowshares and their spears into pruning hooks; nation shall not lift up sword against nation, neither shall they learn war any more.*
>
> *(Isaiah 2:4)*

We confess that the nations which, with the help of God, can transform swords, can also disarm missiles. We bear witness that the Lord our God is a God of peace who wills the well-being of the whole of His creation. He has granted us and all His People a vision of *shalom* for the present time and for the ages to come in which all peoples and nations will dwell together in security.

Yet we acknowledge that this, the very longing for security on the part of the nations, is often used to justify the arms race. The possession of arms by some breeds fear and suspicion among others which they seek to quell by acquiring their own arms. This in turn breeds more fear and suspicion, which results in an escalation of terror rather than the establishment of full security.

We recognize that we ourselves and the peoples of our two nations, and indeed, every man, woman and child in all the world, are caught in this spiral of terror. We perceived that the threat of this escalation is slipping beyond human control. We were then reminded of the Apostle Paul's exclamation that "we wrestle, not against flesh and blood, but against principalities, against powers" (Ephesians 6:12). We confessed that seeking our security through arms is in fact a false and idolatrous hope and that true security can be found only in relationships of trust. These relationships we believe to be possible, for Christ has overcome the principalities and powers (Colossians 2:15).
JESUS IS LORD!

Call to Action
We therefore pledge ourselves and encourage our brothers and sisters:

— to press for the earliest possible approval of the SALT II accords. While we understand that SALT II does not provide for more substantial arms reduction, it does provide a new and essential framework (of parity) for negotiating substantial and equal reductions in SALT III, and further steps in the direction of general and complete disarmament. It promises a new opportunity to consolidate institutions for halting the spread of nuclear weapons. The success of SALT II would open the way to decisive progress on other critical disarmament issues. It would enable our two governments to share more fully in the constructive works of peace in economic, technical and cultural affairs. It would help to promote a new climate of international relations in general.

— to call for a full and general prohibition of: nuclear arms testing; the development and deployment of new nuclear weapon systems; and the production and accumulation of chemical and radiological arms as well as other weapons of mass destruction.

— to support the role of the UN in disarmament negotiations and such international forums as the Special Session on Disarmament and other initiatives in this field. The arms race produces hardships, and lethal dangers, not only for our two countries, but for all nations of the world, especially those having nuclear capability. Therefore, all governments have the right and the duty to participate constructively in the process of disarmament.

— to support ecumenical programmes concerned with disarmament, especially the World Council of Churches Programme for Disarmament and Against Militarism and the Arms Race; and to cooperate with other non-governmental programmes for disarmament.

— to express readiness to unite our efforts for peace and disarmament with the followers of all religions and all persons of goodwill.

— to call upon our churches to make available staff persons and financial resources for disarmament programmes.

— to urge our churches in their teaching and preaching programmes to emphasize the Biblical vision of peace; and also to stress the devastating social and personal consequences of the arms race.

— to give special attention to strengthening and enlarging the community which has been nurtured among the Christians in the USSR and the USA for more than twenty years, and which we have again experienced here, including the possibility of further consultations on disarmament and other visitations of a general nature, as well as joint days of prayer for peace using the Ecumenical Prayer Cycle (World Council of Churches) and respective liturgical materials of the churches involved.

Finally, our sisters and brothers, we call to your attention the authoritative predictions that nuclear war by the 1990's is an increasing probability. In that decade of high risks we will be approaching the end of our millenium. Even now, only twenty years separate us from the moment when we will be called upon to mark prayerfully the bi-millenary anniversary of the coming to the world of our Lord and Saviour, Jesus Christ, the Prince of Peace. How shall we meet that day!? In what state shall we present our planet to the Creator: shall it be a blooming garden or a lifeless, burnt out, devastated land!?

Thus the Lord has set before us again life and death, blessing and curse: therefore choose life that you and your descendants may live.

Metropolitan Juvenaly of Krutizy and Kolomna (Head of the USSR delegation) chairman of the External Church Relations Department of the Moscow Patriarchate, Russian Orthodox Church;

Rev. Alexey Bichkov, General Secretary of the Union of Evangelical Baptists of the USSR;

Protopresbyter Professor Vitaly Borovoy, Representative of the Russian Orthodox Church to the World Council of Churches;

Dr. Alexey Buevsky, Secretary of the External Church Relations Department of the Moscow Patriarchate;

Archbishop Edward Hark, of the Estonian Evangelical Lutheran Church;

Archbishop Kirill of Vyborg, Rector of the Leningrad Theological

Academy, Russian Orthodox Church;

Archbishop Janis Matulis of the Evangelical Lutheran Church of Latvia;

Archbishop Nikola (Maharadze) of Soukoumi and Abhasia, Georgian Orthodox Church;

Professor Alexey Ossipov of the Moscow Theological Academy, Russian Orthodox Church;

Archimandrite Tyran, Representative of the Armenina Apostolic Church in Moscow;

Technical Advisor: **Professor Vladimier Koolagin,** Dean of the Faculty of International Relations of Moscow State Institute of International Relations;

The Rev. M. William Howard (Head of the USA delegation), President of the National Council of Churches of Christ, USA, American Baptist Churches in the USA;

Dr. Claire Randall, General Secretary of the National Council of Churches, United Presbyterian Church in the USA;

Dr. Dorothy J. Marple, Vice-president of the National Council of Churches, Lutheran Church in America;

Bishop Chester A. Kirkendoll, Secretary of the National Council of Churches, Christian Methodist Episcopal Church;

The Very Rev. Vladimir Berzonsky of the Orthodox Church in America, Member of the Governing Board of the National Council of Churches;

The Rev. Arie R. Brouwer, General Secretary of the Reformed Church in America, Member of the Governing Board of the National Council of Churches;

Bishop James K. Mathews of the United Methodist Council of Bishops, Member of the Governing Board of the National Council of Churches;

The Rev. Avery D. Post, President of the United Church of Christ, Member of the Governing Board of the National Council of Churches;

Dr. V. Bruce Rigdon, Professor of Church History, McCormick Theological Seminary, Chicago, Ordained Minister of the United Presbyterian Church, USA;

Ms. Alice Wimer, Executive for International Affairs, National Council of Churches, Member of the United Church of Christ;

Technical Advisor: **Dr. Alan Geyer,** Executive Director of the Churches' Centre for Theology and Public Policy, Washington, D.C., Member of the United Methodist Church.

Military Technology: Issues of Power and Peace

WCC-MIT Conference on Faith, Science, and the Future, July 12-24, 1979
(Part III of Section IX Report)

The history of industrialized societies discloses intimate and complex connections between military technology and the basic institutions of government, economy and science. These connections require the most competent and thorough analysis if the churches are to be effective instruments of God's justice and peace.

Three aspects of this institutional complex may be approached somewhat separately — although the final word must stress their inter-related nature.

A. Relationships between military technology and political institutions.

B. Military demands on science and technology.

C. The churches' challenge to military technology.

A. Military Technology and Political Institutions

A comprehensive picture of connections between military technology and political institutions may be sketched by the following propositions which we believe to be true but which invite continuing discussion and research:

1. The advance of military technology has (paradoxically) undermined the capacity of nation-states to defend their own citizens. (The boundaries of the territorial state are indefensible against nuclear bombs and missiles.)

2. The speed of delivery of nuclear weapons has increasingly curbed the capacity of democratic institutions to share in crisis decisions about national security by reducing the time available for decisions and the number of persons making them. (A crisis response to a missile attack in a few minutes hardly permits parliamentary debate.)

3. The managerial structures of military technology have evolved a new form of government in both capitalist and socialist countries: a pattern in which industrial, scientific, military and political elites collaborate in determining national priorities and allocating resources. (The term 'military-industrial complex' is too simplistic.)

4. The growing complexity of military technology expands the network of vested interests in the development and production of new weapons. (As the variety of technologies and components in modern weapons systems multiplies, the industries and localities affected also tend to multiply.)

5. Early bureaucratic decisions about weapons research and development tend to become increasingly inaccessible to the public and irreversible

in the legislative process.

6. The escalating sophistication of military technology tends to alienate increasing portions of the public from any sense of competence in coping with issues which are left to "the experts." (No area of public policy is more troubled by a widespread sense of powerlessness than defense and disarmament.)

7. The co-opting of intellectual resources by the gross demands of high military technology threatens the autonomy and integrity of academic disciplines and institutions and of public discussion of policy alternatives. (Conflicting loyalties and pervasive secrecy are the lot of many scholars in this field.)

8. Public acquiescence in weapons of mass annihilation threatens mental health by fostering a schizophrenic attitude toward the relation between national security and normal living.

9. The increasing costliness of military technology aggravates the problem of unemployment, not only by diverting government budgets from social programs but by reducing the ratio of employees to expenditures.

10. The massive allocation of resources to military research and development undermines the progress of civilian productivity and weakens a nation's position in world trade in civilian products. (The quality and efficiency of industrial engineering are critically affected by military priorities.)

11. The costliness of high military technology in the 1970s has become a growing stimulus to arms exports: the aim is to reduce unit costs by multiplying production.

12. Transfers of advanced military technology to the Third World can increase the capacity of authoritarian regimes for repression and for inflicting suffering on their citizens.

13. The dynamics of the strategic arms race tend to become increasingly domesticated through the bureaucratic momentum of military technology which acquires an autonomous power not dependent on the behavior of adversary states.

14. Innovations in military technology increasingly threaten to outrun the technology of disarmament. (Strategic weapons are now being developed in which the characteristics of concealment, deception, and mobility may frustrate available instruments of verification and regulation.)

15. The threat of nuclear weapons technology to the life and habitability of all countries deprives non-nuclear-weapon states of political autonomy in matters of their own safety and survival.

16. The assumption of special political prerogatives by nuclear states gives impetus to nuclear options by other states.

17. The more a foreign policy is based on nuclear weapons, the more it tends to substitute technical abstractions for political goals and to become preoccupied with stability and the status quo. (A recent study of nuclear deterrence describes that doctrine as peculiarly appropriate to the "reactive" foreign policy of a status quo power.)

18. The technology of mutual terror holds masses of citizens hostage

to the narrowly conceived interests of political elites. (The traditional moral doctrine of noncombatant immunity affords no protection to ordinary citizens in a nuclear war.)

B. Military Demands on Science and Technology

To account for the massive demands of military programs on science and technology is to survey a wide range of human motives — personal, professional, and national.

Unquestionably, many governmental and military persons, together with many scientists and technologists, sincerely believe that their work in weapons research and development contributes to national security and peace. The relationship of such persons to the churches offers a largely neglected opportunity for engagement in these issues through special ministries of the laity.

In many cases, however, the motives of these and other persons are mixed with careerist ambitions and materialistic life-styles. The result is often a personal and family dissociation from any serious moral concern about the consequences of their research and development. Still more disturbing are the blatant greed and profiteering which often exploit and manipulate public anxiety, fear, and national pride in order to promote new weapons programs. In some countries, the propaganda of militarism is at least as much for domestic consumption as it is for international impact. Such propaganda is repeatedly unleashed in order to sustain the momentum of research and development, production and deployment which has become the dynamic of military technology and the prime engine of the arms race.

Nevertheless, the very real hostilities between militarized states and the increasing possibilities of nuclear war make concern for national security and survival a more legitimate motive than ever. The issue is whether further escalations of the arms race can make any positive contribution to genuine security. The terrible irony of the nuclear age is that the more the superpowers have committed their resources to the idols of deferrence and defense, the more defenseless they (and all other nations) have become. The final Document of the UN Special Session on Disarmament in 1978 declared that nuclear weapons have become "much more of a threat than a protection" for humanity.

Preoccupation with the scenarios of nuclear war has pre-empted the political and scholarly resources which must be devoted to the scenarios of peacemaking. Policy-makers, physical and social scientists, the churches, and the general public need new scripts for the strategies required to reverse the arms race and to construct the institutions of global security and survival.

The new scenarios of peacemaking must confront the fear, insecurity, ignorance, hate and mistrust which fuel the upward thrust of military technology and the arms race. Such strategies must multiply opportunities for personal encounter across adversary boundaries for political and military leaders, scholars, religious groups, and every sector of their societies. While we are very grateful for the multilateral exchange of views at this conference, we earnestly hope that the next WCC Conference of this kind will experience the fullest possible representation of both East and West, South and North.

If total trust of any government, others' or one's own government, is not only difficult but unwise, the works of reconciliation must nevertheless initiate and reinforce relationships of increasing trust and confidence between nations. Disarmament should never be advocated solely on the grounds of "national technical means of verification" and the fictitious claim that no trust is required. Rather, the technology of verification must operate in a political environment in which serious and sustained efforts are made to forge the links of trust.

The possibility of even a minimal degree of trust is frustrated to the extent that weapons production and deployment are captive to "worst case" assumptions. To assume the absolutely worst motives of an adversary is to compound the vicious circle of mistrust and to provide an infinite rationalization for the arms race. In the nuclear era, it is to deny all practical possibility of expressing Christian hope.

The impact of military demands on science and technology is not only to distort the priorities and perceptions of "developed" societies: it is to intensify the pressures of domination upon "developing" societies. The pattern of domination is one in which economic, military, intellectual and cultural interests are closely interrelated. Some of the poorest of "developing" societies are increasingly militarized through collaboration between indigenous elites and the military-industrial-scientific elites of "developed" societies. The distortion of developmental priorities (educational, technological, and social) thus increasingly mirrors the misplaced values and interests of richer countries—but at the heavy cost of frustrating the most elemental human needs of poor countries and even undermining their own authentic security.

A serious international consequence of such distorted priorities and dominance relationships is the disadvantaged position of poorer countries in multilateral disarmament institutions. With the proliferation of UN and other disarmament agencies, the richer and more militarized countries can deploy platoons of experts on weapons systems, nuclear technology, and monitoring devices to represent those countries. The poorer countries cannot easily muster the personnel to represent their governments in all these agencies.

Moral criticism of military technology is often rebutted by citing the benefits of "spin-offs." Among these civilian by-products are flu vaccine, jet aircraft, radars for air safety and meteorology, synthetics, nuclear energy, communications satellites, the astronomical revolution, and urban rapid transit.

It is deeply troubling to ask whether some of these developments would ever have occurred without the high priorities accorded to military technology in research and development. Some of these innovations are clearly ambiguous in their consequences — such as the hazards of nuclear energy and the power of communications to become tools of cultural imperialism. Moreover, the benefits of some spin-offs, such as jet aircraft, tend to be limited to elites and not to benefit the poor majority. We may also ask whether military technology itself, in economic terms, is most efficient in producing civilian benefits, especially in view of the enormous wastefulness of defense industry and its tendencies to aggravate employment problems. Finally, we must ask whether the new generations of strategic weapons which have emerged during the 1970s, such as MIRVs, cruise and mobile missiles, will ever generate substantial civilian benefits. We may well have reached an era of diminishing returns, at best, in which the case for spin-offs will lose its attractiveness altogether.

Nor can we overlook the fact that the process of technological innovation has often been the reverse: civilian inventions which are exploited for military purposes. Steamships, internal combustion engines, aviation, rocketry, computers have all been diverted from humane purposes to the tools of war.

The role of scientists and technologists in confronting the ethical dilemmas and theological imperatives inescapably embodied in these issues deserves special recognition and nurture in the Christian community.

Scientists and technologists must ask themselves whether their careers are instruments of humane service. They must ask themselves how much their very choice of research topics is determined by anticipated funding or rationalized by the hope of spin-offs. They must confront the imbalance of teaching and research resources between the physical sciences with their special claims to costly equipment and the social sciences with their special responsibilities for public policy. More particularly, they must confront the gross disparities between the funding of military research and the funding of disarmament research — as well as the tendency of arms control research to focus more on matters of military hardware than on economic and political processes related to disarmament.

C. The Churches' Challenge to Military Technology

The churches' witness to this complex arena of military technology and its relationships with science, education, industry and politics can hardly be said to be even adequately envisioned, let alone embodied in the life of congregations or denominations or ecumenical networks.

The WCC Programme on Disarmament and Militarism offers a promising framework for constituent churches to become an active presence in this arena. This Programme merits much more substantial support (including funding) if the world church is to have significant impact on governments and scientists on disarmament issues. Local and regional ecumenical centers on disarmament and peace can provide vital links to this Programme.

First and foremost, the churches must undertake new vocational strategies of the laity among scientists, technologists, industrialists, politicians and others who have most access to this arena in their daily work. The meaning and empowerment of their work must be nurtured by a more vocation-oriented learning of the fullness of Christian ethics.

Second, theological education must develop a new cross-professional orientation in which ministers learn to encounter the struggles of the laity for meaningful work and witness as the foundation of their own professional ministry.

Third, in addition to fostering personal exchanges across the boundaries of hostilities between militarized states, the church's world mission must give special place to exchanges in which persons from the poor nations most victimized by the injustices of the rich nations' technological priorities and threats may testify to the human consequences as they see them.

Fourth, local congregations and ecumenical clusters should be prepared to exert strong and competent leadership in the conversion of regional defense industry to civilian purposes.

Fifth, the churches should encourage investments in those enterprises producing humane products and services and not engaged in military production. Thorough and continuing research can provide the information needed for such investment procedures.

Sixth, the churches must celebrate politics as the vocation of all citizens. Humane decisions about the allocation of scientific and technological resources require citizen participation by persons most directly affected. In most countries, the political ethics of our churches require a much more positive development if they are to become redemptive forces in society. The churches can, and do, help to shape the civic values and public opinions which are expressed in governmental decisions about science and technology. Perhaps no other institution can do more to sustain a steadfast public commitment to disarmament and to peaceful and liberating uses of technology.

Seventh, the churches must help their members to understand and support the complex net of interrelated agreements which improve the prospects for eventual nuclear disarmament. In particular, the churches of nuclear-weapons-states must now give forceful emphasis to strategic arms limitations (SALT) and a comprehensive test ban as the indispensable preconditions to halting the spread of nuclear weapons technology. The churches must speak with theological vigor and moral clarity to the injustice and invidious discrimination of the world power structure in nuclear technology. Our colleague from Nigeria, B. C. E. Nwosu, spoke bluntly but fairly to this issue in declaring:

> "Any country that tells you that nuclear energy is bad but refuses to share with you the secrets of commercial solar energy or other alternative technologies should not be taken seriously. Any country that sits on thousands of megaton bombs and harasses you about the dangers of nuclear proliferation should not be considered a friend."

Eighth, the churches should work cooperatively with other religious communities and with non-religious groups to wind down the annihilating trends of military technology and to abolish war itself. The totalitarian nature of weapons of mass destruction has made the whole human family a community of peril which must become a community of hope. Thus have the technical characteristics of the tools of war driven us to acknowledge in our time an ironic fulfillment of prophetic theology: Christ has embraced us all, with every people everywhere, people of every religion and of no religion, because we all belong to God in life and death and life again.

—Alan Geyer, Rapporteur

'Like Lemmings Heading for the Sea'

George F. Kennan made the following address in accepting the Albert Einstein Peace Prize on 19 May 1981 at the Marriott Hotel in Washington, D.C.:

A person would have to be wholly insensitive, or perhaps selfless to the point of saintliness, in order not to be moved by such an honor as the Einstein Foundation is conferring on me today. I am neither of those things; so I am naturally deeply gratified and appreciative.

On the other hand, I cannot help but have my doubts as to whether I have fully deserved it. And for that reason I can look on it only as a mark of confidence and of encouragement — encouragement to myself and to a great many other people — encouragement to continue to do what little may be in our power to assure that we of this generation, here and elsewhere, do not, in deference to our military fears, commit the supreme sacrilege of putting an end to the civilization out of which we have grown, the civilization which has made us what we are, the civilization without which our children and grandchildren can have no chance for self-realization, possibly no chance for life itself.

This, as I see it, is the task to which the Einstein Foundation has devoted itself. Beside it, all personal considerations ought to fade into insignificance. I am grateful for the opportunity to associate myself publicly with this cause. And I am grateful for the admonition which the award implies: the admonition to neglect nothing — no effort, no unpleasantness, no controversy, no sacrifice — which could conceivably help to preserve us from committing this fatal folly.

What *can* we do?

Adequate words are lacking to express the full seriousness of our present situation. It is not just that we are for the moment on a collision course politically with the Soviet Union, and that the process of rational communication between the two governments seems to have broken down completely; it is also — and even more importantly — the fact that the ultimate sanction behind the conflicting policies of these two governments is a type and volume of weaponry which could not possibly be used without utter disaster for us all.

For over 30 years wise and far-seeing people have been warning us about the futility of any war fought with nuclear weapons and about the dangers involved in their cultivation. Some of the first of these voices to be raised were those of great scientists, including outstandingly that of Albert Einstein himself. But there has been no lack of others. Every president of this country, from Dwight Eisenhower to Jimmy Carter, has tried to re-mind us that there could be no such thing as victory in a war fought with such weapons. So have a great many other eminent persons.

When one looks back today over the history of these warnings, one has the impression that something has now been lost of the sense of urgen-cy, the hopes, and the excitement that initially inspired them, so many years ago. One senses, even on the part of those who today most acutely perceive the problem and are inwardly most exercised about it, a certain discourage-ment, resignation, perhaps even despair, when it comes to the question of raising the subject again. The danger is so obvious. So much has already been said. What is to be gained by reiteration? What good would it now do?

Look at the record. Over all these years the competition in the devel-opment of nuclear weaponry has proceeded steadily, relentlessly, without the faintest regard for all these warning voices. We have gone on piling weapon upon weapon, missile upon missile, new levels of destructiveness upon old ones. We have done this helplessly, almost involuntarily: like the victims of some sort of hypnotism, like men in a dream, like lemmings heading for the sea, like the children of Hamlin marching blindly along behind their Pied Piper. And the result is that today we have achieved, we and the Russians together, in the creation of these devices and their means of delivery, levels of redundancy of such grotesque dimensions as to defy rational understanding.

I say redundancy. I know of no better way to describe it. But actually, the word is too mild. It implies that there could be levels of these weapons that would not be redundant. Personally, I doubt that there could. I ques-tion whether these devices are really weapons at all. A true weapon is at best something with which you endeavor to affect the behavior of another society by influencing the minds, the calculations, the intentions, of the men that control it; it is not something with which you destroy indis-criminately the lives, the substance, the hopes, the culture, the civilization, of another people.

What a confession of intellectual poverty it would be—what a bank-ruptcy of intelligent statesmanship—if we had to admit that such blind, senseless acts of destruction were the best use we could make of what we have come to view as the leading elements of our military strength!

To my mind, the nuclear bomb is the most useless weapon ever in-vented. It can be employed to no rational purpose. It is not even an effec-tive defense against itself. It is only something with which, in a moment of petulance or panic, you commit such fearful acts of destruction as no sane person would ever wish to have upon his conscience.

There are those who will agree, with a sigh, to much of what I have just said, but will point to the need for something called deterrence. This is, of course, a concept which attributes to others—to others who, like our-selves, were born of women, walk on two legs, and love their children, to human beings, in short—the most fiendish and inhuman of tendencies.

But all right: accepting for the sake of argument the profound iniquity of these adversaries, no one could deny, I think, that the present Soviet and American arsenals, presenting over a million times the destructive power of the Hiroshima bomb, are simply fantastically redundant to the purpose in question. If the same relative proportions were to be preserved, something well less than 20 percent of these stocks would surely suffice for the most sanguine concepts of deterrence, whether as between the two nuclear super-powers or with relation to any of those other governments that have been so ill-advised as to enter upon the nuclear path. Whatever their suspicions of each other, there can be no excuse on the part of these two governments for holding, poised against each other and poised in a sense against the whole northern hemisphere, quantities of these weapons so vastly in excess of any rational and demonstrable requirements.

How have we got ourselves into this dangerous mess?

Let us not confuse the question by blaming it all on our Soviet adversaries. They have, of course, their share of the blame, and not least in their cavalier dismissal of the Baruch Plan so many years ago. They too have made their mistakes; and I should be the last to deny it.

But we must remember that it has been we Americans who, at almost every step of the road, have taken the lead in the development of this sort of weaponry. It was we who first produced and tested such a device; we who were the first to raise its destructiveness to a new level with the hydrogen bomb; we who introduced the multiple warhead; we who have declined every proposal for the renunciation of the principle of "first use"; and we alone, so help us God, who have used the weapon in anger against others, and against tens of thousands of helpless non-combatants at that.

I know that reasons were offered for some of these things. I know that others might have taken this sort of a lead, had we not done so. But let us not, in the face of this record, so lose ourselves in self-righteousness and hypocrisy as to forget our own measure of complicity in creating the situation we face today.

What is it then, if not our own will, and if not the supposed wickedness of our opponents, that has brought us to this pass?

The answer, I think, is clear. It is primarily the inner momentum, the independent momentum, of the weapons race itself—the compulsions that arise and take charge of great powers when they enter upon a competition with each other in the building up of major armaments of any sort.

This is nothing new. I am a diplomatic historian. I see this same phenomenon playing its fateful part in the relations among the great European powers as much as a century ago. I see this competitive buildup of armaments conceived initially as a means to an end but soon becoming the end itself. I see it taking possession of men's imagination and behavior, becoming a force in its own right, detaching itself from the political differences that initially inspired it, and then leading both parties, invariably and inexorably, to the war they no longer know how to avoid.

This is a species of fixation, brewed out of many components. There are fears, resentments, national pride, personal pride. There are misread-ings of the adversary's intentions — sometimes even the refusal to consider them at all. There is the tendency of national communities to idealize themselves and to dehumanize the opponent. There is the blinkered, nar-row vision of the professional military planner, and his tendency to make war inevitable by assuming its inevitability.

Tossed together, these components form a powerful brew. They guide the fears and the ambitions of men. They seize the policies of governments and whip them around like trees before the tempest.

Is it possible to break out of this charmed and vicious circle? It is sobering to recognize that no one, at least to my knowledge, has yet done so. But no one, for that matter, has ever been faced with such great catas-trophe, such inalterable catastrophe, at the end of the line. Others, in earlier decades, could befuddle themselves with dreams of something called "victory." We, perhaps fortunately, are denied this seductive prospect. We have to break out of the circle. We have no other choice.

How are we to do it?

I must confess that I see no possibility of doing this by means of dis-cussions along the lines of the negotiations that have been in progress, off and on, over this past decade, under the acronym of SALT. I regret, to be sure, that the most recent SALT agreement has not been ratified. I regret it, because if the benefits to be expected from that agreement were slight, its disadvantages were even slighter; and it had a symbolic value which should not have been so lightly sacrificed.

But I have, I repeat, no illusion that negotiations on the SALT pat-tern — negotiations, that is, in which each side is obsessed with the chimera of relative advantage and strives only to retain a maximum of the weaponry for itself while putting its opponent to the maximum disadvantage — I have no illusion that such negotiations could ever be adequate to get us out of this hole. They are not a way of escape from the weapons race; they are an integral part of it.

Whoever does not understand that when it comes to nuclear weapons the whole concept of relative advantage is illusory — whoever does not un-derstand that when you are talking about absurd and preposterous quanti-ties of overkill the relative sizes of arsenals have no serious mean-ing — whoever does not understand that the danger lies not in the possibility that someone else might have more missiles and warheads than we do but in the very existence of these unconscionable quantities of highly poisonous explosives, and their existence, above all, in hands as weak and shaky and undependable as those of ourselves or our adversaries or any other mere human beings: whoever does not understand these things is never going to guide us out of this increasingly dark and menacing forest of bewilderments into which we have all wandered.

I can see no way out of this dilemma other than by a bold and sweep-ing departure — a departure that would cut surgically through the exagger-ated anxieties, the self-engendered nightmares, and the sophisticated mathematics of destruction, in which we have all been entangled over these recent years, and would permit us to move, with courage and decision, to the heart of the problem.

President Reagan recently said, and I think very wisely, that he would "negotiate as long as necessary to reduce the numbers of nuclear weapons to a point where neither side threatens the survival of the other."

Now that is, of course, precisely the thought to which these present observations of mine are addressed. But I wonder whether the negotiations would really have to be at such great length. What I would like to see the President do, after due consultation with the Congress, would be to propose to the Soviet government an immediate across-the-boards reduction by 50 percent of the nuclear arsenals now being maintained by the two superpowers — a reduction affecting in equal measure all forms of the weapon, strategic, medium range, and tactical, as well as all means of their delivery — all this to be implemented at once and without further wrangling among the experts, and to be subject to such national means of verification as now lie at the disposal of the two powers.

Whether the balance of reduction would be precisely even — whether it could be construed to favor statistically one side or the other — would not be the question. Once we start thinking that way, we would be back on the same old fateful track that has brought us where we are today. Whatever the precise results of such a reduction, there would still be plenty of overkill left — so much so that if this first operation were successful, I would then like to see a second one put in hand to rid us of at least two thirds of what would be left.

Now I have, of course, no idea of the scientific aspects of such an operation; but I can imagine that serious problems might be presented by the task of removing, and disposing safely of, the radioactive contents of the many thousands of warheads that would have to be dismantled. Should this be the case, I would like to see the President couple his appeal for a 50 percent reduction with the proposal that there be established a joint Soviet-American scientific committee, under the chairmanship of a distinguished neutral figure, to study jointly and in all humility the problem not only of the safe disposal of these wastes but also the question of how they could be utilized in such a way as to make a positive contribution to human life, either in the two countries themselves or — perhaps preferably — elsewhere. In such a joint scientific venture we might both atone for some of our past follies and lay the foundation for a more constructive relationship.

It will be said: this proposal, whatever its merits, deals with only a part of the problem. This is perfectly true. Behind it there would still lurk the serious political differences that now divide us from the Soviet government. Behind it would still lie the problems recently treated, and still to be treated, in the SALT forum. Behind it would still lie the great question of the acceptability of war itself, any war, even a conventional one, as a means of solving problems among great industrial powers in this age of high technology.

What has been suggested here would not prejudice the continued treatment of these questions just as today, in whatever forums and under whatever safeguards the two powers find necessary. The conflicts and arguments over these questions could all still proceed to the heart's content of all those who view them with such passionate commitment. The stakes would simply be smaller; and that would be a great relief to all of us.

What I have suggested is, of course, only a beginning. But a beginning has to be made somewhere; and if it has to be made, it is best that it should be made where the dangers are the greatest, and their necessity the least. If a step of this nature could be successfully taken, people might find the heart to tackle with greater confidence and determination the many problems that would still remain.

It will be argued that there would be risks involved. Possibly so. I do not see them. I do not deny the possibility. But if there are, so what? Is it possible to conceive of any dangers greater than those that lie at the end of the collision course on which we are now embarked? And if not, why choose the greater — why choose, in fact, the greatest — of all risks, in the hopes of avoiding the lesser ones?

We are confronted here, my friends, with two courses. At the end of the one lies hope — faint hope, if you will — uncertain hope, hope surrounded with dangers, if you insist. At the end of the other lies, so far as I am able to see, no hope at all.

Can there be — in the light of our duty not just to ourselves (for we are all going to die sooner or later) but of our duty to our own kind, our duty to the continuity of the generations, our duty to the great experiment of civilized life on this rare and rich and marvelous planet — can there be, in the light of these claims on our loyalty, any question as to which course we should adopt?

In the final week of his life, Albert Einstein signed the last of the collective appeals against the development of nuclear weapons that he was ever to sign. He was dead before it appeared. It was an appeal drafted, I gather, by Bertrand Russell. I had my differences with Russell at the time as I do now in retrospect; but I would like to quote one sentence from the final paragraph of that statement, not only because it was the last one Einstein ever signed, but because it sums up, I think, all that I have to say on the subject. It read as follows:

> *"We appeal, as human beings to human beings: Remember your humanity, and forget the rest."*

The SALT II Treaty

HEARINGS
BEFORE THE
COMMITTEE ON FOREIGN RELATIONS
UNITED STATES SENATE
NINETY-SIXTH CONGRESS
FIRST SESSION
September 6, 1979

*Statement of Dr. Alan Geyer,
Representing the Council of Bishops
and the Board of Church and Society of the
United Methodist Church, Washington, D.C.*

Mr. Chairman and members of the committee: My name is Alan Geyer. It is my privilege today to testify on behalf of the Council of Bishops of the United Methodist Church and also on behalf of our denomination's Board of Church and Society. I am not myself, a bishop, I regret to say, although some of my best friends are bishops. I am a political scientist whose main teaching and research have been in international relations, with a special interest in arms control and disarmament. I am also an ordained minister, which many folks imagine is incompatible with being a political scientist or a political anything. My present position is Executive Director of the Churches' Center for Theology and Public Policy, an ecumenical study center here in Washington. I wish to state clearly that I am not speaking today for that Center but only for my own denomination.

Last April, the Council of Bishops adopted "A Resolution on SALT II and Commitment to Disarmament" which urged approval of the SALT II Treaty. That resolution also expressed determination "that the American people and their government must not fail to make positive decisions for disarmament in the days just ahead." The text of the resolution is attached to this testimony and I shall make continuing reference to it in my remarks today.

Several weeks ago I heard a private complaint from one of our government's key officials in SALT affairs. He said, with great vexation, that the churches have waited much too long to get into the action on nuclear arms issues — and that even now they bring mostly a dilettantism to the really hard choices.

I could not argue with him — except to say that there is a new serious-ness about disarmament on the part of many church leaders and local con-gregations, as many members of the Senate and the House are beginning to discover in their constituencies. The survival of the human race is, at last, becoming a theological issue. In fact, it is hard to think of a more fun-damentally theological issue.

If the nuclear arms race really does raise serious theological questions, it should point us toward mysteries which we cannot pretend fully to under-stand. And, truth to tell, we do not understand very much about the human consequences of nuclear technology, or about the dynamics of political power in a nuclear age, or about the limits of human rationality in coping with nuclear crisis.

Our national security debates in these late 1970s have once again become preoccupied with strategic scenarios of nuclear war. The SALT II hearings themselves have too often been turned into a platform for pro-moting the further development of offensive nuclear weapons and military budget increases. These hearings and the general public require a more ade-quate framework of political vision and humane policy if the SALT process is to be an effective instrument of peacemaking.

Our religious communities are clearly summoned to lift up some alter-native scenarios: some new scripts for the strategies of peace. Scenarios in which both our real security and our very survival are more surely promised than they are by the fatuous assumption that we'd be better off with still more and bigger and better nuclear weapons than the 32,000 already in the U.S. arsenal. Scenarios in which our leaders muster the wit and the will to draw us away, at last, from these grisly apprehensions of total terror which make mental health and normal living impossible for us all. Scenarios which appeal to "the better angels of our nature."

Deep beneath the military mathematics of the SALT debate are some searing questions of moral wisdom.

What, if anything, would we not do to 260 million Soviet people, or to our own people and institutions, or to all Earth's peoples, for the sake of promoting our military technology and our perceptions of our own prestige? Do we have enough vision of our creaturehood in God's good Creation, or of the humanity even of our enemies, or of the things that really make for peace and security — any redeeming vision which may yet spare us all from the Great and Final Firestorm?

The political setting in this country for discussing these questions right now is hardly auspicious. We are heavily burdened with political cynicism, wounded pride, Cold War hallucinations, loss of common purpose, and manipulation of all of the above by lushly funded propaganda from mean-spirited interests.

I wish to raise four broadly political questions which should be basic to the SALT II debate. Each of these is morally loaded precisely because it is political, and not simply technical.

Questions

(1) What moral claims, if any, do the Soviet government and people have against us — and what do we do about them?

(2) What are the moral claims of non-nuclear-weapon states against both the Soviet Union and the United States — and what do we do about them?

(3) What view of the meaning of our own security do we bring to arms limitation issues?

(4) Can we make a national decision on SALT II without further corrupting the integrity of our domestic politics?

Answers

(1) You do not have to overlook the repressive habits of Russian governments, or the opportunism of Soviet foreign policy, or their Avis complex about catching up with the U.S. in strategic weapons to ask whether the SALT debate isn't plagued with very crude images of the Russians as our enemies. One such crudity is to ignore obvious Soviet motives in avoiding a war even more devastating than World War II and in reducing the terrible economic burdens of the arms race. Another crudity is to attribute irresistible force to Soviet penetration of such societies as Afghanistan and Ethiopia — thus failing to see how bogged down the Soviets now are in coping with national and religious forces in those societies. Still another crudity is the unwillingness to recognize how many concessions the Soviets have actually made on SALT and other disarmament questions.

After all, in SALT I, they did agree to exclude U.S. bombers and NATO forward-based systems from the accords.

In SALT II, they agreed to come down from the 1974 Vladivostok launcher limit, which means scrapping 250 of their own launchers capable of devastating all our major urban areas. They changed their positions to accommodate demands on sharing a common data base; permitting one new land-based missile system; defining the size of "new" missiles; limiting land-based missiles to 10 warheads; permitting the U.S. to deploy long-range cruise missiles from our bombers, then permitting an "average" limit of 28 cruise missiles per bomber after proposing a limit of only 20; stipulating that the Backfire will not be upgraded into a long-range bomber nor will its production rate increase.

One of our senior U.S. negotiators has reported that "all the major moves" on concessions have come from the Soviet side. While some Americans complain of appeasing the Russians, we may well suspect that there is honest perplexity in Moscow as to what more they must do to appease the Americans.

In short, our antipathies to many aspects of Soviet politics and policy must not blind us to the very human seriousness of Soviet leaders about avoiding nuclear war — a seriousness which transcends all ideologies and cultures.

(2) The moral claims of many other nations — in fact, of all nations —

are at stake in the SALT process.

There is no greater sense of inequity in the world today than that felt by nations which have renounced nuclear weapons for themselves and, under U.S. and Soviet pressure joined the Non-Proliferation Treaty of 1978. But they joined only because of a clear promise by the superpowers, written into that treaty, that there would be an end to all nuclear testing and steady progress in reducing nuclear arsenals. Next year's second Review Conference on that treaty could witness the collapse of effective international cooperation in halting the spread of nuclear weapons if it convenes with neither a SALT agreement nor a comprehensive test ban.

Mr. Chairman, I attended the First Review Conference on the Non-Proliferation Treaty in Geneva in May 1975 and I served as head of this country's non-governmental observers there. That conference, just six months after President Ford met Chairman Brezhnev in Vladivostok, heard repeated assurances that a SALT II accord was just ahead. Those assurances were offered in the face of understandable protests from non-nuclear-weapon states that the Non-Proliferation Treaty was increasingly an intolerable instrument of invidious discrimination.

Now, more than four years later, can we really suppose that a refusal to ratify SALT II on the eve of the Second NPT Review Conference will promote the safety or security of this nation? Is there any more likely circumstance of nuclear war than the threat or use of nuclear weapons by any of a dozen other states which already possess, or could soon possess, them in a world of uncontrolled proliferation?

It is primarily because of this perverse linkage between the vertical spiral of strategic arms and the horizontal spread of nuclear arms that the United Nations General Assembly last fall voted 127-1 (only Albania voting No) to urge the earliest possible conclusion of the SALT II accords. That doesn't mean universal enthusiasm for SALT itself: it does mean that the non-fulfillment of SALT II is almost universally viewed as the greatest obstacle to progress on all the other issues on the world's disarmament agenda.

(3) Perhaps our most basic ethical concern in national security policy is not a conflict between principles and politics: it is the question as to how we conceive political reality.

Do we really believe, for instance, that more and bigger nuclear weapons have a redeeming effect on our insecurities, or that "strategic superiority" is still a politically meaningful term in nuclear policy? A much more useful perspective has been suggested by Henry Kissinger in an uncharacteristic moment of modesty and perplexity (which was one of his wiser moments) when he blurted out: "What, in the name of God, is strategic superiority? What is the significance of it politically, militarily, operationally at these levels of numbers? What do you do with it?"

The ultimate contradiction of the nuclear age is that the more we have committed our substance to the idols of defense and deterrence, the more defenseless we have become. Our insecurity has been compounded by every new escalation of military technology. Not only have our national boundaries become indefensible against nuclear attack: offensive technology increasingly threatens to outrun the technology of arms control itself. As ingenious and even redundant as our present verification systems may be, they can be overtaken by still more exotic offensive weapons if we do not develop more peaceable political relationships and reverse the dynamics of the arms race. There is no technical escape from the requirements of reconciliation.

Not only has our defenselessness been compounded militarily: nonmilitary threats to our security — resource exhaustion, ecocatastrophes, inflation and massive poverty and human degradation — all are severely aggravated by the arms race.

As our power to destroy has grown, our power to conserve and to create has shrunk.

SALT II can be a step toward greater security if, as the Council of Bishops has said, the US and USSR proceed "immediately after the approval of SALT II to negotiate substantial reductions in nuclear weapons in SALT III and succeeding agreements."

If, however, this treaty's "disturbingly limited" provisions are used to push on with still more devastating weapons and with thousands of additional nuclear warheads, we cannot believe that our national security will really be served. The Council of Bishops declared themselves "persuaded of the hard truth declared by the United Nations Special Session on Disarmament that nuclear weapons constitute 'much more of a threat than a protection' for the future of humanity."

(4) Our domestic political integrity is very much on trial in the SALT II decision.

One of the sorriest episodes in our political history was a whole series of extravagant pay-offs for SALT I. The director of the Arms Control and Disarmament Agency was dismissed, along with his top aides. The Agency's budget was sharply cut. Both research and public affairs functions were gutted. And the SALT II negotiations have, from the beginning, been burdened with promises of new weapons systems made at the time of SALT I: full-scale MIRV deployment, cruise missiles, Trident submarines.

The consideration of SALT II on its merits has, I personally believe, been made much more difficult by a series of decisions about weapons, budget, and personnel, as well as by official and unofficial rhetoric about Soviet policy.

I regret very much having to report my own impression that the prospects for public support of SALT II were badly damaged by the Administration's own anti-Soviet talk during the spring and summer of 1978. In fact, there was more than alarmist talk. There was the first public cruise missile test. There was stepped up planning for MX mobile missile development. There was a revival of evacuation planning for civil defense. There was a highly publicized mock anti-Soviet maneuver in Texas, attended by the President. In the early fall, a general was named to succeed Paul Warnke at the Arms Control and Disarmament Agency. All of these happenings tended to reinforce public hostility toward the Soviet Union — yet all of them were rationalized as efforts to consolidate support for SALT II.

Even before SALT II was signed in Vienna and before these hearings began, the White House had decided that the MX mobile missile had become a domestic political necessity if SALT II were to be ratified. The tragedy of this most costly and ominous development is that it could have been avoided politically if the public had been engaged on the merits of SALT II during 1978.

The United Nations Special Session on Disarmament in May and June of 1978 offered a timely opportunity to engage the public on the issues of nuclear arms control and disarmament. In fact, the mobilization of public opinion was clearly the prime purpose of the Special Session. But the President declined even to attend, the United States offered no significant policy initiatives, and the Special Session became a non-event for the American public. Yet these decisions, too, were rationalized as political necessities for the sake of SALT II.

Whatever political games may be played in support of SALT II, we must also be candid about the degree to which treaty opponents have cheapened the debate by the hard selling of raw fantasies, not only about the Soviet Union but also about American groups committed to arms limitation. One of the silliest canards is being spread by the American Security Council's Coalition for Peace Through Strength: the claim that there is a $100 million pro-disarmament lobby led by the National Council of Churches and the Coalition for a New Foreign and Military Policy. Those of us who have tried for years, without success, to get the National Council to fund at least one modestly-paid staff person on disarmament issues — and who are familiar with the subsistence style of the latter Coalition — have reason to wonder whether the inadequacy of the American Security Council's political research may help to explain the vain imaginings of their strategic analysis.

If there is any set of issues which ought to lift the level of political debate in this country to the highest levels of honesty and integrity — and a clear-eyed view of the common good — it is these issues of national security and human survival.

Now I must conclude this review of the moral ambiguities of SALT II. I wish to share with this Committee the fruit of a U.S.-Soviet disarmament consultation in Geneva last spring, in which I was privileged to participate, along with governmental and church leaders from both countries. A major product of that consultation was the very first joint U.S.-Soviet theological statement on any policy issue, a statement which has since been warmly endorsed by both the Council of Bishops of the United Methodist Church and the Governing Board of the National Council of Churches. The benediction of that statement was written mostly by a Russian Christian and ends with a familiar and terribly appropriate text from Deuteronomy:

"Finally, our sisters and brothers, we call to your attention the authoritative predictions that nuclear war by the 1990's is an increasing probability. In that decade of high risks we will be approaching the end of our millenium. Even now, only twenty years separate us from the moment when we will be called upon to mark prayerfully the bi-millenary anniversary of the coming to the world of our Lord and Saviour, Jesus Christ, the Prince of Peace. How shall we meet that day!? In what state shall we present our planet to the Creator? Shall it be a blooming garden or a lifeless, burnt out, devastated land!?

"Thus the Lord has set before us again life and death, blessing and curse! Therefore choose life that you and your descendants may live!"

NOTES

Chapter 1
1. Martin J. Sherwin, *A World Destroyed: The Atomic Bomb and the Grand Alliance* (New York: Alfred A. Knopf, 1975), 7-8.
2. *Ibid.,* 228.
3. Joseph Nogee, "The Diplomacy of Disarmament," *International Conciliation,* January 1960, 280. See also Alva Myrdal, *The Game of Disarmament: How the United States and Russia Run the Arms Race* (New York: Pantheon Books, 1978).

Chapter 2
1. Walter Millis and James Real, *The Abolition of War* (New York: The Macmillan Company, 1963), ix-xv.
2. George H. Quester, *Deterrence Before Hiroshima* (New York: Wiley, 1966).
3. Benjamin S. Lambeth, "Soviet Strategic Conduct and the Prospects for Stability" (London: International Institute for Strategic Studies, *Adelphi Paper 161,* Autumn 1980), 31.
4. Quoted in Bernard Brodie, *War and Politics* (New York: The Macmillan Company, 1973), 377.
5. Robert S. McNamara, *The Essence of Security* (New York: Harper and Row, 1968), 53.
6. Thomas Schelling, *Strategy of Conflict* (Cambridge: Harvard University Press, 1960), 188.
7. Michael Howard, "The Relevance of Traditional Strategy," *Foreign Affairs,* January 1973, 262.
8. James Fallows, *National Defense* (New York: Random House, 1981), 39.
9. Lawrence Freedman, "The Rationale for Medium-Sized Deterrence Forces" (*Adelphi Paper 160,* Autumn 1980), 52.
10. Richard Barnet, *Real Security* (New York: Simon and Schuster, 1981), 39.
11. Laurence Martin, "The Determinants of Change: Deterrence and Technology" (*Adelphi Paper 161,* Autumn 1980), 9.
12. Curt Gasteyger, "The Determinants of Change: Deterrence and

the Political Environment" (*Adelphi Paper 161,* Autumn 1980), 2.

13. Alexander L. George and Richard Smoke, *Deterrence in American Foreign Policy: Theory and Practice* (New York: Columbia University Press, 1974), 605.

14. Martin, 10.

15. Quoted in Robert C. Batchelder, *The Irreversible Decision: 1939-50* (New York: The Macmillan Company, 1961), 61-2.

16. Philip Green, *Deadly Logic: The Theory of Nuclear Deterrence* (New York: Schocken Books, 1968), 226.

17. Brodie, 479-95.

18. *Ibid.,* 496.

19. *Ibid.,* 381.

20. *Ibid.,* 398-9.

21. *Ibid.,* 488.

22. Maxwell Taylor, "Can We Depend on Deterrence?" *The Washington Post,* June 30, 1981, A17.

23. Fred Iklé, "Can Nuclear Deterrence Last Out the Century?" *Foreign Affairs,* January 1973, 267-85.

24. Wolfgang K. H. Panofsky, "The Mutual Hostage Relationship between America and Russia," *Foreign Affairs,* October 1973, 109-18.

25. Raymond Aron, *Century of Total War* (New York: Doubleday and Company, 1954), Chapter 8. Quoted in McGeorge Bundy, "Strategic Deterrence Theory Thirty Years Later: What Has Changed?" (*Adelphi Paper 161,* Autumn 1980), 6.

26. Lewis C. Bohn, "Is Nuclear Deterrence Really Necessary?" *War/Peace Report,* November-December 1972, 7-8.

27. Barnet, 93.

28. Hedley Bull, "Future Conditions of Strategic Deterrence" (*Adelphi Paper 160,* Autumn 1980), 16.

29. B. C. E. Nwosu, quoted in Alan Geyer, "The EST Complex at MIT," *The Ecumenical Review,* October 1979, 378.

30. Martin, 10.

31. Gasteyger, 6.

32. *North-South: A Program for Survival* (Cambridge: MIT Press, 1980) is the report of the Independent Commission on International Development chaired by Willy Brandt. The five primary threats to human survival emphasized by the commission are: economic disaster, mass hunger, nuclear annihilation, environmental catastrophe, and political terrorism. Chancellor Brandt's introduction links military spending with development

in four comparative illustrations, cited at the end of Chapter 6 in this book.

33. Roger Fisher, *International Conflict for Beginners* (New York: Harper and Row, 1969), 106.

34. Michael Walzer, *Just and Unjust Wars* (New York: Basic Books, 1977), 283.

35. George and Smoke, Chapter 21.

36. *Ibid.,* 613.

37. Karl Deutsch, *The Nerves of Government* (London: Free Press, 1963), 70. Quoted in Green, 144.

38. Henry Kissinger, *The Necessity for Choice* (New York: Harper and Row, 1960), 40-1.

39. Green, 216.

40. *Ibid.,* ii.

41. Bull, 15.

42. George Kennan, "Like Lemmings Heading for the Sea," Appendix C.

43. Stanley Hoffmann, *The State of War* (New York: Frederick A. Praeger, 1965), 215.

Chapter 3

1. Nigel Calder, *Nuclear Nightmares* (New York: Penguin Books, 1981), 142. See also Robert C. Aldridge, *The Counterforce Syndrome: A Guide to U.S. Nuclear Weapons and Strategic Doctrine* (Washington: Transnational Institute, 1979).

2. Fallows, 143.

3. Calder, 149-50.

4. Bundy, 6.

5. Walzer, 279-82.

6. Hoffmann, 216.

7. Richard Rosecrance, "Strategic Deterrence Reconsidered" (*Adelphi Paper 116,* Spring 1975), 23.

8. Taylor, A17.

9. Bernard Brodie, *Strategy in the Missile Age* (Princeton University Press, 1959), 391.

10. Carl Kaysen, "Keeping the Strategic Balance," *Foreign Affairs,* July 1968, 672.

11. Quoted in Robert A. Gessert and J. Bryan Hehir, *The New Nuclear Debate* (New York: Council on Religion and International Affairs, 1976), 24.

12. Calder, 142.

13. Quoted in Desmond Ball, "Counterforce Targeting: How New?

How Viable?" *Arms Control Today,* February 1981, 8.
14. Herbert York, *Race to Oblivion: A Participant's View of the Arms Race* (New York: Simon and Schuster, 1970), 180.
15. Michael Howard, "Return to the Cold War?" in *America and the World 1980* (New York: Council on Foreign Relations, 1981), 465.
16. Bundy, 10.

Chapter 4
1. Quoted in Ralph Lapp, *Arms Beyond Doubt* (New York: Cowles, 1970), 68.
2. York, 180, 234-7.
3. *Ibid.,* 237, 239.
4. Michael Mandelbaum, *The Nuclear Question: The United States and Nuclear Weapons 1946-1976* (Cambridge University Press, 1979), 199.
5. John G. Stoessinger, *Henry Kissinger: The Anguish of Power* (New York: W. W. Norton, 1976), 85.
6. Strobe Talbott, *Endgame: The Inside Story of SALT II* (New York: Harper and Row, 1979), 146-7.
7. Editorial, "Arming for Arms Control," *The New York Times,* July 17, 1981, A 22.
8. Quoted by Senator Edward M. Kennedy in address to annual meeting of the Arms Control Association, February 20, 1979.
9. Quoted in Louis Beres, *Apocalypse: Nuclear Catastrophe in World Politics* (University of Chicago Press, 1980), 4.
10. William Epstein, *The Last Chance: Nuclear Proliferation and Arms Control* (New York: Free Press, 1976), 288.

Chapter 5
1. Interview, March 2, 1981.
2. Ralph Earle II, "Arms Control Lessons of the Carter Administration," *Arms Control Today,* March 1981, 4.
3. William Epstein, "Stopping A-Bombs," *The New York Times,* August 6, 1981, A 23.
4. Mason Willrich and John B. Rhinelander (eds.), *SALT: The Moscow Agreements and Beyond* (New York: Free Press, 1974), 267, 269.
5. Henry Kissinger, *White House Years* (Boston: Little, Brown and Company, 1979), 549.
6. "ACDA: Today and Before the Purge," *Defense Monitor,* August 1974.

7. Richard Burt, "The Scope and Limits of SALT," *Foreign Affairs,* July 1978, 753.

8. Quoted in Talbott, 35.

9. Burt, 754.

10. Jan Lodal, Letter to *The New York Times,* April 12, 1977, 29.

11. Robert G. Kaiser, "New SALT Agreements Attacked by Senator Jackson," *The Washington Post,* November 30, 1976, A10.

12. See especially *SALT II Senate Testimony,* Section on "Case Histories," by Ambassador Ralph Earle II, July 10, 1979 (Department of State Current Policy No. 72A), 30-2; a four-part series by Don Oberdorfer in *The Washington Post,* May 10-13, 1974; and Strobe Talbott, *Endgame: The Inside Story of SALT II* (New York: Harper and Row, 1979).

13. Among several accounts I have published on the NPT review conferences, the most extensive appeared in *Worldview.* See "The Nuclear Question Explodes," September 1975, and "NPT II: No Miracles in Geneva," December 1980.

14. Lincoln Bloomfield, "Nuclear Spread and World Order," *Foreign Affairs,* July 1975, 746.

Chapter 6

1. See my earlier analysis of the military-industrial complex in Charles Wolf, Jr., Roger Fisher, and Alan Geyer, *Is America Becoming Militarized?* (New York: Council on Religion and International Affairs, 1971).

2. Marshall D. Shulman, "Arms Control in an International Context," *Daedalus,* Summer 1975, 53.

3. Quoted in Duncan Clarke, *Politics of Arms Control: The Role and Effectiveness of the U.S. Arms Control and Disarmament Agency* (New York: Free Press, 1979), 32.

4. Henry Fairlie, "Why the Cultivated Man of Affairs Is a Rarity in America," *The Washington Post,* August 2, 1981, C3.

5. Karen Rothmyer, "Citizen Scaife," *Columbia Journalism Review,* July/August 1981, 47.

6. Stephen Rosenfeld, "Defense: Another Great Leap Forward," *The Washington Post,* July 24, 1981, A13.

7. *Ibid.*

Chapter 7

1. Robert Johansen, *Toward a Dependable Peace: A Proposal for an Appropriate Security System* (New York: Institute for

World Order, 1978).

2. Gene Sharp, *Exploring Nonviolent Alternatives* and *The Politics of Nonviolent Action* (Boston: Porter Sargent, 1970, 1973).

3. Charles E. Osgood, "Reciprocal Initiative," in Richard A. Falk and Saul H. Mendlovitz (eds.), *Disarmament and Economic Development* (New York: World Law Fund, 1966). For a systematic extension of Osgood's approach, see Gordon Shull, "Unilateral Initiatives in Arms Control," in *Ohio Arms Control Study Group: Selected Papers* (Columbus: Mershon Center, Ohio State University, 1977).

4. Alan Geyer, "Disarmament: A Losing Cause in Need of Rescue," *Christianity and Crisis,* May 15, 1978, 112.

5. Wilder Foote (ed.), *Dag Hammarskjöld, Servant of Peace: A Selection of His Speeches and Statements* (New York: Harper and Row, 1962), 180.

6. *Ibid.,* 305-6.

7. Barnet, 118.

8. Foote, 132.

9. Herbert Butterfield, *Christianity, Diplomacy, and War* (New York: Abingdon-Cokesbury Press, n.d.), 68.

Chapter 8

1. Karl Barth, *Evangelical Theology,* quoted in Hans Küng, *Truthfulness: The Future of the Church* (New York: Sheed and Ward, 1968), 87.

2. Hans Morgenthau, "The Purpose of Political Science," in James C. Charleswoth (ed.), *A Design for Political Science: Scope, Objectives and Methods* (Philadelphia: The American Academy of Political and Social Science, 1966), 69.

3. Küng, 15.

4. André Dumas, *Political Theology and the Life of the Church* (Philadelphia: Westminster Press, 1977), 76-7.

5. *Ibid.*

6. Küng, 142.

7. *Ibid.,* 22-25.

8. My longtime concern about the debilitating effects of a "realistic" theology of history upon politics was explored in my Ph.D. dissertation which, in abridged form, was published as my first book, *Piety and Politics: American Protestantism in the World Arena* (Richmond: John Knox Press, 1963).

9. Reinhold Niebuhr, *The Structure of Nations and Empires* (New

York: Charles Scribner's Sons, 1959), 259.

10. Dennis P. McCann, *Christian Realism and Liberation Theology: Practical Theologies in Creative Conflict* (Maryknoll, N.Y.: Orbis Books, 1981).

11. William Temple, *Christus Veritas,* 139, quoted in Donald Baillie, *God Was in Christ* (New York: Charles Scribner's Sons, 1948), 106.

12. Teilhard de Chardin, *Hymn of the Universe* (New York: Harper and Row, 1965), 144.

13. Teilhard de Chardin, *The Divine Milieu* (New York: Harper and Row, 1960), 141.

14. Herman Kahn, *Thinking About the Unthinkable* (New York: Horizon Press, 1962), 85.

15. Gerhard Leibholz, "Memoir," in Dietrich Bonhoeffer, *The Cost of Discipleship* (New York: The Macmillan Company, 1963), 30.

16. Nicholas Berdyaev, *Slavery and Freedom* (New York: Charles Scribner's Sons, 1944), 21. Quoted in Walter G. Muelder, *Moral Law in Christian Social Ethics* (Richmond: John Knox Press, 1966), 101.

17. Herbert Butterfield, *International Conflict in the Twentieth Century* (New York: Harper and Brothers, 1960), 45.

18. See Appendix A for the full text of "Choose Life."

19. Paul Hume, "JFK Center 'Mass' is Show of Faith" (special from *The Washington Post*), *Chicago Sun-Times,* September 9, 1971, 78.

INDEX